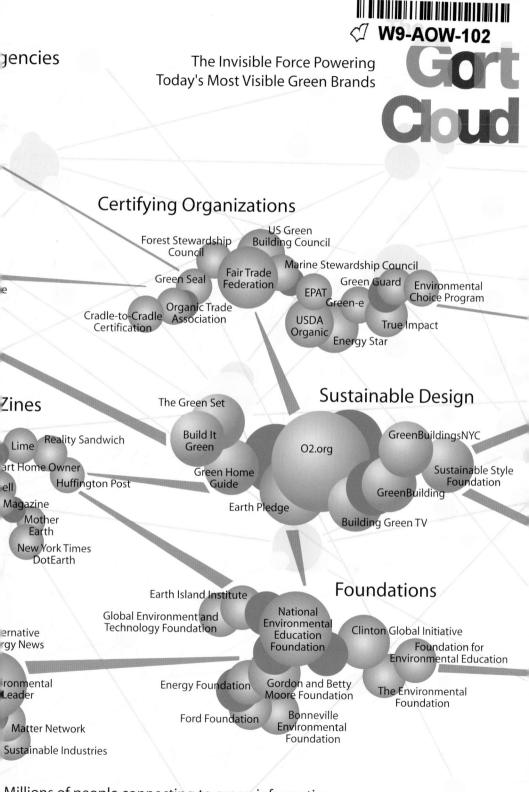

gencies

The Invisible Force Powering
Today's Most Visible Green Brands

W9-AOW-102

Gort Cloud

Certifying Organizations

Forest Stewardship Council

US Green Building Council

Green Seal

Fair Trade Federation

Marine Stewardship Council

Green Guard

Environmental Choice Program

EPAT

Green-e

Cradle-to-Cradle Certification

Organic Trade Association

USDA Organic

True Impact

Energy Star

Zines

The Green Set

Lime

Reality Sandwich

art Home Owner

ell

Huffington Post

Magazine

Mother Earth

New York Times DotEarth

Sustainable Design

Build It Green

Green Home Guide

O2.org

GreenBuildingsNYC

Sustainable Style Foundation

GreenBuilding

Earth Pledge

Building Green TV

Foundations

Earth Island Institute

Global Environment and Technology Foundation

National Environmental Education Foundation

Clinton Global Initiative

ernative gy News

Foundation for Environmental Education

ronmental Leader

Energy Foundation

Gordon and Betty Moore Foundation

The Environmental Foundation

Ford Foundation

Bonneville Environmental Foundation

Matter Network

Sustainable Industries

Millions of people connecting to green information
through a vast, interconnected community.

THE
Gort Cloud

THE
Gort Cloud

*The Invisible Force Powering Today's
Most Visible Green Brands*

RICHARD SEIREENI
with Scott Fields

CHELSEA GREEEN PUBLISHING
WHITE RIVER JUNCTION, VERMONT

Project Manager: Emily Foote
Developmental Editor: Joni Praded
Copy Editor: Laura Jorstad
Proofreader: Nancy Ringer
Designer: Peter Holm, Sterling Hill Productions

Printed in the United States of America
First printing, December 2008
10 9 8 7 6 5 4 3 2 1   08 09 10 11 12 13 14

Our Commitment to Green Publishing
Chelsea Green sees publishing as a tool for cultural change and ecological stewardship. We strive to align our book manufacturing practices with our editorial mission and to reduce the impact of our business enterprise in the environment. We print our books and catalogs on chlorine-free recycled paper, using soy-based inks whenever possible. This book may cost slightly more because we use recycled paper, and we hope you'll agree that it's worth it. Chelsea Green is a member of the Green Press Initiative (www. greenpressinitiative.org), a nonprofit coalition of publishers, manufacturers, and authors working to protect the world's endangered forests and conserve natural resources. *The Gort Cloud* was printed on 55-lb. Natures Cream, an FSC-certified, 30-percent postconsumer-waste recycled paper supplied by The Maple-Vail Book Manufacturing Group.

Please see page 309 for complete Green Press Initiative environmental-impact statement.

Printed by The Maple-Vail Book Manufacturing Group using their exclusive *THINK*Tech™ printing process with ultra-low VOCs and energy-free curing. *THINK*Tech™ reduces energy consumption by more than 70% when compared to traditional web offset printing.

Library of Congress Cataloging-in-Publication Data
Seireeni, Richard, 1949-
 The Gort Cloud : the invisible force powering today's most visible green brands / by Richard Seireeni with Scott Fields.
   p. cm.
 Includes bibliographical references and index.
 ISBN 978-1-60358-061-8
1. Green marketing. 2. Green products. 3. Green movement. I. Fields, Scott. II. Title.

HF5413.S45 2009
658.8--dc22

2008044095

Chelsea Green Publishing Company
Post Office Box 428
White River Junction, VT 05001
(802) 295-6300
www.chelseagreen.com

To Mother Earth and three of the creatures she has cared for:
Elaine, Tiber, Echo.
And to my parents, Bob and Terry, who taught me to think for myself.

CONTENTS

Introduction: The Gort Cloud?

Imagine a place where a budding green business can get all the support and experienced help it needs. A place that can supply partners, and investors, and distributors. Imagine that this place can also telegraph a product message in exactly the right tone to key stakeholders and the most influential early adopters.

This place is what I call the Gort Cloud — the vast but invisible community that has the power to make or break green brands. It is a unique force that I discovered in the process of interviewing and researching the many ecopreneurs profiled in this book. It has few counterparts in other business spheres.

Knowledge of this unorganized but interconnected network is critical to anyone involved in making, marketing, or selling eco-friendly products and services. That's because green products are examined, commented on, and shared within this community — at little or no cost. Products that are "endorsed" by environmental experts, bloggers, trendspotters, and first adopters in the Gort Cloud do better than those that are not.

When green business leaders have examined the chart of the Gort Cloud (reproduced on the endpapers of this book), the lights go on. They get it. They recognize it as a map of the sometimes difficult but familiar terrain that they have had to navigate to build their businesses. As they wrap their heads around it, they can appreciate the opportunities within it. Their desired partners and customers become visible, as do the threads connecting them.

So whether you're an entrepreneur weighing the risks and rewards of entering the green sphere, or a marketing or communications consultant, or simply a student of modern business practices, knowledge of the Gort Cloud, coupled with the experiences of the firms profiled here, will give you insights on how to build a successful green business — and provide the world more options in the coming Age of Sustainability.

An Interdependent Community of Green Businesses and Their Customers

> Thousands of candles can be lit from a single candle,
> and the life of the candle will not be shortened.
> — *Prince Gautama Siddhartha, the Buddha*

I was some six months into research for this project before the light went on. Originally, I was going to write a book about ecopreneurs — the enterprising businesspeople who are launching green products and building more eco-friendly companies. It was going to be a book about the brand builders for the Age of Sustainability. As a specialist in brand consulting, I believed this was the perfect subject, because it allowed me to use my knowledge and experience to explain how pioneering businesspeople are creating products, identifying customers, and getting the word out in the still tiny but hotly competitive green marketplace. The hope was that such a book would serve as a guide to other would-be ecopreneurs, encouraging more and more businesses to commit to environmental and social responsibility. As a person concerned about the planet, I thought this would be the perfect combination of career, experience, and passion.

Then I realized that the stories of the ecopreneurs I was interviewing had as much — if not more — to do with the larger community that supports them and on which they are dependent.

This is still a book about ecopreneurs and their experiences, but it is also a book about this growing but largely invisible community of eco-conscious customers, partners, and other stakeholders who are also committed to a more sustainable economy. In an effort to make this green community more tangible and more visible to green business leaders, I call it the Gort Cloud.

Without the vision — and the risk — of this new breed of eco-conscious entrepreneur, we would not have today's growing list of socially responsible and sustainable products. We wouldn't have the Prius, the compact fluorescent bulb, or a gallon of low-VOC YOLO Colorhouse paint. Of course, anything short of pure asceticism may be bad for the earth, but we are much better off with business leaders who weigh the environment, humanity, and profitability equally, instead of viewing the planet as both larder and waste pile. So the focus of this book is on the difficult decisions my subjects have made to balance performance and cost in the quest to meet the expectations of their customers and everyone — and everything — that shares this planet. It's about how they have translated these benefits into brand positions and unique selling propositions that are designed to establish credibility and build market share — without stretching the truth, something we call greenwashing. It's also a book about the marketing techniques these entrepreneurs and their partners have used to target audiences and raise awareness.

Throughout the book, I let my subjects speak for themselves because they are the most convincing evangelists for their own stories. These are colorful people with a gift for salesmanship and storytelling. And it was difficult to choose among case studies. The longer I looked, the more great candidates I found. The list kept growing and growing. In the end, I selected businesses that would represent a range of industries and a variety of experiences. It was also important to include some of the most venerable brands in the green marketplace as well as some of the newest and most experimental. In the process, I've taken the risk that some may not survive until the publishing date. Indeed, one company, Nau, was forced to close its doors and then was miraculously saved by an angel investor just as I completed this book. As a result, this story has become a particularly instructive one in dealing with adversity.

As Woody Allen has said, "Eighty percent of success is showing up." All of the men and women profiled in this book showed up when it was time for business to do things differently, and that is what's most important. They are all pioneers forging paths for others to follow. This is also my hope — that this book will embolden more brave pioneers to give us more sustainable product choices in the future.

What this book is not.

This project was not intended to convince anyone that there is a problem. Rachel Carson, Al Gore, Jared Diamond, and many others have done a great job of sounding the alarm. This is also not a book about sustainable economics or the argument for profitability associated with more sustainable business practices. The case for this has been made in books like *Cradle to Cradle*, *Eco-Economy*, *Harvard Business Review on Business and the Environment*, *The Sustainability Revolution*, *The Ecology of Commerce*, *Green to Gold*, and, of course, the mighty opus on the subject, *Natural Capitalism*.

This is also not a book about sustainable manufacturing processes or green technologies or about eco-design, although all of these have a bearing on brand positioning and marketing. These subjects are covered in a host of books, including *The Clean Tech Revolution* and *The Philosophy of Sustainable Design*.

Nor is this a personal how-to-be-greener handbook. For that information, I would refer readers to the *Whole Earth Catalog* of the twenty-first century, *Worldchanging*, edited by Alex Steffen, or any of the many well-written green guides available in print and online.

This book is more focused. It's written for anyone interested in exactly how others have built green brands and how they've developed a following.

Lester Brown recently updated his series of books with *Plan B 3.0: Mobilizing to Save Civilization*. Well, the business leaders profiled in this book are trying to do just that. Their stories present a practical insider's guide to building and marketing a successful green company.

Discovering a network.

As I was busy sourcing information on these companies and their markets, I continually came across families of similar organizations, all sharing some aspect of sustainability. They included individual green businesses and green business alliances; advocacy groups; nongovernmental organization (NGO), government, and education Web sites; bloggers; trendspotters; social networks; certifying groups; technical libraries; news organizations; green guides and shopping sites; authors' sites; and so many others. Some deal with green building, others with organics. Some are focused on transportation, or energy, or water conservation, or waste. Some groups concentrate on a single focused subject, like the Slow Food movement or the development of next-generation car batteries. Others deal with broad issues, like global warming and climate change. While many of these groups are backed by large organizations or institutions with substantial budgets, others are one-person shows fueled only by personal energy. There's a wealth of information in this network, and it comes in all forms and sizes and, of course, in different shades of professionalism. But the one thing they share is that they all have a bearing — greater in some cases, lesser in others — on the fortunes of enterprising green businesses. The network supplies a simultaneous source of credibility, endorsement, and echo effect, which is a critical aspect of viral marketing.

For each of the Web sites representing these groups, there are one, or ten, or hundreds of people contributing. On the other side of the screen, there are hundreds, thousands, even tens of thousands of people viewing the information. It's a huge network when you include everyone contributing and everyone viewing, but we will never know how huge. It will be forever expanding and, therefore, unquantifiable.

Despite the fuzzy nature of the beast, I realized that this vast network is connected. People know one another. They share information. The longer they've been there, the more organizations and people they are interconnected with. They form alliances and cross-discipline exchanges. The leaders in each of these nodes in the network know many of the others, either virtually or in person. On this point, the network is not limited by the Internet but facilitated by it. The Internet provides convenient glue, but the contents spill out into the real world. Members of the community show up at the same conferences and trade shows. They collaborate on presentations and research. They weigh in on one another's concerns, and they offer commentary on their thoughts and musings in a kind of ad hoc peer review process. They are called on to band together on certain issues. And . . . they have the power to make or break new green products by virtue of their collective oversight. In a sense, they act as a kind of *Consumer Reports* or *Good Housekeeping*, offering a critical review process for new green products and technologies. Techies would describe it as a gateway process.

The Gort Cloud has enormous power.

Take the Swiffer disposable mop that was promoted by its designer as a green product in 2007 chiefly because it doesn't require soap and water.[1] The green network immediately went to work and lynched it for greenwashing. People simply weren't buying the trade-off between less water use and more landfill waste. Whether or not the Swiffer is, in fact, a green product has been the subject of much debate. Both TreeHugger.com and Inhabitat.com, two popular green trendspotters, investigated the product claims, and their investigations were reprinted in the mainstream media, including *BusinessWeek*. The designers of the Swiffer defended themselves,[2] but damage was done. Swiffer became the poster child for greenwashing. Procter & Gamble, the maker, was stung.

Nestlé, too, hit a bump in the road when attempting to jump on the green bandwagon. The owner of several major bottled water brands, Nestlé rolled out a "new eco-shaped" bottle that uses 30 percent less plastic; the firm touted its newly packaged bottled water as eco-friendly. Green bloggers around the country accused Nestlé of putting lipstick on a pig. Instead of placating environmentally concerned consumers, the company actually drew more attention to the waste built into bottled water, a product easily replaced with plain old tap water.[3] In an effort to avoid similar criticism, Fiji Water, which ships its product from the South Pacific, launched a major PR campaign in 2008 touting its carbon measurement and offset program.[4] And with this, I cannot help invoking the cliché, "Carrying coals to Newcastle?"

BP has also felt the sting of this green network. SourceWatch.org, PRWatch.org, CorpWatch.org, USPIRG, and others have chided BP for its claims of environmental stewardship. When the company once named British Petroleum changed its tagline to "Beyond Petroleum," watchdog groups posted negative story after negative story on the Internet. Headlines read, BP'S $200 MILLION GREENWASHING CAMPAIGN: BEYOND PETROLEUM OR BEYOND PREPOSTEROUS? and GREEN WORDS, DIRTY DEEDS. Much later, OilWatchdog.org busted BP for quietly toning down its green rhetoric as it invested in Canada's highly controversial tar sands extraction. The green network is full of watchful eyeballs and poison pens.

After these episodes and a few others, very few of us in the brand, marketing, advertising, and public relations world were unaware of the negative effects of fudging environmental credentials. The network had spoken, and there were consequences.

The anatomy of a network.

So I began to play in the network myself. I started categorizing the various groups by type of organization and by mission. I began to introduce myself to some of the key authors, and we began a dialogue. I participated with others via membership, contributions, or literary exchanges. Some of the green news sites published my articles, and I made a point of reading their postings regularly. I bookmarked them, downloaded them, tracked them. Like a teenager trapped in Facebook or Dungeons & Dragons, I've become glued to this network with thousands of friends and colleagues who share similar ideals. When I see a promising organization emerge, like the EcoMom Alliance, I make virtual introductions to other individuals in the network. "Kimberly, you might like to meet Blake Mycoskie from TOMS Shoes. For every shoe bought, he gives one to needy kids in South America." "Blake, this is Kimberly Pinkson of the EcoMom Alliance. She's connecting eco-conscious mothers all over the globe. You may have common interests." A friend teased me for running a dating service. Well, maybe — in the sense of creating business relationships.

I began to think of this particular green network as something tangible, with a mission and with a collective membership of like-minded people. It wasn't a single community. It wasn't a movement. It defied easy definition. And in my opinion it needed its own name, so I called it the Gort Cloud.

The inspiration for that moniker lies in the Oort cloud, named after the astronomer Jan Hendrick Oort, who guessed at its existence. The Oort cloud is a vast field of stellar debris that orbits the solar system. It is a thousand times farther out from the sun than Pluto and mostly made up of comet nuclei, so, obviously, we can't see the Oort cloud. We can only detect it electronically and view its effects, mostly in the form of the occasional comet it tosses back into our neighborhood. The mass of the Oort cloud is huge, greater than the mass of the earth, but it's invisible to us. Totally invisible. This seems to perfectly describe the Gort Cloud, a vast green network made up of untidy bits that is most easily detected through electronic means and that has a huge effect on the evolution of green business. Thus, a term was coined.

Now, to be clear, none of my business subjects has thought of this green network quite the way I have, but most have intuitively felt its existence and interacted with it. They have all been unwitting players in the Gort Cloud — this invisible network that connects thousands of environmentally aware people. In building their companies and developing their products, the Gort Cloud has played a role. For Spencer Brown at Earth Friendly Moving, it has been trendspotters and green news channels that have spread the word about his eco-friendly alternative to the cardboard moving box.

Gary Hirshberg of Stonyfield Farm has used dialogue with the organic blogosphere to help explain the complicated trade-offs in sourcing organic milk, the chief ingredient in his yogurt. Both Portfolio 21 and Southwest Windpower have hired egg, a Seattle-based brand communications company, to handle their communications. Egg, in turn, targets participants in the Gort Cloud to deliver its clients' messages, although it would deny knowing of a Gort Cloud by name — until I got the firm involved in this book, of course. Egg, by the way, is one of the pioneers in providing communications services to sustainable brands. The company itself has a large perch on a specific node in the Gort Cloud.

One of the most adept Gort Cloud navigators among my subjects must be Jeffrey Hollender, founder and CEO of Seventh Generation. He is profoundly aware of the players in this universe and regularly reaches out to them. The scope of his outreach touches Native American advocates, forestry and chemical industry watchdogs, various players in the health food and green grocery industry, and many others. Nearly as active but newer at the game is Tom Szaky of TerraCycle, who spends nary a dime on advertising, instead relying on an in-house PR team to mine channels within conventional media and the Gort Cloud, where he is rewarded with endless newsbytes.

In the automotive arena, I chose to profile Tesla Motors and a plug-in hybrid advocacy group called CalCars.org. Felix Kramer's advocacy group divides its time between outreach to the real world and collaboration within the virtual world of the Gort Cloud. Tesla Motors has done a fantastic job of conventional PR, but for every print write-up, there are countless mentions on industry blogs and among automotive trendspotters that are also aspects of the Gort Cloud.

I'll spare you a synopsis for every one of my subjects, but even the venerable Dr. Bronner, the magic soap maker who caught the train to sustainability in the 1940s, has unwittingly made use of the Gort Cloud in surprising ways. The backpacking community that often turns its passion for the outdoors into environmental action has long used Dr. Bronner's as toothpaste, deodorant, insect repellent, body wash, and nonpolluting cookware soap. As modern outdoors lovers now use the Internet to search and share, praise for this product continues to echo around the Gort Cloud.

As far as business is concerned, the Gort Cloud is like a versatile multitool. On the one hand, it is an enforcer of credibility standards. Individual green businesses may argue about how extreme or nitpicking that oversight should be, but I think all would agree that the Gort Cloud functions as a watchdog against unwarranted claims or greenwashing. On the other hand, the Gort Cloud can be a partner. It can provide technical information and insights into consumer preferences; it can link manufacturers with respected distributors and retail partners; and it can help get the word out to a highly focused audience and the influencers within that audience.

As you read the case studies in this book, you'll see just how seriously these businesses factor the Gort Cloud into their green business strategy.

The Rise of the Ecopreneur

Education is the path from cocky ignorance to miserable uncertainty.
— *Mark Twain*

The world has known many pioneers — people with extraordinary vision who have addressed social imperatives with intuition, imagination, scientific breakthroughs, technological inventions, product innovations, and plain old business savvy. They were and are revolutionaries of the business sort.

Abraham Darby is a good example. He's credited with starting the Industrial Revolution in 1709. Darby was the enterprising Quaker who figured out how to smelt iron with coke instead of the more costly charcoal. Working in a small town on the River Severn in central England, Darby used his cheap iron, instead of brass, to cast inexpensive cooking pots for the poor. Although it would be a couple hundred years before brands like Cuisinart and Magic Chef would become well known, Darby's pots were harbingers of the modern, mass-produced consumer goods we find in a Target store today. Under the direction of his son and, later, his grandson, Darby's Coalbrookdale works produced a number of world firsts, including cast-iron rails, iron wheels, steam cylinders, steam locomotives, iron boats, and, most famously, the first iron bridge. Over time, the Severn Gorge area was transformed into a hive of foundries, kilns, and factories producing the goods, and the pollution, that the modern era is famous for.

The Industrial Revolution marked a turning point in human social history, like the invention of farming or the rise of the city-state. It unleashed a torrent of inventions and technologies that increased labor efficiency, reduced product costs, improved transportation, increased international trade, and ultimately led to the primacy of the modern corporation — and all without central direction or government control. There was no conductor leading this band of innovators. It just took off on its own.

Unfortunately, the Industrial Revolution had a price.

Mass production demanded a steady flow of raw materials that soon began to outstrip the earth's ability to replace them. Processing these raw materials often required brute-force processes that taxed natural systems and produced toxic wastes that no one bothered to deal with properly. Industrialism also demanded cheap fuel, mostly in the form of wood, coal, and petroleum. The by-products of burning these fuels are soot and greenhouse gases. When the climate-change denial industry, which was financed and then abandoned by the likes of ExxonMobil, attacks Al Gore's inconvenient truths, it forgets that industrialization has also resulted in the loss of natural habitats and fisheries; an increase in extinctions; industrial and agricultural substance poisoning; a popu-lation explosion; social injustice; ozone depletion; urban sprawl; defor-estation; the draining of natural aquifers; the introduction of invasive species, like kudzu, Africanized honeybees, and zebra mussels; the loss of indigenous culture; obesity and related illnesses; regional wars for limited natural resources; toxic dumps; increased incidence of asthma and other autoimmune diseases; cancer; increased risk of radiation exposure; sewage spills; smog; red tides; land, space, and ocean litter-ing; contaminated runoff and oil spills; and global pandemics, including AIDS and influenza. Clearly these are problems with far greater propor-tions than just global warming, and they are not going to be solved by recycling soda bottles. It will take a lot of people, especially business-people, making incremental changes on their own without the direc-tion of central authorities – just as the Industrial Revolution was set in motion without central direction.

While the First World's standard of living and personal longevity are certainly better than in Darby's time, the earth has paid a heavy price for the miracle of modern consumerism. We are paying the piper for the gift of prosperity. From the mercury poisoning at Minamata Bay in Japan to the Superfund sites in America to the perpetual smog over Beijing, we have managed to foul our own homes in the name of progress. Even the Inuit people of northern Canada and Greenland are not immune, as industrial contamination has risen to health-threatening levels in Arctic fish and mammals. Tony Soprano put it rather bluntly: "You don't shit where you eat."

Luckily and perhaps not too late, we who are old enough have also witnessed two other revolutions: the technology revolution, sometimes referred to as the third Industrial Revolution, and the digital communications revolution, which has produced the Internet, with immediate mass dissemination of raw and unfiltered information. It's this flood of information that has led to a worldwide recognition that something must be done if we are to sustain and spread the quality of life many of us enjoy today. As in Darby's time, a few enterprising folks see opportunity in a different kind of future.

The people responsible for transforming the theory of sustainability into the practice of sustainable business and, then, into viable and desired brands are the ecopreneurs I will profile in this book. Of course, there are many, many more than I had the time or the space to profile properly. Nevertheless, the total list of American sustainable business pioneers is still quite small. It's a small community of like-minded entrepreneurs who generally know one another and continually run into one another at conferences and on speaking tours. And like Darby's village in Shropshire, England, the ecopreneurs in America are found concentrating in places like Burlington, Vermont, and Portland, Oregon, and San Francisco. From these and other bases, they are diligently building green brands.

Green Branding 101.

Each of the businesses profiled in this book has built its brand and designed a marketing program around commonly accepted principles. I'll refer often to these principles. For those who may be unfamiliar with brand and marketing terminology, I've included this basic introduction to brand-building theory.

Definition + Purpose + Advantages + Audience + Personality = Brand Position

These are the components that describe a brand and differentiate it from competitors. Collectively, this is called a **brand position**. It can be thought of as the summation of a brand strategy — the plan a company uses to position itself against other products and services. Brand positions can change or evolve over time, just as market situations do.

The **definition** defines a product or service category, such as energy, transportation, or home appliances. These definitions can get pretty narrow — say, the manufacturing specialty for space shuttle O-rings used on external fuel tanks. In cases like this, a company might be in a class by itself. The definition carves out a marketplace and identifies both customers and competitors. The definition also defines suppliers, the pool of qualified employees, support specialists, the distribution channels, and appropriate communications media. It's the playground a business chooses to play in.

The **purpose** describes a need and how a business serves the need by providing a product or service. Some brand consultants combine *definition* and *purpose*, as they are closely related, but there is a difference in my mind. The purpose tends to define a company's mission: to serve humanity with better medicine or to provide the most luxurious driving experience, for example. For one of my clients in Japan, the mission was to provide the highest-quality basic sportswear at the lowest price. The company is called UNIQLO, and it has built a successful international brand around that simple idea.

Advantages are not as obvious as you would think. A company may value certain "advantages" very highly only to discover that its customers value other things. For instance, an automaker may be very proud of its air-conditioning, but car buyers expect air-conditioning. For a car buyer, air-conditioning is a table stake. It's what is required to simply get in the game. A modern car must have AC. In this sense, advantages are in the eye of the beholder. *Drivers of preference* are a way to sort out the meaningful advantages from the not so meaningful. Drivers of preference define the things that will cause a particular customer to pick one product over another, and those things can be bona fide advantages or simply a perception that was skillfully conjured up by a marketer or advertising agency. So there are tangible drivers of preference, like bigger, faster, better, cheaper, and there are intangible ones, like "It looks cool, so I want it."

This leads to the notion of benefits versus attributes. We've all heard the saying, *Sell the sizzle, not the steak.* In other words, it is more effective to describe an advantage in terms of the benefit the customer will enjoy. The makers of Tide can describe its eco-friendly package as concentrated, an attribute, or as a benefit — weighs less, cleans more, costs less, better for the environment. Interestingly, Landor Associates, the big branding firm based in San Francisco, conducted research in 2006 suggesting that at least 58 percent of people did "not care about environmentally friendly practices, including recycling, corporate social responsibility, or natural and/or organic ingredients."[1] For these people, green was not a driver of preference. But there's a flip side to this. Forty-two percent apparently did care, and that's a sizable market — especially if those customers are early adopters who fuel trends.

But what a company does, the market it competes in, the things it makes, and its product advantages represent only one side of the equation. On the other side is a pairing with customers who want these things. Designing for the desires of the CEO is rarely successful. A company must understand who the stakeholders are and what they want. This helps define the **audience**, and there can be multiple audiences, each with a different set of wants and needs. They are not necessarily just customers. Audiences can also be the critical press, resellers, investors, employees, or anyone with a stake in the success of the brand. Of particular interest to marketers are the influencers within these audiences — the people whose choices influence others. Targeting influencers among customers is the poor person's alternative to mass marketing. It can also be the smart person's alternative, because it takes relatively fewer dollars to reach a focused group with a highly focused message. This precisely describes the importance of the Gort Cloud. All those eyeballs following product stories in the Gort Cloud belong to a green brand's most cherished target customers — what the *New York Times* has called Magic People, the early adopters and trend-spreaders.[2]

Take that 2006 Landor study mentioned before. It was updated a year later, and things had definitely changed.

> The results of the 2007 ImagePower® Green Brands Survey, conducted by WPP's Landor Associates, Penn, Schoen & Berland (PSB) Associates and Cohn & Wolfe (C&W) ... indicate a shift in the U.S.'s collective consciousness — green is no longer an issue marginalized to fanatical environmentalists; nearly all Americans display green attitudes and behaviors versus a year ago. The survey was conducted by PSB's Internet Surveys Groups (ISG) and represents a sample of the American and British populations for their respective perceptions of green and its effect on branding and marketing. The survey also found that 40% of the U.S. population feels that the leading issue driving concern

around the environment is global warming, while 20% blame themselves for the state of the environment.

A similar survey conducted in 2006 indicated that most U.S. consumers were unfamiliar with the concept of green and how their actions affected the environment. The results of the 2007 survey, however, not only show how Americans' attitudes have changed, but also bring to the forefront business imperatives for corporations currently in the green space, or considering entry. No longer can corporations just say they offer fuel-efficient vehicles, organic foods or energy-efficient products — it is now a cost of entry in many industries and corporations need to begin thinking ahead.[3]

There is an important lesson here. First-to-market brands that designed for and marketed to the early adopters in 2006 reaped benefits only a year later in 2007 as awareness spread.

Companies and/or the things they make are often described in anthropomorphic terms — *reliable, trustworthy, sexy*. Remember when it was all the rage to call software robust? This is the process of imbuing a brand with **personality**. One competitor may describe itself as having stamina while another calls itself versatile. Another form of personality description is mimicry. A smaller competitor may describe itself as "just like the bigger, better-known brand" — but cheaper. Personality can bring a brand or company to life in the hope that we will like it — the way we admire certain people. But there also people we don't like. That's why greenwashing is so bad. It implies that the brand is an exaggerator at best, a liar at worse.

The total of these attributes — description, purpose, advantages, audience, personality — suggests a **brand position**, and there can be many different and possibly equally effective positions, but smart companies usually elect to pursue one position strategy at a time. Sometimes the brand position is articulated as a tagline. Wal-Mart changed its tagline after nineteen years to "Save money. Live better." Admittedly a bit boring, but the change came with a change in brand strategy that emphasized not just "Always low prices" but also the promise of an improved lifestyle — and this leads to yet another aspect of brand positioning.

A company's brand position can also be thought of as a promise. It's the promise inherent to the brand that certain things will be delivered as claimed, which is why credibility is so crucial to brand trust and why the Gort Cloud can be so important to green brands trying to win that trust. Stakeholders must reasonably believe the claims. So, in a sense, it is customers, not managers, who give a company "permission" to make certain claims. Take that earlier example of BP. Despite a massive advertising campaign, British Petroleum has had a very hard time convincing the core greenies that it's "beyond petroleum." The less informed public might buy the brand promise, but BP hasn't convinced the growing number of green-aware consumers — at least not yet.

So how might this brand positioning formula apply to a company seeking a green advantage? Here is a hypothetical example.

Brand positioning for a hypothetical green company.

An apple is an apple is an apple, unless, of course, it is a certified organic apple, grown locally without pesticides and thus not harmful to the people who work in the orchard or who consume the apple. Perhaps the grower also uses biodiesel to fuel her trucks and pays a fair wage to her immigrant workers. Perhaps she has a water collection facility and uses solar power to take her operation off-grid for most of the year. And perhaps she sells only at the local farmers' market so she can market her apples near their peak ripeness. These would be the advantages or benefits of buying this apple over a conventionally grown and possibly imported apple sold at a large supermarket chain.

So who is the target customer for these special apples? Well, maybe not Landor's 58 percent. They would be happy with the conventionally grown apple. The price for the conventional apple would be lower and the grocery store closer. But maybe 2 or 3 percent of an urban population would be interested and go out of their way to buy fresh, organic, locally grown produce at the farmers' market on Sunday morning. Because price can be an upward limiter on desirability, the grower has cut out the middlemen in an effort to contain costs and lower price. This special apple may, in fact, be cheaper than the conventional one sold at the big-box grocery store — and it may taste better without having to be put in a brown paper sack to ripen. For this target customer, it is a win-win situation. Now comes the tough part. There are several vendors at the farmers' market selling similar apples, all within sight of one another. All are selling the same quality, at more or less the same price, and each comes from a certified organic grower. The definition, purpose, and advantages may all be the same. This is where personality comes into play. Brand personality can also be referred to as brand culture. Brand personality defines the emotional mission that is driving a brand. When all things are equal, the personality of a brand can make all the difference, especially to certain segments within the target audience.

Our make-believe apple grower is the head of her farming clan. Her family has owned its farm for five generations. Her husband died several years ago from cancer associated with exposure to pesticides and other farming risks. The family's business was also hard hit by the Alar scare of 1989, when *60 Minutes* broadcast a faulty Environmental Protection Agency report that the ripening spray was a health risk. Sales plummeted 50 percent. She was left with four boys to raise on her own and the threat of losing her farm to an aggressive corporate farming operation that was eyeing vulnerable properties in her county. She read up on organics, including all the associated issues: genetically engineered food, irradiation, wax coatings, unfair imports. She saw an opportunity to break the economic crunch of higher production costs and the shrinking margins offered by the wholesalers and apple-processing companies. It took years to rid her farm of pesticide residue and learn how to deal with orchard pests without resorting to harmful and expensive sprays. This is a motivated seller with a mission to provide for her family and protect her way of life.

She markets her apples as Jean & Sons Family Organics. She appears regularly on Evan Kleiman's *Good Food* show on National Public Radio. She's a member of the Organic Consumers Association, which encourages organic, permaculture, and biodynamic farming techniques and supports local farmers throughout the country in addition to campaigns for health, justice, and sustainability. Her focus is not just on organics. She is intensely concerned with soil quality, erosion control, farm pollution, and energy efficiency. She's even taken steps to encourage biodiversity and reduce the problems associated with monoculture by mixing trees other than apple trees and other plants into her orchard. She's built a green brand.

Her sons work the farm and help her sell at the market. She's published a cookbook on how to use apples to sweeten stews or add moisture to baked goods, and how apple cores make excellent mulching material. Jean has built a green enterprise with a credible brand position that helps describe things that are otherwise invisible to the customer. In this case, one apple may appear as good as another, unless, of course, it comes from Jean's farm.

A resonant brand position is that essential ingredient that makes a brand real and tangible not only for customers but also for employees, partners, investors, the media, and peers. It's the underlying story that describes the focus and the commitment behind an ordinary apple or a ream of recycled copy paper or an energy-efficient lightbulb.

Visualizing a Network of Shared Interests

A community is like a ship; everyone ought to
be prepared to take the helm.
—*Henrik Ibsen*

The community of environmentally concerned people is vast; and, while there is no formal organization, I have found it convenient to think of the Gort Cloud in terms of clusters of common interests or common functions. In the following section, I'll take some time to describe some of these clusters and introduce you to a few of the people behind them, but keep in mind that a total accounting of relevant sites and individuals is unknowable. As former secretary of defense Donald Rumsfeld said, ". . . there are known knowns; there are things we know we know. We also know there are known unknowns; that is to say we know there are some things we do not know." The Gort Cloud is a known unknown.

The earliest warnings and calls for action came from people like Robert Thomas Mathus (1766–1834), Ralph Waldo Emerson (1803–1882), Henry David Thoreau (1817–1862), John Muir (1838–1914), Lucy Braun (1889–1971), Rachel Carson (1907–1964), and Jacques Cousteau (1910–1997). Add to this the literature of the Romantic Age, ushered into England by poets William Wordsworth and Samuel Taylor Coleridge in 1798. Their work delivered a message of reconciliation between man and nature — ideas that sharply contrasted with the Enlightenment that placed man above nature — and were delivered through the mass medium of the time, which was English poetry. Similar themes can be found in Chinese and Arabic poetry and in Japanese haiku, but one of the most famous of these allegories concerns the abuse and subsequent redemption of a man who betrays a gift of nature. That story is Coleridge's "The Rime of the Ancient Mariner."

These writers, who raised awareness of nature and the need to preserve it, laid the groundwork for the modern environmental movement, but they are not part of the Gort Cloud because, well, they're all dead. They don't provide active support to modern green brands, but they did inspire organizations that do, like Greenpeace, the Natural Resources Defense Council, the Environmental Defense Fund, Earth First!, the Nature Conservancy, the World Wildlife Fund, the Sierra Club . . . even the Earth Liberation Front.

These were joined (sometimes reluctantly) by government agencies, most particularly the EPA, the Food and Drug Administration, and the US Department of Agriculture's National Organic Program, among others. Their efforts have been bolstered by certifying organizations like the US Green Building Council's LEED program, the Forest Stewardship Council, EPEAT (Electronic Product Environmental Assessment Tool), the Rainforest Alliance, Green Seal, Fair Trade, California Certified Organic Farmers, and many others. Working with these groups are countless academic, scientific, and social action groups that provide the research and technical knowledge to make sustainable programs effective. In more recent years, the chorus of concern has been channeled into new business and economic models championed by green business leaders, sustainability experts, and economists. At the grassroots level, we have bloggers and social movements that promote sustainable lifestyles. Large corporations have also heeded the call. The US Climate Action Partnership is a relatively new group made up of some enlightened and perhaps self-serving Fortune 500 companies that are lobbying the US government for remedial action. We even have large and successful conventions where sustainable businesses meet and exhibit their wares. All of these organizations represent aspects of the Gort Cloud, and while most of them are not there to serve business, they do interact and collectively support green business initiatives.

A partial outline of the Gort Cloud might look something like the listing on page 22.

Of course, this list is just that — a list. You must then imagine the organizations and Web sites that occupy these categories. I've attempted to make this more clear with the chart mapping the Gort Cloud, reproduced on the endpapers of this book. Nevertheless, the real force in the Gort Cloud is people, and it is surprising how small this leadership community still is. Most of the driving personalities behind the green network are known to the others. Following are a few profiles of some of these green organizations and their leaders.

Some Components within the Gort Cloud

Providers
Green Business & Manufacturing
Retail
e-Commerce Sites
Brick-and-Mortar Stores
Eco-Travel
Environmental Quality Consultants
Carbon Offset Programs
Ecosystem Services

Provider Support
Designers & Inventors
Think Tanks & R&D
Foundations & Grant Makers
Green Operations Advisors
Supply Chain Audit & Integrity
Legal & Compliance
Financial & Investing
Employee Health & Relations
Product & Materials Testing
Facility Design
Brand & Marketing Consultants
Printing, Packaging, POS
Distribution Systems
Training & Education

Rule Makers & Watchdogs
Government Agencies
NGOs
Certifying Organizations
Investigative Reporting
Whistleblowers

Advocacy Groups
Green Business Alliances
Issue Advocates
Citizen and Community Action Groups
Government Policy

Special-Interest Authorities
Climate Change
Energy
Transportation
Air Quality
Water & Aquifers
Waste Management, Recycling, Reuse
Oceans & Fisheries
Wildlife & Ecosystems
Food & Agriculture
Extraction Industries
Health & Medicine
Family & Children's Welfare
Green Building
Sustainable Fashion
Personal Care & Household Products
Fair Trade

Eco-Tech
Eco-Capitalism & Sustainable Economics

Information Disseminators
Trendspotters
Green News Organizations
Educators & Institutions
Authors & Thinkers
White Papers & Exposés
Documentary Producers
Bloggers & Podcasters
Green Media
Publications
Book Publishers
Radio
Television
Public Relations
Outdoor Advertising
In Store
Alternative Media
Banners & Click-Thrus
Web 2.0
Green Guides
Databases & Exchanges

Green Search Engines

Social Networks
Professional Networking
Common Interests
Membership Clubs

Lifestyle Movements

Reuse, Recycle
Safe Disposal
Resell/Donate

In-Person Exchange
Conferences & Seminars
Trade Shows
Events & Festivals
Exhibits & Demonstrations

Competitions

Campaigns and Fundraisers

Education & Career
Green Technology
Green MBA & Law
Research
Parenting & Child Education
Citizen Action Workshops
Job Boards and Headhunters

The Trendspotters

When I lay out the Gort Cloud in a schematic, I view it as a network of synapses — little nodes of processing energy interconnected to all the others either directly or indirectly. This is especially true of the trend-spotters who are the ever-watchful, all-seeing, all-knowing eyeballs that thrive on a stream of tips sent in by a network of volunteer tipsters. The trendspotters are very important to green businesses because they have the ability to announce — and therefore promote — new products and services to primary audiences and key influencers, including other, more conventional media. Like drummers in the forest, their messages are picked up and repeated far and wide.

Three of my favorites are TreeHugger, Inhabitat, and Springwise, but there are many more. TreeHugger has earned boasting rights as the deepest and most venerable of the bunch. Founder Graham Hill and his team deliver all kinds of environmental information through a variety of channels, including their Web site, a blog, newsletters, forums, podcasts, video segments, and their own radio show. TreeHugger was bought in 2007 by Discovery Communications, parent company of the Discovery Channel, the Science Channel, Animal Planet, and other cable properties, and contributes to Discovery's Planet Green channel. The most famous eco-journalist to emerge from TreeHugger is Simran Sethi, an Indian American woman who has co-created and hosted video and audio content for TreeHugger, NPR, and the Sundance Channel. She is a prolific presenter and has collaborated with Al Gore on seminars and podcasts. Simran is now a highly visible television eco-anchor — perhaps even the most visible.

Inhabitat.com has a sweet spot for design and architecture. Its mission is "tracking the innovations in technology, practices and materials that are pushing . . . design toward a smarter and more sustainable future." The site was founded and is led by Jill Fehrenbacher, a designer, journalist, and Columbia grad student. Inhabitat has a wide following and is itself part of a mini network of spotter sites that share information. It is often the first to report on innovative designs and design ideas. The echo effect from Inhabitat is substantial.

Of particular interest to marketers is the fact that sites like Inhabitat will accept appropriate banner ads. To make the process of buying ads easier, Largetail — a network of like-minded online publishers — offers advertisers the chance to buy promotion packages that will get their ad on a number of trendspotting sites, including Cool Hunting, Thehappycorp, Refinery 29, Format, LVHRD, Beautiful Decay, PSFK, JC Report, Lost At E Minor, V Magazine, Turntable Lab, the Winger, and Inhabitat. Most of these sites are not necessarily focused on green issues, so they may fall outside the Gort Cloud, but the idea of bundled marketing could be a harbinger for other sites in the green community.

Starting in 2002 and headquartered in Amsterdam, Springwise .com tracks worldwide business ideas and posts the best to its site. Springwise boasts a network of more than eight thousand spotters. Not all ideas are eco-friendly, but there is an obvious bias toward those that are. The editor is Liesbeth den Toom, who has a background in law. A posting on Springwise, Inhabitat, TreeHugger, or other trendspotting sites is much noticed and virally exchanged. All three use advanced Internet technology, such as RSS feeds and YouTube-style videos, and all three derive a portion of income from banners and clickable ad links.

Green Business News

Performing roles similar to trendspotters but with a more rigorous journalism style are the online green business news organizations, which include GreenBiz.com, EnvironmentalLeader.com, and SustainableBusiness.com, among others. These outlets tend to focus exclusively on green business news, while other popular green news sites like the Environmental News Network (ENN.com) and TreeHugger deliver content that is broader and more popularly based.

GreenBiz.com is part of a family of sites held under the parent Greener World Media, Inc. The mission of founders Joel Makower and Pete May is "to provide clear, concise, accurate, and balanced information, resources, and learning opportunities to help companies of all sizes and sectors integrate environmental responsibility into their operations in a manner that supports profitable business practices." That's a mouthful, but the goal is to furnish the information business leaders need to make the leap to an Age of Sustainability. Greener World Media has used its various sites to align with other important organizations in the Gort Cloud. ClimateBiz.com works in partnership with Business for Social Responsibility. GreenerBuildings.com works in partnership with the US Green Building Council, the certifying agency for LEED accreditation. GreenBiz extends its reach through electronic newsletters and electronic feeds known as Green Buzz. Joel Makower is a prolific essayist and the editor of the *State of Green Business* annual report. He is also a consultant with GreenOrder, a business sustainability adviser. Pete May and Joel Makower have built a multifaceted news organization that delivers focused information to industry segments.

It's hard to describe any green business news organization as old, but ENN is one of the oldest, having been around for about fifteen years. CEO Lincoln Norton's mission has been to edit the flood of green business news down to the most relevant and bite-sized pieces for executive consumption. Environmental Leader occupies a similar niche and is led by publisher and managing editor Paul Nastu. SustainableBusiness.com is headed by Rona Fried and offers focused information for investors and a green job board in addition to supplying a stream of green business news.

Trendspotters and green business news outlets are primary vectors for raising awareness of new green products and services, but along with that potential awareness comes scrutiny. These sites have reputations to protect.

Green Search Engines

Green search engines are one of the newest Internet phenomena. Some donate a portion of revenue to green causes, while others will tip a search in favor of qualified green businesses and suppliers. EcoSearch, GoodSearch, GoodTree, Flock Eco-Edition, Green Maven, Green Planet Search, and EcoSeek are just few.[1] Green search engines may turn out to be the glue that binds the Gort Cloud together in the future.

Social Networks

The majority of organizations in the Gort Cloud and particularly those with Internet sites have a component of social networking or viewer outreach built into them, but there are some sites that stress the social networking component and actively strive to build communities. Change.org, 2people.org, GUSSE, Care2.com's Healthy & Green Living section, GreenOptions.com, and the Nature Conservancy's Groupspace are just a few examples. DoTheRightThing.com, Playgreen.org, Hugg .com, and Fivelimes.com may fall into this category, as they enable user postings in a Digg- or Wikipedia-style format. Each operates slightly differently, and each may contain aspects of a news outlet, a trendspotter, and a green guide. One thing they share is the ability for visitors to interact with the site and become involved with other members in a virtual community.

Acccording to David Wigder of Marketing Green, "For green marketers, social networks provide a compelling channel to communicate with consumers that have an affinity for green or are at least open-minded enough to listen."[2] Marketing Green has identified six different types of social networks: interaction, utility, commitment, shopping, engagement, and activism. As you can guess, each type creates community around a different need.

The EcoMom Alliance is a particularly good example of a true social network because it clearly defines a community with a common interest, bringing mothers together around environmental health and safety issues. The site acts as a catalyst for moms to form local, issue-oriented groups and then meet regularly in their neighborhoods. Founder Kimberly Danek Pinkson helps women harness the power of their purse to affect business decisions. The potential power of this young organization to influence green business decisions was recognized in a front-page *New York Times* article in early 2008.

Online Magazines

Related to social networks, trendspotters, and news outlets are sites I would compare more closely to online magazines. These sites perform many of the same functions, but the difference is in their presentation style, which is similar to that of a magazine with features and stories. A few examples are Lime.com, GOODMagazine.com, and RiverWired. com. Many print magazines also maintain an online presence with a strong green bias, including *National Geographic's Green Guide*, *Mother Jones*, *Plenty*, *Utne Reader*, *Science Magazine*, *HG*, *Real Simple*, *The Ecologist*, and *E Magazine*. Add to this list the green book publishing industry that includes my publisher, Chelsea Green Publishing Company. Online or in print, the green publishing industry is the primary distributor of new ideas and insights on the coming Age of Sustainability.

Lifestyle Movements

Another category within the Gort Cloud describes organizations that define and promote an aspect of sustainable living as a movement. Four particularly good examples are Lifestyles of Health and Sustainability, better known as LOHAS; Worldchanging.com; the Slow Food movement; and (Still) Made Here.

LOHAS is one of the pioneering organizations with regard to consumer awareness. The group describes itself as "a market segment focused on health and fitness, the environment, personal development, sustainable living, and social justice." Founded in 2000, LOHAS was created by lifestyle products company Gaiam and the Natural Marketing Institute (NMI) as a way to describe a consumer segment dominated by "cultural creatives." LOHAS produces trade shows, conferences, a journal, a news site, and a list of approved partners in its business directory that confers credibility on those businesses and products. Product developers and marketers have made ample use of the term in defining a customer base that the NMI estimates at "19 percent of adults in the U.S., or 41 million people," but it has grown into something more than a convenient term for demographers. LOHAS has turned into the definition of a social movement, that is directly responsible for consumer product resources such as Whole Foods. LOHAS has become a particularly powerful movement in Japan, where it was introduced by Kazumi Oguro and became a household word to describe anything natural and healthy.

Worldchanging is a kind of *Whole Earth Catalog* for the twenty-first century. Executive editor and cofounder Alex Steffen's mission was driven by the awareness of climate change issues made famous by Al Gore's *An Inconvenient Truth* and the desire to give people access to actionable resources and knowledge. As stated in its manifesto, "The tools, models and ideas for building a better future lie all around us. Plenty of people are working on tools for change, but the fields in which they work remain unconnected. The motive, means and opportunity for profound positive change are already present. Another world is not just possible, it's here. We only need to put the pieces together" — which is what *Worldchanging* attempts to do. The current site began as an ambitious printed tome, referencing everything green. Its title is both a description of the problem and a call to action.

The Slow Food movement was launched in Italy in 1986 by Carlo Petrini, a food writer who wanted to combat fast food and the disappearance of local food traditions — and to get people back in touch with the food they eat, where it comes from, and the role food choices play on the world stage. Petrini originally organized the Slow Food movement in response to the opening of a McDonald's on the Spanish Steps in Rome, but the protest struck a chord. The movement grew within Italy and branched out into more than 122 countries around the world, becoming the first organized faction of the broader Slow movement. Preserving local, sustainable, safe, and culturally rooted food choices is at the heart of the Slow Food movement.

Related to the Slow Food movement is (Still) Made Here, a trend well described by Trendwatching.com as "the comeback of all things local, all things with a sense of place, and how they're surfacing in a world dominated by globalization."[3] A number of books have been written on the subject, including *Animal, Vegetable, Miracle* by Barbara Kingsolver, *A Year Without 'Made in China'* by Sara Bongiorni, and *The 100-Mile Diet* by Alisa Smith and James MacKinnon, with local enterprises supported by the eat.shop series of guide books. This idea goes far beyond the notion of shopping at local farmers' markets and encourages the growth of local industry and crafts — an ideal strongly supported by a group of financial institutions profiled later in this book. The brand advantage of (Still) Made Here can be substantial for greenies who are concerned for the viability of their local economies and way of life.

Authors and Thinkers

There are some really smart and peripatetic thinkers contributing to the discussion of sustainability. They include Jared Diamond, author of *Collapse* and *Guns, Germs, and Steel*; Lester Brown, who has written multiple editions of *Plan B* and is founder of both the Worldwatch Institute and the Earth Policy Institute; Paul Hawken, the cofounder of Smith & Hawken, head of the Natural Capital Institute, and author of many seminal books on eco-commerce; Amory Lovins and L. Hunter Lovins, authors and cofounders of the Rocky Mountain Institute, which promotes "efficient resource use and policy development"; Andrés R. Edwards, author of *The Sustainability Revolution*; Al Gore, about whom we need not say more; Bill McDonough and Michael Braungart, who coauthored *Cradle to Cradle*, one of the most influential books on the business community; Daniel Esty and Andrew Winston, who wrote *Green to Gold*, a book that makes a powerful financial case for going green; as well as Gary Hirshberg, Yvon Chouinard, Ray Anderson, and other business leaders who have written about their personal experiences with ecopreneuralism. There has been a lot of ink spilled on this topic — including this book. The reason I include these writers and thinkers in the Gort Cloud is because they are often credited by otherwise conservative business leaders for their personal environmental awakening. They have influenced business managers to change corporate agendas.

NGOs, Government Agencies, Certifying Organizations
As mentioned earlier, there are literally hundreds of nongovernmental organizations, federal and state agencies, and various certifying groups that directly influence green business. Whether it's through the bully pulpit, rules and regulations, or enforcement of standards, these groups shape the dialogue among green entrepreneurs. Even the Federal Trade Commission publishes a list of guidelines for marketing green products.[4] Their collective influence often comes down to basic everyday consumer choices: *Do I buy that farm-raised salmon or that certified fresh-caught halibut? Which laptop is more eco-friendly? Should I choose all-natural or certified organic? Which plastic baby bottle is safest — and while I'm on the subject, is that milk or formula safe? Is it better to buy local and conventionally grown or imported and organic? Which car has the best overall mileage?* Through scientific study, monitoring, and policy decisions, these organizations have a profound influence on what products are available and which are deemed more desirable from an environmental standpoint. They can be kingmakers.

To add weight to their work, many offer certification and/or endorsement. Their logos become much sought-after medals of credibility, like the Good Housekeeping Seal.[5] A few of the more visible marks we commonly come across are the Marine Stewardship Council, Energy Star, Green-e, the Rainforest Alliance, Dolphin Safe, the European Eco-label, the Plastic Bottle Material Code System, the USDA's National Organic Program, and the Forest Stewardship Council. In fact, there has been such a profusion of these labels that recent research suggests that confusion is settling in. GreenBiz.com has noted, "Interestingly, the Natural Marketing Institute's 2007 LOHAS Consumer Trends Database report determined that not all eco-labels have the same impact. In fact, consumers indicate that they are more likely to make eco-friendly purchase decisions if the eco-labels are also widely recognized and trusted brands in [and] of themselves. Familiar labels for programs like the EPA's Energy Star have a more significant influence on consumer behavior than others."[6] However, within the Gort Cloud where the audience is more educated on the issues, these endorsements continue to rain gold. (Detailed information on green labels is available at *Consumer Reports*: www.greenerchoices.org/eco-labels.)

Green Retailers
Without a doubt, retailers are also the kingmakers for consumer products, whether online or bricks-and-mortar, but they are especially critical for green products. All across the country, specialized green goods shops have opened. In Southern California, where I live, we have a well-known home improvement, furnishings, and gift shop called Livingreen with stores in Culver City and Santa Barbara. Ellen Strickland is the founder and co-owner and has a rich background including educational programming and exhibit design. Livingreen has a great system for comfortably introducing customers to the complicated trade-offs in choosing among green products. It's a rating system called Shades of Green that "offers customers an easier way to judge the various levels of green or sustainable elements in their product selection." Because trust is such an important part of a brand's green promise, having a trusted shop owner recommend a product is pure gold for the brand. Livingreen carries at least one of the brands covered in this book, YOLO Colorhouse.

Of course, the importance of health food stores can never be understated. Whole Foods and Wild Oats are now the dominant players, but they were preceded by countless local co-ops. These stores are largely responsible for the green consumer goods market, because they made buying green easy, convenient, and part of everyday life.

In addition to dedicated green shops is a growing list of mainstream retailers that provide specially selected products. The Home Depot is a pioneer in this category with its Eco Options product line. For earth-conscious shoppers, the Eco Options label makes it easier to shop green. TerraCycle is at least one brand covered in this book that is sold under the Eco Options banner.

In the virtual world, there are a dizzying number of eco-friendly shops and product directories: Green Home, Green People, Green Living, Buy Green, et cetera. Of course, they don't all have the word *green* in the name, but a lot do, and they tend to sell a lot of the same well-known products. A site that promises to be just a little more distinctive will be launched in late 2008 by Priscilla Woolworth, an heir to the founder of Woolworth's, one of the original department stores. Priscilla is an artist and mother with very special, very eclectic taste. Her site, PriscillaWoolworth.com, will offer basic green products for people who don't live close to a Whole Foods, as well as unique, internationally sourced, eco-friendly kitchen, garden, and gift products.

The importance of a trusted channel for retail sales adds yet another facet to the Gort Cloud's power to support green business strategies.

Think of it as a giant green Rolodex.

Of course, this is just a snapshot of the rich cast of characters that inhabit the Gort Cloud, and there are many more in so many more categories. Some of these category leaders have emerged from the business side, while many others have carved out territory in regulatory agencies, NGOs, the media, and social networks. Knowing who is most relevant to a particular green business is a key component in stakeholder outreach. These people can also be a rich source of information, technical assistance, and potential partnerships.

The realization that a large and complex green community exists should be no surprise to anyone, but knowing that it can be quantified, understood, designed for, and communicated to is the key to building a successful green brand.

Marketing Magic
Dr. Bronner's Magic Soap

THE CHALLENGE

Emanuel Bronner, a third-generation soap maker, rabbi, and eccentric spiritual guru who eschewed industrial chemicals decades ahead of his time, is the godfather of today's green brands. His all-natural line, Dr. Bronner's Magic Soaps, out of Escondido, California, was embraced by the counterculture in the 1960s and has been going strong ever since.

Now grandsons David and Michael Bronner and their uncle Ralph are charged with expanding the company's vision — and market share. How can they do this while still connecting the brand to its original iconoclastic image?

THE SOLUTION

With its roots in a nonconformist founder, Dr. Bronner's exploited a tiny niche in the counterculture and then doggedly grew it. The eccentricities of the man became the brand's compelling backstory for generations of new customers. It's a unique form of differentiation by perpetuating a kooky image in a conformist age.

Just as Dr. Bronner did, his family members travel the country to hand out samples, building one loyal customer at a time. Now that the Internet Age has arrived, they continue the tradition of personal contact through highly personal digital communications.

Dr. Bronner's has become a product icon among green-aware consumers and a mark of authenticity for retailers entering this category, who may carry some of the newer brands, like Seventh Generation or Method, but Dr. Bronner's remains a mainstay. The company's current efforts to fight for tougher organic certifying standards continue to lift its standing. This has caused distribution channels to naturally expand.

Today the brand name Dr. Bronner's Magic Soap echoes throughout the Gort Cloud — among consumer advocate groups, at government and certifying agencies, within the various sustainable lifestyle movements, and with social networks, particularly those with a large following of women who are concerned about family health.

In the spirit of the old-time traveling salesman.

Dr. Bronner's Magic Soap makes use of its very deep backstory to differentiate itself as a venerable, if unorthodox, company with a superior product that has withstood the test of time since 1858. This founder's story enshrines Dr. Emanuel Bronner, whose first act of branding was to put the *Dr.* on his name without earning a degree. In reality, he was a rabbi, a self-styled philosopher, and a third-generation master soap maker from an Orthodox Jewish family in Heilbronn, Germany, who had developed a secret soap-making process. The formula remains confidential to this day.

Emanuel, rebelling against his father, emigrated to the United States in the late 1920s. The soap factory he left behind was eventually lost in a forced sale to the Nazis, and the elder Bronner was murdered in the concentration camp at Buchenwald, with other relatives meeting a similar fate elsewhere. In the United States, Emanuel worked as a consultant to American soap companies at a time when these enterprises were beginning to convert to the synthetic formulas that make up many modern body care products. Bronner, a man concurrently behind and ahead of his time, was opposed to the use of petrochemicals, warning of their negative effect on people and the planet.

"The mantra of the day was *Better living through chemistry*," explains Emanuel's grandson Michael Bronner, who along with his older brother David runs the company today. "They were making pesticides and plastics and artificial fertilizers, and here's my grandfather saying, 'You gotta watch out for this stuff . . . you may think it's a step in the right direction, but it could come back to haunt you.' And so, in a way, he was very forward thinking. Because he appreciated time-honored formulas."

Emanuel Bronner: Spreading a message of unity, loudly.

Emanuel Bronner was on a lifelong spiritual mission (his Hebrew name means "search for truth"). He espoused the view that a prophet arrives on earth every seventy-six years, inspired by Halley's comet, to bring man back to God. These prophets, to name a few, are thought to have included Moses, Jesus, Muhammad, Hillel, Lao-tzu, and Gautama, the Buddha.

The doctor's obsessive passion was sometimes mistaken for mental illness, due in part to his tendency to rant about his opinions. "He was often yelling," says Michael Bronner.

In 1947, while giving a talk on the importance of free speech at the University of Chicago, Bronner was detained by authorities, who eventually contacted his sister, then living in Rhode Island. She agreed to commit her brother to the Illinois State Asylum in Elgin. There he underwent shock treatments, says Michael, for what they saw as his "crazy beliefs that we're all children of one divine source, and we will destroy ourselves if we don't realize this."

Bronner ultimately escaped the asylum after stealing twenty dollars out of his sister's purse when she was visiting. He headed west, thereafter referring to the mental institution as the time he spent in a "concentration camp." "I think he did have some slight schizophrenic tendencies that were exacerbated by the asylum's persecutory environment," says David.

Michael adds, "He ended up setting up shop in Pershing Square in Los Angeles, which was a hotbed of political activity at the time. He was a very passionate speaker. People would come and listen to him."

Product storytelling with a spiritual message.

As the company's Web site states, "Bronner's essential vision and philosophy were born out of the fate of his family and the Holocaust, and are emphatic that we are all children of the same divine source: People must realize that we are 'All-One!' and that the prophets and spiritual giants of the world's various faith traditions all realized and said this."

"Constructive capitalism is where you share the profit with the workers and the earth from which you made it," the site continues in its summary of Bronner's teachings. "We are all brothers and sisters, and we should take care of each other and spaceship earth!"

Following his speeches in Pershing Square, Bronner would hand out a bottle of peppermint soap made with his family's secret formula. "People would come for the soap because it was so darn good, and then leave and not always listen to him," Michael says.

It wasn't long before Dr. Bronner was putting his "Moral ABC" message on the bottle labels. "Whereas no 6 year old can get by without learning the ABC's, no 12 year old can get by without learning the moral ABC's," he was fond of saying. He didn't waste any space, squeezing in as much text as possible, eventually adding well over two thousand words per bottle. To this day, approximately thirty thousand words of the doctor's teachings are spread across the range of the company's products.

A hit with hippies.

When the late 1960s hit and a new counterculture erupted, Dr. Bronner's eco-friendly soaps and his peace-loving message found their audience.

The product "became successful for all the reasons that it wasn't successful before," says Michael Bronner. "The quality was always good, but you had this packaging that included my grandfather's spiritual message that was completely anti-corporate."

The soap "was never advertised, yet everybody seemed to know about it . . . like it arrived on the scene by magic, appearing in backpack after backpack," Michael continues. In addition, "it was a soap that could be used for anything . . . It was biodegradable, good for the earth . . . you could jump into a nearby lake and use it," which is what I used it for back then. We always had a bottle of Dr. Bronner's in our packs when we went hiking in the Pacific Northwest.

Dr. Bronner's 18-in-1 Pure-Castile Soap, as it was called back then, became a sought-after product for those in the know, spreading to hippie communes across the United States. "If you were a part of that world, you knew Dr. Bronner's soaps," David Bronner explains. "It was like a club. The fact that it wasn't advertised was a big advantage."

Whether consciously or unconsciously, Dr. Emanuel Bronner knew his nonconformist, antiestablishment target audience well enough to understand that using conventional channels to reach them would not work. That is still largely the company's understanding now.

Keeping a loyal customer base happy.

As the members of the counterculture have grown up and aged, many have stayed loyal to the Dr. Bronner's product. David and Michael Bronner, who were not alive in the 1960s, do their best to keep this market segment satisfied.

"Making our soaps is similar to making wine — you can have the same ingredients, but it'll turn out a little bit differently depending on where those ingredients come from, where they're grown, such as the peppermint coming from a different field. Especially with a natural product, there can be variation," Mike Bronner explains. "People will call us up and ask about it because they want to know what's going on. They'll say, 'What did you do with *my* soap?' So while you're always supposed to improve a product, no one lets you change it."

Because they're not of the '60s generation, the brothers are also fighting the perception that "we're trying to milk the product and the profits out of our grandfather's legacy," Michael explains. "If we raise our prices, no one understands that our materials cost twice as much as they did before — they just think that we've gone for a cheaper grade, that we're selling out in some way. I get pretty strongly worded e-mails calling us out, saying, 'You've lost a customer forever!' or 'You sold out!' exclamation point, exclamation point, exclamation point."

"All you can really do," he continues, "is write these people back and say something like, 'Our peppermint oil did change a little bit when we went organic. It now comes from India so it has a little bit more of an edge.' And sometimes they'll e-mail back and they'll say, 'Wow, keep up the good doctor's work.'"

Keeping the legacy alive.

David and Michael Bronner attempt to keep their grandfather's spiritual message alive while at the same time relegating it to the background. They work to keep the brand associated with truth and goodness and respect for the planet but attempt to stay away from promoting a religious -sounding message.

"I very much respect my grandfather for his beliefs and for the cosmic vision he had . . . his urging people to break free of whatever barriers confine them . . . to reach out to others [who] may not share our same cultural or religious perspective on things . . . to be mindful of the environment," explains Michael Bronner. "But that is not part of how we brand ourselves these days. We're a secular company. We don't get into religious discussion." The company does send out a booklet on Emanuel Bronner's philosophy, *The Moral ABC's*, to customers who ask for it.

The Bronner brothers believe they are keeping their grandfather's social mission alive, albeit in a different way than he did. "What the whole thing meant to him was very much what he put on the label," explains Michael. "He wanted those words to find their way into everybody's mind on Planet Earth so that they could interpret them and come together."

"The ideas behind that label are very sound," Michael continues. "And those ideas are ones of environmental sustainability and of social accountability and responsibility. By going organic, we've achieved the environmental aspect of my grandfather's mission. And by going Fair Trade, we're on our way to fulfilling his social mission."

Putting a little magic in the name.

In 1972, when *Esquire* did a piece on Dr. Bronner's product, it topped the article with a headline reading DR. BRONNER'S MAGIC SOAPS. The headline caught on among the target counterculture audience. Never missing an opportunity, the company adopted it first as a promotional slogan and later as the company name itself.

"Dr. Bronner's Magic Soaps is a brilliant name, and the funny thing is that we didn't even give it to ourselves," Michael Bronner explains. "It was a user-defined product name."

In Michael's analysis, "*Dr.* gives you an aura of authority. *Bronner* is a real person. *Magic* gives it some intangible aspect. It's intriguing. And then *Soap*, well, that's what it is. So every word definitely is there for a reason."

I might also add that the name invokes the counterculture, having become something of an advantage of late as so many of that movement's precepts, especially when it comes to organic products and the environment, are becoming mainstream attitudes.

Making the message personal.

In addition to including his spiritual pronouncements on the labels, "my grandfather put his home phone number on every single bottle of soap he sold," Michael Bronner continues. It reminded customers that "this is a real person, not [an imaginary] Dr Pepper, who would answer the phone if you wanted to call and talk to him" about the product or his message.

Emanuel's son Ralph Bronner, David and Michael's uncle, who lives in Wisconsin, is keeping this personal touch alive today, still intent on winning over customers one by one. "With my uncle Ralph, you can see that the apple hasn't fallen far from the tree," explains Michael. "He's the more Buddha-like representation of my grandfather. He packs his van up with soap and his guitar, and just goes around the country, stopping at health food stores, where he plays songs, talks to people, and gives hugs — everything always ends with a hug. He's just one of the most engaging people you'd ever meet."

Ralph has gone so far as to stage a one-man off-off-Broadway show in New York City in which he talks about his family and their product.

A rich and full-bodied advantage.

An important differentiator of the Dr. Bronner's product has always been its concentrated richness. Michael Bronner calls his family's soap "the best-feeling soap in the marketplace," as well as the thickest. "Nothing gets you cleaner than this stuff," he says.

Most soaps attain a 20 percent concentration, while Dr. Bronner's, through its trade-secret process, raises it to 39 percent. The Bronner product is three times as concentrated as Dial. According to Michael, "Whenever anyone calls to complain about the thickness, we say, 'Well, we can make a lot more money by selling the same soap at half the concentration.'"

The concentration is one reason why Dr. Bronner's caught on in the outdoor recreation market. That's how I personally became acquainted with the product — on camping trips with my family when I was a kid. You could take a lot of it in a small bottle, and you didn't have to worry about polluting the lake or river you were visiting. We used it for everything from brushing our teeth to cleaning burned trout off the cooking pans.

"When I go to outdoors shows to promote the soap, I say you can use it for everything you need," says Michael Bronner. "And because it's superconcentrated, it's gonna last you the entire weekend. Just leave everything else at home."

"If you look at the simplicity of the ingredients, there's nothing that's proprietary," he continues. "The materials are things you can just buy yourself, mix yourself. Granted, you'd need some equipment, but the equipment is out there. People have it."

Nevertheless, no one can seem to duplicate Dr. Bronner's soap to the concentration level that the Bronner process is able to attain.

In addition, because the Bronner name is established and has a following, the brand is able to thrive with little advertising support. "We can put all of our money into the cost of the material," Michael explains, noting that any company that wanted to compete would have to pay a premium in advertising costs in addition to buying the expensive ingredients.

Try it. You'll like it.

Perhaps because of its unrivaled effectiveness, Michael Bronner maintains that sampling has always been, and remains to this day, "by far the most important way to sell our soap." The company gives out small packets at markets such as Whole Foods. "When you try it — even if you try it without any packaging from a clear bottle — it would blow your mind. It's that good."

"Everything else that we're doing [in terms of marketing] is incidental" compared with "getting the soap in people's hands," Michael continues. "We raised the prices 20 percent when we went organic, and then raised them 10 percent to support our Fair Trade initiatives. And we didn't lose any sales. Yes, a lot of people dig the fact that it's organic, people dig the fact that we're going Fair Trade, but more than that I think it was just extremely undervalued soap. People have been willing to pay 30 percent more for it because it's that good."

Michael himself has been visiting Trader Joe's franchises to tout the product. "Nobody knew our soap at Trader Joe's. And one day I gave everybody there a sample of the two-ounce, and now 70 percent of them are buying it. That's all we needed to do — let them try it. Of course I told them the story about it and they grooved on the message, but by and large it's the quality of the soap."

This viral-marketing approach to developing business goes well with the company's sponsorship of charitable and musical events, especially when the Dr. Bronner's product can be included in gift packets and put "into the hands of potential customers," Michael says.

The company does free product distribution at organic body care trade shows as well. "The two biggest shows for us are the Natural Products Expo East and Expo West," Michael Bronner says. In addition, the company participates in expositions overseas, including the largest organic trade show in the world, held in Nuremberg, Germany. "In order to get in, you have to pass all these product specifications," Michael explains. Consequently, Dr. Bronner's is one of just two US companies allowed to participate.

By design, a slim marketing budget.

"We spend very little money on marketing. Whereas if you buy something like Estée Lauder, the majority of the money you spend is going [to the marketing budget]. With us, most of the cost of the product is actually for the materials themselves." In fact, while the company does spend some money for PR, it spends close to nothing on advertising. The entire budget for 2008 was a paltry twelve thousand dollars, used to purchase ads in trade publications.

"In 2003, when we went all organic, it was the first time we advertised to the consumer," says David Bronner. "We were telling our customer why the price was going up." The company placed ads in "every kind of New Age, natural health, vegan, vegetarian magazine you'd find in a health food store. What I realized after we did that was there was a lot of waste doing that kind of thing."

For reaching the consumer directly, Dr. Bronner's now relies on in-store shelf talkers and tag talkers. "The only promos that really make sense are these retailer POS [point-of-sale] ads," David adds.

"Our whole branding strategy comes down to the integrity of the message," explains Michael Bronner. "Not branding for the sake of branding but just to do things that we feel really passionate about and informing our customers that this is what the company, what we're all about, and tying that in to the product itself."

For its PR needs, Dr. Bronner's retains the Mintwood Media Collective, which describes itself as "a worker owned and operated public relations firm in Washington DC" providing "low-cost public relations work for non-profit social justice groups." Dr. Bronner's is the collective's only for-profit client, the account managed by Mintwood's Adam Eidinger. "Adam is as well spoken as they come," says Michael. "He's the master of the guerrilla marketing effort . . . not marketing through normal channels, but through direct action and demonstrations." Says David, "Adam's practically an employee of ours."

"I've been involved in Dr. Bronner's overall marketing strategy since 2003," Eidinger says from Washington. "This brand is held up as a model company when it comes to having a biodegradable [and earth-friendly] product. We've found that what benefits the business benefits the world at the same time."

Nevertheless, "you have to do something to get press, you have to make news," he continues. "Just launching a new project is not going to do it." Luckily for Eidinger, the Bronners are a wellhead of news, especially the kind that easily echoes around the Gort Cloud.

Carrying on the family tradition by embracing activism.

Founder Emanuel Bronner had two sons and a daughter, his infirm wife passing away when their oldest son, Ralph, was seven. During her illness, and then after she died, Emanuel left their children in a series of fourteen orphanages and foster homes in order to pursue his mission. He was given to bragging that he sacrificed his children in order to unite Spaceship Earth.

Nevertheless, his sons eventually became involved in the company, his youngest son, Jim, in charge of production and business matters, and Ralph, as earlier mentioned, in the role of company spokesperson. During that time, Emanuel slowly lost his vision, eventually calling himself "the happiest blind man on earth."

Jim Bronner "took the company to fiscal discipline [and] efficiencies and gave it a business logic it didn't have," explains David Bronner about his father. But just one year after Emanuel died in 1997, Jim passed away, too. David and his brother Michael took over management duties.

David seems to be following in his grandfather's and uncle's footsteps in serving as a spokesperson for the brand mission. Says Michael, "My brother is a big activist. He's the one who's out there on the front lines."

Promoting Fair Trade.

"In terms of branding, the issues themselves come first. We're very involved with Fair Trade because we think it's important for society, not because of the marketing benefit," Michael Bronner says. "Nevertheless, we're very excited about the fact that we've gone Fair Trade. We're the first body care company to convert all existing product and business to do it . . . and telling that story is branding."

It should be pointed out that there is a big difference between Fair Trade and Free Trade. Free Trade is the exchange of goods between countries without government-imposed restrictions. This, of course, allows companies to avoid the taxes and regulations in richer countries while exploiting the lack of such costs and safeguards in poorer countries. The Fair Trade movement welcomes trade but with procedures that ensure that workers and their environment are not harmed in the process.

In 2005, the company announced a plan to achieve 95 percent use of organic and certified Fair Trade raw materials by 2007, a goal it has now reached. "This is all very important for our marketing. It gives us a real quantifiable product attribute," Michael says. "Our customers feel like they own the soap."

"We want to leverage the products to advance our causes, and Fair Trade is a huge one," notes David Bronner. "It's an opportunity to promote the concept of Fair Trade. And then it kind of comes back around to publicize the product itself."

"It was hard for us to point the finger at other industries that are not Fair Trade when we weren't Fair Trade ourselves," explains Adam Eidinger. "Fair Trade is good for the brand because people feel like it's a guilt-free product."

The company has been putting money behind its message all over the world. In Sri Lanka, Dr. Bronner's built a coconut mill that recently went online, as well as an organic fertilizer plant for the local farmers. The mill cost the company more than $1 million but greatly improved the working conditions in the area.

Tackling the Israeli–Palestinian conflict.

In the Middle East, Dr. Bronner's primary Fair Trade olive oil source is the Palestinian Canaan Fair Trade project in the West Bank, but the firm has also partnered with Jewish and Arab-Israeli sources for the Bronner's soap products. It makes certain that farmers are paid a fair price and that the entire supply chain is organic. It footed the bill for organic certification for farmers on the Palestinian side.

The Middle East program, which has converted many small olive farmers to organic methods, is the subject of a short documentary piece, *Olive Oil from the Holy Land*, which was aired on the PBS *Foreign Exchange* program on Earth Day in April 2007. It is also prominently featured on the company's Web site with a link from the home page. Called Sindyanna, the cooperative is run by Palestinian and Israeli women who make and market olive oil soap, za'atar spice, and carob syrup, in addition to organic extra-virgin, cold-pressed olive oil.

In the film, Hadass Lahav, a Jewish woman who helps run the Sindyanna project, says, "I think what people in the US should understand — it's not enough to say, 'I'm for the peace.' We have to change the basic situation . . . What Dr. Bronner's does is show that the solution for the Middle East starts from real economic opportunities." Chimes in Michael Strauss, a Jewish farmer, "We have come to the conclusion that unless we find a way not only to mix the oils, but to mix our lives, there is no future for either of us."

Dr. Bronner's was originally the cooperative's largest buyer. Within a year of formal Fair Trade certification and validation sponsored by Dr. Bronner's, however, the soap company was responsible for just one-tenth of the overall volume exported. The remainder went to buyers in Europe. Dr. Bronner's had jump-started a process.

Fighting for truth in marketing organic.

David Bronner is also leading the charge when it comes to fighting for truth in organic labeling. He was on the Organic Trade Association (OTA) Personal Care Taskforce and now chairs the Composition Committee for the NSF personal-care "Made with Organic" standard that replaced it. He's something of a "bull in a china shop" on the issue, according to his brother Mike.[1] (The prestigious Ann Arbor–based NSF — formerly the National Sanitation Foundation and not to be confused with the National Science Foundation — is a nonprofit that develops standards and provides product certification in the fields of public health and safety.)

In fact the OTA tried to kick him off the program back in 2003 as he was trying to stiffen organic certification rules. According to a release issued at the time from the Organic Consumers Association, "Dr. Bronner's Magic Soaps of Escondido, California, the largest seller of natural soap in the U.S., will be locked out of PCTF discussions this fall just as a new organic standard will be developed for eventual recommendation to the Department of Agriculture's National Organic Program (NOP). According to several members, the company is being removed for speaking out against watering down standards for bodycare."[2]

The Dr. Bronner's Web site slams so-called natural body care companies that make "a mockery of organic principles" by "using standard formulations based primarily on conventional synthetic ingredients to which secondary organic ingredients are added," and/or by "using conventional natural instead of certified organic essential oils for scent." The site takes particular issue with products that are "in part or wholly derived from petroleum."

"It's the Wild West out there," Michael Bronner says. "You can call anything organic and get away with it. You have all these buyers who are assuming that body care products must be organic if they're labeled organic, just like this soup I'm buying is organic because it says so." Well, in the case of the soup, it's true. In the case of body care products it's not, so when consumers see *true* organic products, they often pass them by for less expensive "organic" products — which are, in fact, less expensive because they are not really organic.

"We're always trying to get out the message that we're the real deal, that we're certified by the USDA's National Organic Program," explains David Bronner. ". . . A lot of these products that are making these organic claims are more or less the same old conventional products with some organic window dressing." The Dr. Bronner's Web site urges "the natural bodycare industry to clean [its] house." It details tricks of the body care trade so that consumers can easily detect greenwashing.

In doing this, David is using the power of the Gort Cloud to educate and mobilize consumers, while at the same time enhancing and protecting truly sustainable brands — some of which may turn out to be his direct competitors. Awareness of his message is elevated by the company's actions and then explained on the Web site. Bloggers and green news media, including industry news outlets like *Natural Foods Merchandiser*, pick up the story and spread it around.

Dr. Bronner's points out that its products are "certified by the USDA's National Organic Program, which consumers rightly trust to ensure the integrity of organic labeled products." The Web site also comes down hard on the Bush administration's USDA for its attempt "to interpret the National Organic Program so as to kick out personal care companies that actually make certified organic lotions, balms and other products certified to National Organic Standards."

"The USDA seal is the only way that truly organic personal care products such as ours can be distinguished versus misbranded 'organic' products," the site maintains. "The National Organic Program is for all products that comply with the program, that truly support sustainable organic agriculture and ecological processing without unnecessary synthetic ingredients."

Heading for an organics showdown.

David Bronner predicts that "there will be a lot more drama with organics" in the near future. "Things are headed for a showdown," he says. "Although we're not sure exactly how long it's going to take."

Dr. Bronner's is suing competitors for failing to live up to their organic label and brand claims, which at a minimum mean that main cleansing and moisturizing ingredients are based on organic, not conventional or petrochemical, material. "But we don't really want to go down that path," says David. "If companies contractually commit to reformulate to meet their organic claims, or drop their claims, we're happy not to have to proceed to litigation."

As of this writing, no agreement is in place. According to a *Forbes* May 1, 2008, report, "A lawsuit filed by All One God Faith — which does business as Dr. Bronner's Magic Soaps — this week accused 13 cosmetic competitors in the washing game of false advertising through the misuse of the label 'organic' on their products. The suit was filed in California Superior Court in San Francisco. Dr. Bronner's accuses these companies, which include Kiss My Face, Stella McCartney America, Estée Lauder, and Hain Celestial Group, of using petroleum-based ingredients in their potions. That, according to Dr. Bronner's, means they are falsely advertising themselves as organic manufacturers."

According to Organic Food Standards, products can be claimed as "100 percent organic" when they are certified 100 percent organic. If products are made 95 to 100 percent organic, they may be labeled "organic," and between 70 and 95 percent organic, they are labeled "Made with organic ingredients." Any non-organic ingredients are strictly regulated and cannot, for instance, contain petrochemical compounds.

Because Dr. Bronner's must use USDA-allowed alkali (sodium hydroxide for the bars and potassium hydroxide for the liquids) to make oils and soaps, as all soap makers do, the organic ingredient level of its products is 82 percent. "So we can't call our product 'Organic Soap' versus 'Soap Made with Organic Oils' in accordance with the law," explains Michael Bronner. "So we are creative about it. We say, 'As organic as soap gets.'" Still, "I don't think it packs the punch we want it to," he continues. "At the same time, a company like Nature's Gate Organics, which is not certified, makes all these really nice-sounding, more direct organic claims than we do . . . because we obey the letter of the law."

This particular episode is a good example of how stories will echo around the Gort Cloud. In a well-written piece in the online magazine *Reality Sandwich*, Jill Ettinger writes that the Bronner brothers are taking on the cosmetic and body care industry precisely because the skin is a nutrient-absorbing organ, just like the intestines. Put the wrong thing on your skin, and you are poisoning yourself. This, according to Ettinger, is why Dr. Bronner's is leading the demand for truth in packaging. It's more than fair competition. It's a matter of life and health.[3]

A motivated PR partner.

Whenever industrial hemp and cosmetics organic certification issues come up in the media, Dr. Bronner's is likely referenced as a company that is on the front lines in pushing to enact change. "We're kind of like the fighting soap company," says Adam Eidinger. "We've been fighting the federal government since 2001 with legislation and lawsuits."

As David Bronner likes to say, "We're trying to effect change in areas of influence that we have. We don't need to look for an environmental project outside our own company's backyard to support. We should look at everything we're doing and involved in, and fix those first."

When it comes to the Fair Trade issue, Eidinger has been working hard to make certain that the company's actions have been noticed in the press over the past several months. This is despite the fact that the Bronner brothers themselves don't push him to do this.

"There is not too much pressure from the Bronners to get press for the company specifically," Eidinger says. "In fact, they're always telling me to emphasize the issues as the priority."

"I'm under strict instructions not to use spokesmodels," he continues. "We're not taking a picture of a beautiful woman washing herself with soap. The family won't allow the modern minimalist text and beautiful woman looking in the mirror, or sitting in the bathtub. They don't believe in it."

Does this hurt Dr. Bronner's in terms of sales? "If they wanted to sell a billion dollars' worth of soap, yes this hurts them," explains Eidinger. "But they're not interested in being Proctor & Gamble or Johnson & Johnson." Nevertheless he cautions, "If we don't have a public face, the company will eventually shrink."

"Money isn't driving this company," he continues. "What's really driving this company are the loyal customers and the message on the bottle. If David and Michael's interest were making money, they'd be doing this completely differently. But they'd be losing something. They're very lucky to have this family soap-making tradition of making the best product for the fairest price possible for everyone involved."

Eidinger proves his point by referencing the many buyout offers the Bronners have turned down. "Any firm of this size — topping twenty million in sales, and being top in their category — has people coming by to ask to buy them out. It would destroy the company."

The Dr. Bronner's story told as documentary.

Dr. Bonner's Magic Soap Box is a feature-length documentary made by director Sara Lamm that played in art-house theaters across the United States during 2007 to very positive reviews. The Bronner family cooperated but had no financial involvement with the project, and all of them were interviewed. Ralph Bronner gets the most screen time as he travels the country as a one-man sales force for the product. He tells prospective customers that the peppermint soap will tingle all over their bodies — and warns them to "watch your undercarriage."

"It tells our family's story in all of its aspects, light and dark . . . the sunny and shadow sides," Michael Bronner says, referencing the section where the film discusses the period of his life in which Emanuel Bronner seemed to be running from his Jewish heritage and, in fact, married a woman who was "by and large, anti-Semitic."

"It's such an honest depiction," Michael says. "In a way it's more promotional than a promo piece we might have done. People watch it and they realize there's no way we would actually make it ourselves or commission somebody to make it. I think people really get moved by it."

The film's release delivered a boost in Dr. Bronner's sales. "The weekend it premiered on the Sundance Channel — it showed about three or four times — our [Internet store] orders increased by about 500 percent," says Michael. "It's the easiest way for us to view a spike in interest in our soaps — through our Web store. We generally have 30 to 50 orders on any given weekend, and we had 350 [during that weekend.]" Normally, Web sales account for 3 percent of total Dr. Bronner's business.

The company has received "all kinds of publicity" from the film's opening in cities around the United States, Eidinger says. "I don't think all that many people have seen the movie, but there's been a whole lot of positive press written about it."

"We didn't know Sarah [Lamm] had all this access — we didn't realize it would be anything other than a small private project," says David Bronner. "And I'm kind of conflicted about the film — my family history, all the good, bad, and ugly up there. It has this real authentic feel."

The documentary, in fact, helps build the Dr. Bronner's brand image in just the way it needs to be built — with an authentic and independent-film feel.

"We're one of the last independent personal care companies of any size," says David Bronner. "We try to keep it real. We try to communicate that we're a brand that's not just about soap, but about a lot of other things, too."

Company culture that sticks to its counterculture history.

Dr. Bronner's has a history of treating its staff remarkably well — a tradition that has held ever since Dr. Emanuel Bronner encouraged nude sunbathing out on the office terrace. "Don't worry, I'm blind, I won't see anything," he told a new employee on her first day of work when encouraging her to take off her clothes.

The Bronners have put a five-to-one cap on salaries, meaning no executive can make more than five times what the lowest-paid fully vested employee earns.

"As the company grows, employees are being rewarded," explains Eidinger. "Everyone gets bonuses — factory workers get bonuses. I never had a ten-thousand-dollar bonus in my life until I worked for these guys." The company gives out bonuses even in years when it sees little profit, he says.

When Dr. Bronner's does have profits, one-third of before-tax moneys are, on average, donated to charitable causes, with the remaining going to business development, debt servicing, and taxes.

Going mainstream?

Dr. Bronner's has grown significantly under the leadership of the Bronner brothers. Its peppermint soap is not only the top-selling natural soap in the United States but has twice the sales of its nearest competitor. Yearly sales have increased from $4.5 million in 1997, when Emanuel Bronner died, to approximately $22 million — and climbing — by mid-2008. "We're not taking advantage of the [green] wave, we're part of the wave," says David. "And we're preparing for the explosion. This is going mainstream in a very big way."

Dr. Bronner's is the number-one body wash and soap in the organic body care category at CVS. Starting in 2008, it will be available at Target, in the retailer's new natural personal care section, in what Eidinger is calling "a major gamble."

An American counterculture institution goes international.

Dr. Bronner's also began to expand globally in 2003. The international market now accounts for between 11 and 12 percent of all sales.

"Europe's kind of a tough nut to crack," says Michael, thanks to competition from natural body care products that have been around for more than a hundred years, as well as to Europeans' tendency to associate American products these days with the Bush administration era. "So the fact that you're an American company does not get you very much mileage in Europe."

In Asia, however, things are different. "Natural products are very much in an infancy stage there, or maybe late infancy stage, so we're getting there on the ground floor," says Michael. "And also, they love English."

In Japan, the company is one of the top body care product sellers, and Dr. Bronner's is the number-one product when it comes to natural soaps. "Organic is used much more to sell beauty in Japan," explains David. "Crucially, the climate and skin types in Japan work very well with our soaps as a facial wash, and the magic's derived from the fact that it's gentle and effective. Some soaps are effective and really get out the makeup and the dirt. And some are really gentle, but few are both. In the Japanese market, they use that angle to pitch our soaps to the twenty- to forty-year-old women as a makeup facial wash. And they sell our soaps at roughly three and a half times the price that we do here."

Sixty years and counting.

In 2008, Dr. Bronner's marked the sixtieth anniversary of Emanuel Bronner's founding of the company. Being first to market earned them iconic status in an otherwise dynamic category. Nevertheless, the family is not content to worship a vision of the past; the Bronners continue to tweak their products, defend their standards, and expand their market.

SUMMARY: DRIVEN BY VISION

Dr. Bronner's was there at the very beginning, before sustainability, Fair Trade, organic, and healthy were popular — even before the first Earth Day celebrated awareness and a movement. The founders and their product are the real deal. Their quirkiness and steadfast commitment to values have enshrined the brand as "green among greens." And as with other companies you will read about in this book, Dr. Bronner's has enjoyed steady and entirely acceptable growth while maintaining product standards and building social responsibility programs. Though it takes a little magic to create a successful green brand, there is nothing illusionary about the concrete business rewards — when the work is done with a pure vision.

So, while neither the Gort Cloud nor the Internet existed when Dr. Bronner's was founded, the heirs have made ample use of these connections — in getting the word out about misleading natural and organic labeling, in reaching out to new and younger customers with a message of sustainability, and in promoting their world vision of peace and healthful living.

The Consummate Pitchman
Earth Friendly Moving

THE CHALLENGE

Spencer Brown had just moved his office when he had an epiphany. All the boxes and packing materials that he'd just bought, he realized, were going straight into a landfill when he was done. On the spot, he invented a new business model, renting recyclable moving boxes for a buck a week.

But how would he change an entrenched industry and the habits of the moving public?

How could he remove an important source of income from traditional movers and storage companies?

Most important, how would he get the word out and convince people there was a better, more efficient, and ultimately cheaper way to move?

THE SOLUTION

Spencer is a born pitchman with the chutzpah of P. T. Barnum. By the force of his personality and the will of a seasoned inventor and entrepreneur, he would charge into the moving industry with an earth-friendly alternative.

He would address a core need with a simple, conveniently delivered moving box that was priced right. This would be his wedge product, the item that would gain the most immediate awareness. It wouldn't hurt if he colored it a vivid green.

He would turn his product distribution system into customer touchpoints, where prospective customers could be educated and convinced by the decisions of their neighbors. His delivery trucks and his drivers would become the primary means of BizDev outreach.

He would concentrate on the influencers among his target audience with one-on-one exchanges, triggering viral word-of-mouth awareness — one neighborhood at a time. He would hunt his prospective customers down where and whenever they made themselves available, at yoga studios, green or healthy living retail stores, and farmers' markets and via his Web site and newsletters.

Spencer would also curry goodwill and recognition from the eco-conscious media and trendspotters in the Gort Cloud. In the days after just one mention in TreeHugger, hits to his Web site soared. That mention led to others and still others. Awareness swelled. Today Spencer is a well-known pioneer in green moving and is often asked to speak on green business causes.

Most important, Spencer Brown would turn Earth Friendly Moving into a cause, not a commodity. Instead of the price-driven, dog-eat-dog world of traditional moving, he would turn the drudgery of moving day into an Earth Day moment — a chance to do right by the environment.

A green epiphany.

Spencer Brown was moving his design studio from his home office in Ladera Ranch, California, to Huntington Beach in 2005. Among the possessions of this tireless forty-year-old product designer were the plans he'd drawn over the last twenty years — plans and patent files for products such as the Dress with Dignity magnetic clothing system, Hand Candy Soap that fizzed and foamed in your hands as you washed, the Pediatric Pal, a decorated shield that hid the needle on a syringe, reducing fear in young patients, and high-performance, ocular adjustable swim goggles. Every one of his many inventions, which are available at Target, Home Depot, and many other national chain stores, had been a success in that it changed consumers' perceptions and helped them with daily life.

Spencer was now a millionaire many times over.

Perhaps his very fertile mind was looking for something new to invent that day, or perhaps it was just that he needed a distraction, but something disturbed him when he looked at the 150-plus cardboard boxes stuffed with his belongings — and these packing supplies were expensive, about eight hundred dollars' worth. He began to wonder where the boxes would end up. He guessed correctly that they were destined for a landfill, at worst, or an inefficient recycling process at best.

The image of 40 feet of stacked cardboard boxes in a landfill stayed with him. Later that week, while at a restaurant in Orange County's Little Saigon, Spencer had what he calls his ah-ha moment. He wrote the AH-HA on a paper place mat he still has to this day. Along with a drawing of boxes that were stacked for speedy loading and transport and the phrase RENTAL — 1 WEEK are the words GINGER and LIME, next to translations into an Asian language.

Spencer says about the moment: "In addition to coming up with the next great disruptive industry, I was learning Vietnamese."

Disrupting an embedded industry.

It is helpful to examine the industry — or more correctly, the industries — that Spencer was intending to disrupt. What kind of competitive landscape was he planning to enter?

Everyone moves at some point in their lives, generating tons of waste in the form of cardboard boxes and packing materials. It's one reason why the average US citizen uses up to twenty tons of basic raw materials annually, and why the total yearly waste for all Americans would fill a convoy of garbage trucks long enough to wrap around the earth six times, or reaching halfway to the moon.

In fact, 40 percent of all that waste is made up of paper and cardboard. This is despite the facts that most cardboard contains a substantial amount of recycled paper and that approximately 70 percent of cardboard is recycled — unless, of course, the price of gas continues to go up. Then recycling actually declines because of the cost of moving all that cardboard around. Nevertheless, trees are still cut down to be made into paper boxes with a very short life span that often end up in the ground where they cannot be used again. Spencer adds, "Cardboard has a huge impact in landfills as the glues that bind the paper are not water-based and this chemistry leaches into and contaminates the water table."

It also takes enormous resources to recycle cardboard boxes — sorting, transporting, washing, agitating back down to pulp, and then remanufacturing into new boxes. When McDonough and Braungart speak of "cradle to cradle," this is not what they have in mind. Spencer notes, "Each time a box is recycled, only 40 percent is usable, and 60 percent is waste. Also, each time we reuse material, the end product is of lesser quality at a higher price, forcing industry to look at virgin materials, like old-growth trees."

In the average move, boxes are furnished by the movers, providing an opportunity for extra revenue in a highly competitive and low-margin industry. Spencer estimates that upward of 40 percent of profit comes from the sale of these moving products. Storage facilities, now ubiquitous on the American landscape, sell boxes as well as bubble wrap and tape. The same thing goes for U-Haul or Penske Trucks, as well as UPS, Staples, Kinko's, the box-and-ship outlets, or anyone selling packing materials.

This is the industry Spencer began to chase in 2005, and he called his alternative Earth Friendly Moving. But despite the name, he had no intention of becoming the green Atlas Movers or the green Starving Students of Orange County. He didn't want to be a mover at all. Nevertheless, the nature of his idea — to rent out reusable moving boxes made of recycled plastics — would put him in direct competition with the entire moving industry.

Moving quickly to build goodwill.

Over the past two decades, the moving industry has changed dramatically. Until the early 1980s, movers were mostly a reliable, union-organized lot employed by a few dominant national moving companies that controlled, and perhaps fixed, pricing and shipping terms. All that changed with the Household Goods Transportation Act of 1980, which allowed interstate movers to issue binding or fixed estimates, opening the door for thousands of new moving companies to enter the industry. This forced an intensification of competition and changed the playing field from services to price. As prices dropped, already slim profit margins grew slimmer.

Some of the new companies weren't exactly playing by the rules. Rogue movers began hijacking freight as part of a new moving scam. Customers would be quoted lowball prices to get them hooked, but then the prices would rise significantly just before the goods were delivered. The victims were forced to pay the premium if they wanted to see their furniture again. This very thing happened to me when my family moved from New York to LA in 2002. As a result of deregulation, the public's perception of this industry has gone downhill.

Spencer's big idea not only suggested a more eco-friendly way to move but also provided him with an opportunity to shine a bit of goodwill on an industry associated with waste, unexpected cost, and the risk of scams. Going green enabled Spencer to build a moving industry brand with what authors Daniel Esty and Andrew Winston call an "eco-advantage."

Spencer Brown: The P. T. Barnum of moving boxes.

Spencer Brown is a certified genius, as evidenced by his IQ and the Stanford-Binet tests during his school years. He grew up in Orange County when it still had orange groves and when *Democrat* was still a dirty word. His father, a successful children's dentist in Cerritos, drove him to Cal State Long Beach when he was fifteen years old because high school just wasn't challenging enough.

"What is this *kid* doing here?" the older college students would ask. "Who's that guy, your dad?"

Spencer's academic brilliance was clear. His history professor called his socioeconomic analysis of the fall of the Roman Empire phenomenal. Later, at UC Santa Barbara, his friends coined the nickname Spenovator for his constant flow of ideas. He had his first business experience there, too, cornering the market on bead necklaces, a staple at UCSB.

Explains Spencer: "I bought all the leather strap there was to buy in India. If you wanted leather strap, you had to come to me." With his outsized personality and nonstop energy, Spencer Brown also turned out to be a great salesman.

Building permanence in a cardboard world.

Brown's moving epiphany led him to examine the life cycle of cardboard. He discovered that the rising cost of energy was making the recycling of cardboard boxes ever more expensive. It had become so expensive, in fact, that it was now cheaper to manufacture cardboard out of virgin forests than out of recycled material.

He set out to eliminate cardboard boxes from the moving business vocabulary. His first stop was the Orange County landfills, where he entered with a camera in his pocket, slipping it out when the coast was clear. "The emissions, the burning, the bugs — it's just a terribly disgusting environment. That's why people don't want landfills in their communities. They want to shove them aside."

The problem, Spencer soon realized, doesn't lie with landfills, but with what fills them. "The waste management industry has been trying to minimize the impact of these horrible places," he explains. "They're experimenting with various processes. They've started to learn how to separate what is biodegradable from what's not."

Spencer was struck by the fact that so much of the refuse was in the "what's not" category. What especially struck him were those brightly colored anaerobic plastic bottles that are projected to last well past fifty thousand years. Those bottles were once filled with bathroom cleaner, dishwashing liquid, laundry detergent, and countless other sturdily packaged products. Perhaps there was another use? "What makes these containers so unique is that you can't break them," he says. "They don't leach and they don't leak. In the 1960s, we called them miracle plastics."

Brown chopped up several bottles made of HDPE #2 high-density polyethylene, ground them into bits, and then, with much difficulty, figured out how to melt them into small pellets that could be melted again and molded into the shape of a box. He was well on his way to launching a new business enabling Americans to move without using cardboard.

"I put a bunch of money on the table, and everyone told me I was crazy," he says. "One woman [I know] called me an idiot."

On the day he officially founded Earth Friendly Moving, Spencer, known for bringing his inventions to market in less than two years, made a commitment that his moving boxes would be in operation within just twelve months. He achieved that goal in nine, attributing the company's quick success, at least in part, to his natural ability to streamline.

Creating a visible eco-advantage.

"I love being simple," Brown explains. Simplicity, it would turn out, would become his brand's eco-advantage, a differentiating message he targets not only toward his core audience of the environmentally aware but also to potential audiences outside of it. "I try to do things in the least number of steps possible, and people appreciate that because there's already too much noise out there, too many choices, too many industries vying for attention. People are saying, 'Strip it down and provide me with something that's easy to understand, that I can adapt to my lifestyle quickly, that's convenient and makes me feel good.'"

Brown designed a box that would require the melting and remolding of seventy-four reclaimed plastic bottles. He placed ergonomic, foam-wrapped handles on each side of the lid attachment that rotated a hundred degrees away from the box, and he incorporated a spring-hinged lid, all designed to reduce wrist strain. He also made the boxes stackable, reducing truck loading and off-loading time by 50 percent. He called the new box a RecoPack, short for "Recycled Ecological Packing Solution."

Manufacturing the RecoPack proved more difficult than Spencer anticipated. Many companies he approached told him it couldn't be done, and others said it would never be cost-effective. He finally connected with Applied Plastics Inc. in the Midwest, which didn't say no. Instead the company's CEO, Carl Gortime, flew into Orange County's John Wayne Airport, examined the storyboards and patents, nosed into Spencer's background, and announced that his company would take on the job.

Says Gortime about his decision to take on the production of the RecoPacks, "I asked around about Spencer Brown. He had a reputation for tenacity, but for doing it with grace and dignity. There was just something about him. I knew he'd make it work."

Defining a market.

The United States is still very much a country on the move. One-fifth of all Americans change their residence every year, representing seventy-four million people moving from here to there. The average US resident will move a total of sixteen times over his or her lifetime — about once every five years.

Before putting his boxes in the marketplace, Brown conducted a study of how cardboard moving boxes are acquired. Tracking 656 moves, he found that less than 1 percent of Americans reuse their existing stored boxes; only 4 percent contact friends, family, and Craigslist to find used boxes; 6 percent acquire used boxes from their place of employment; and 7 percent drive to a grocery store to see what's available for free.

According to Brown's statistics, that leaves better than 80 percent of Americans who buy new cardboard boxes. They pay an average cost of $450 per move, up 250 percent from just four years ago. The average time spent locating these boxes is an astonishing nineteen and a half to thirty-four hours, due in part to the tendency to purchase an inadequate amount of packing material on the first trip, forcing return visits to the store for more. The research he shared with me seems to back this up.

Explains Spencer: "We can watch *Desperate Housewives* on an iPod, trade stocks in real time with a PDA, and use GPS technology to navigate the urban sprawl. Yet we seem to insist on remaining stuck in the past when it comes to packing and moving materials."

Creating a product vocabulary that tells a story.

Spencer Brown removed large loads of plastic detergent jugs out of landfills in the western states, shipping them to a site in Nevada where they were cleaned, scrubbed, and finally ground into billions of plastic flakes. This material was sent to Applied Plastics, where it was molded into boxes with a life expectancy of ten years, at which point 96 percent of the material could be recycled again.

Applied Plastics churned out fifteen thousand RecoPacks in three consumer-friendly sizes. The boxes are now bright green but were initially gray because that was the easiest color to dye from mixed plastic sources. Earth Friendly began renting them out for a buck a week — which is, as Spencer likes to point out, less than fifteen cents a day. Demand grew quickly. Within six months, his company had ordered more than fifty thousand durable, reusable moving boxes.

To distribute the boxes to customer doorsteps, Spencer built the largest biofuel truck fleet in the nation over the course of two years. True to his environmental mission, he purchased six big rigs and thirty-four smaller vehicles, all with two fuel tanks, one tank for the biofuel B100 and the other for waste vegetable oil. Each truck as well as his own biofuel Mercedes is painted a vivid, not wimpy, green. As the cost of diesel has been going up and up, Spencer has begun searching for non-food-generated biofuels made from algae, switchgrass, or WVO (waste vegetable oil).

Brown was well on his way to building a sustainable brand with all the right qualities, not just eco-qualities. He was pulling plastic out of landfills, turning it into a superior moving box that could be reused, and distributing the boxes with veggie-oil-powered trucks. The price was right. The product design was superior. It was delivered to the door and picked up on order. It made the customers feel good because they were doing something positive for the environment. Recent experiences have shown that just being green doesn't get you far. The product must also meet customer expectations and be competitive. Brown's products accomplished both.

Though he did not know it at the time, he was also fitting into the objectives of the Zero Waste movement, as promoted by groups such as the Zero Waste Alliance and Zero Waste America. This movement, an aspect of the Gort Cloud, urges American businesses to look at trash as a cash-generating asset and advocates the idea of separating organic from inorganic compounds, with the inorganic returned to industry for reuse.

Spencer's trucks and big rigs double as mobile stores, with plenty of Earth Friendly Moving literature to hand out to passersby. They are also power plants on wheels, capable of generating the electrical energy required to shred packing paper at the delivery site. Stored in compact rolls on the truck, the recycled paper — a product named Giami, which means "friends of the earth" in Latin — is fed through a shredding device that turns it into a honeycomb stuffing. This paper packing material is 70 percent cheaper to make than the petroleum-based bubble wrap it replaces, and just as effective. Spencer first saw the material at a local Williams-Sonoma and tracked it down.

Spencer mentions, "We make a point of taking customers on the rig to show them this system as a way of getting them to talk about it . . . and they love to say that they were on this truck that runs on veggie oil that makes electricity to make this paper. It's a great story and people love to talk about it."

Other elements of the Earth Friendly all-in-one moving package include storage bags made from recycled boat sails, as well as RecoCube packing pellets — made from nontoxic recycled paper sludge — that take the place of Styrofoam peanuts. "After use, the pellets can simply be tossed in the yard, where they'll compost, helping to feed trees and grass," Brown explains. He makes a point of stressing that industrial paper sludge is highly toxic, but that he uses the safer newsprint type that "has zero toxins and is easy to bind with pectin, minerals, and vitamins."

Perhaps the most unique of Earth Friendly's products are the Poopy Pallets on which the RecoPacks sit when they're delivered or picked up from a site. One of the landfills Spencer visited specialized in baby diapers, receiving between thirty and forty tons a month. Much of the diaper material was sent out of the landfill to be recycled, but the outer shells, made of plastic, were incinerated because no use for them could be found. Spencer realized he could combine this material with industrial-waste plastic to produce the pallets. Each of the thirty thousand Poopy Pallets that Earth Friendly has produced to date contains seven hundred recycled diaper shells.

Interestingly, another company in the Portland, Oregon, area has developed a diaper that can be safely flushed down the toilet along with the waste. This enterprising eco-company is gDiapers, and with luck, maybe gDiapers will dry up Spencer's source for Poopy Pallets. Spencer would love that.

An infectious can-do culture of optimism.

Brown became Earth Friendly Moving's first deliveryman, sometimes rising at 4:30 AM to make certain his customers got what they wanted. He still does deliveries, generally keeping it to ten orders per week and concentrating on the commercial clients — the labs, the corporations, the colleges, the design houses, and perhaps a celebrity or two.

"This is physical work," he explains. "I sweat delivering boxes. My employees see I'm in this thing with them, and my customers see my passion up close. People are blown away when they see me loading boxes. It's genuine and respected. The celeb clients love to talk green with me, and I try to educate them on what they can do with their influence as tastemakers and motivators for doing the right thing."

Spencer's sweat — and enthusiasm — exudes the culture of his business. And the culture, which binds the employees, partners, and customers to the company, comes out of the Earth Friendly mission — to reduce waste while making moving easier.

Brown also learns from his customers when he delivers to them, hence the all-in-one-package approach that Earth Friendly offers. "I've discovered that consumers don't want to hunt for packing materials because they don't have the time," he explains. "They don't want to drive around using up gas to locate cardboard boxes. They want to look for a button on the Internet that says 'I'm moving' and press it. They want to say, 'I want the Number 3 combo, super-size and hold the pickles.'"

That's branding simplicity again, and it goes straight to the driver of preference, which is brand-speak for that special thing that resonates with and makes a difference to the customer. When it comes to locating moving boxes, the driver of preference is always convenience.

Getting the word out via the Gort Cloud.

When Brown set out to build his firm, his first goal was to define and isolate his target customers — not the whole range of potential customers, but the ones who influence others. He decided to create a positive, fast-moving, viral-marketing campaign seeded by word-of-mouth referrals from first adopters. In his case, these were the environmentally aware who would snatch up his business as another way to fulfill their commitment to a healthier planet.

"The best way to reach green consumers is viral marketing," Brown says in a perfect description of the power of the Gort Cloud. "The green community talks. They love to share and expose their new finds. It's all about being in this self- and group-education process that is amplified by the connectivity of the Internet. The information resonates superfast and with huge impact. We delivered the RecoPack to one customer and in six months we had seventy-four hundred deliveries. If you have truly done your work, and you haven't just tried to sugarcoat or greenwash your product, then you'll zoom, because there's such a pent-up demand for green alternatives."

Brown took his displays to yoga studios, where he was well received. He'd tell whoever would listen that it was time to create a new paradigm for moving, that it was time to fight off big oil, to be that much less dependent on it. He sparked a whole lot of interest and found many new customers.

Brown then turned to the "lighter greens" — consumers who may take a little convincing. He spoke about the new company on Earth Day in school classrooms full of children who, he hoped, would tell their parents that there was a right way to move. More than one nine-year-old insisted that his family use Earth Friendly boxes so vociferously that the parents finally caved in.

Invariably, the kids would also chat it up with their friends on MySpace. Earth Friendly found itself part of the online social networking community. When a young man named Jeff posted a short article about Spencer's box rental company on TreeHugger.com, Earth Friendly had one million hits on its Web site within three days. The company's servers crashed. Of these million visitors, seventy-five thousand joined the Earth Friendly e-mail list. One of those visitors was me.

"It was overwhelming," says Spencer. "All of a sudden, you know you've made it . . . but now you have to make sure you can prove to the marketplace you're a viable business, that you're worthy of all the praise you're getting. Everyone's watching."

Today, Spencer has received attention through a number of channels. Yelp, a product and services review site driven by customers, boils over with praise for Earth Friendly Moving. The business scored No. 1 on EnviroMedia Social Marketing's Greenwashing Index — 1 is good, 5 is worst. Spencer was the Grand Prize Winner of the 2008 Keen Footwear Stand-Up Competition that recognizes environmental efforts. His business was listed as one of the top ten eco- and sustainability business ideas for 2007 by the trendspotter Springwise, which generated over 9 million hits to his Web site. He was named entrepreneur of the month in Orange County in 2007 and again in 2008 — the first ever green entrepreneur and the first ever back-to-back winner. He was featured in *USA Today Weekend* with 26 million copies that generated 300,000 e-mails in one day. And on and on. It should be clear to anyone reading this that going green definitely has a silver lining.

Reaching out to customers.

By examining the moving process, Spencer identified five target customer rings, which are reached through the brand's primary touchpoints — the primary contact points between a customer and a brand.

For an airline, the touchpoint might be the tail of the plane seen parked at the airport, or the sound of the ticket agent's voice on the phone. The touchpoints for Earth Friendly Moving include:

- The distributed flyers,
- The Earth Friendly Web site,
- Spencer Brown's appearances,
- The free media publicity,

- His well-developed e-mail newsletter list,
- The person-to-person referrals, and
- The bright green trucks and boxes.

At the center of Earth Friendly's customer rings are the customers who hear about the brand and hire the service. The second ring includes those customers' friends and family, who hear about Earth Friendly's special service from them. The third ring comprises neighbors, at both the old and the new locations, who see the green Earth Friendly trucks out the window. The fourth ring includes the real estate agents and/ or landlords; the fifth, those lookie-loos who invariably wander by the truck and ask what's going on.

Brown makes certain that the trucks are always well stocked with Earth Friendly literature in several varieties, one piece targeted to the neighbors, another to real estate and leasing agents, and a third to apartment building owners and managers. "We use a frame of reference, as each group has their own trigger points . . . so when they read these target marketing pieces they connect with it. They tell me that the information resonates with them, and they feel connected to what we are doing."

Brown has approached some very large apartment building owners for marketing purposes. "If you want to find people who move, go to an apartment community," he explains. "There's constant turnover for many different reasons." Recently, Brown approached the Irvine Company. With 11,700 units and an average occupancy rate of less than twelve months, the company was spending between six and seven hundred thousand dollars a year to remove tenants' moving waste. Spencer convinced the firm to recommend Earth Friendly Moving to its tenants.

As for free exposure in the media, Brown is turning into a master. He has been featured in local press articles as well as on TV and the Web. Recently, he was featured with three interviews on MSN.com in which he detailed information about his company and gave advice about marketing green products.

"The green community tends to be very difficult to market to," Brown explains on MSN. "They're very aware. They're very educated. To date, this has been the most difficult group to convince, and that makes it the best challenge, that makes it very satisfying."

"You have to walk the talk," he continues. "You have to make the greenest product you can, and communicate that with specific facts. You also have to demonstrate what the eco-impact is of your product. You can't assume that the consumer, being green, will make that connection. You also have to demonstrate with specifics how this product will save them time and money. They're not going to spend more money on your product just because it's green."

Spencer takes every opportunity to amplify his media exposure with e-mail notices he blasts out to his customers and supporters. He will also mention other green products and services in a kind of informal co-marketing program that takes advantage of a common customer base.

Storytelling and the art of the sell.

Spencer's daughter describes her dad as a "trash-digging tree hugger." His son calls him "the green box guy." Both children love to spend time with their father, who takes a very hands-on approach to parenting. He tries to be a role model. One reason he started this business was to show his kids that, as stewards of the environment, we must all do something to protect it. Perhaps most importantly, Spencer teaches his children how to think, instead of what to think.

That's similar to the attitude he has when it comes to his clientele. "I'm not telling people anything. I'm just making them think," he explains. "You need to get people to stop and look and use their brain a little . . . you need to give them intellectual stimulus, something to figure out. Once they solve the riddle, they'll start discussing it with their friends."

This jives with everything I've learned about brand theory. If people work just a little harder to discover and understand the brand, they will become co-owners of the brand.

"We don't rent boxes, we tell a story," Brown says. "That story is interesting enough and factual enough that people know it's right. It's not like a fantasy. We all throw things into the recycle bin. Now we can see what can happen with what we're recycling. We can see a tangible result — the detox of the landfills."

The story Spencer tells begins with Earth Friendly's claim that for every hundred Earth Friendly moving boxes manufactured, five hundred pounds of landfill is removed, including seventy-four hundred hard-to-recycle plastic bottles. And for every hundred boxes rented, another five hundred pounds will be saved because it will give Earth Friendly the funds needed to go back to the landfill to pull out more.

Brown also reminds potential customers that the rental of a hundred Earth Friendly boxes saves three hundred pounds of trash from entering the landfills. This figure comes from calculating the materials needed for an average move, including a hundred cardboard boxes, which at 2.5 pounds per box adds up to 250 pounds, plus 70 pounds of packing materials such as tape, Styrofoam, or dish packs. Use of the RecoPacks also saves three trees, because it takes three trees to produce a hundred recycled cardboard boxes — only 30 percent of the material used is actually made from post-consumer cardboard waste.

"When you do the math, we have removed over 740,000 bottles to make the first ten thousand RecoPacks," Spencer says. "Imagine one million RecoPacks . . . spread the word and we'll be there in no time."

CEP (chief executive pitchman).

Brown serves as his own marketing and PR department, constantly spreading the word with phrases he's coined himself: "Do-it-yourself pack and move solutions"; "Delivered right to your door"; "Moving made simple"; "What moves you"; and the company's primary tagline, "A buck a box a week." He believes that the most effective line has been, "Think about it: Without trees, we're fish out of water." Just recently, he introduced a new e-mail address: rentagreenbox.com.

In fact, Brown is always looking for that next effective line, that special thing that resonates with and makes a difference to the customer. In brand-speak, we call this the unique selling proposition. Although a recent Landor Associates study concluded that most people don't care about the environment, some people care a lot, and the number of people who do care is increasing while the number of those who don't is decreasing. Playing the long-term game, Spencer would seem to be on the right side of this equation.

To drive home his message, Spencer came up with five icons in the international signage style to represent delivery, stacking, packing, moving, and pickup. "When people see [our] little man, they associate him with finding a bathroom, so they feel relief," he explains. "That's what we want people to feel when they use our moving products."

"I believe that society reads in icons now," Spencer continues. "The last generation, before computers took off, communicated in broad concepts that would then funnel down to smaller concepts. Now it's a reverse funnel effect. You start with just an image, just a picture . . . and it represents the broader idea."

Brown was very aware of branding opportunities from the beginning. The first step was branding the company green, literally and figuratively, and that meant finding the right green. Spencer wanted it to be fresh and positive. He studied color palettes for a month, ultimately coming up with a lime green that felt urban and edgy. "That green is the Coca-Cola red of our brand," he explains. "There's a certain look to our green."

Spencer bought a 1981 Mercedes-Benz, converted it to vegetable oil, and painted it in the eco-green color he'd chosen. He added a metallic finish to emphasize that green doesn't have to be boring, and then added the EARTH FRIENDLY MOVING name in big letters. He still drives this Mercedes everywhere he goes. It's his message delivery vehicle.

As the business grew, he purchased eleven more Mercedes, all vintage 1981 to 1985, converting them to run on vegetable oil. His "eco-sales agents" drive the vehicles on all their calls. Every car has a personalized license plate with messages such as RECYCLE IT, RECOPACK, GO GREEN GO, and I LOVE TRASH.

The cars cannot be missed. "What we're saying is, 'Look at us,'" Spencer explains. "This is an obnoxious company. This is a disruptive company. And we're having fun."

Brown has turned to ad agencies on occasion, developing several print ads, generally employing the image of a gas mask to represent what the world will become if we don't do something about carbon emissions. "We want to make potential customers ask themselves, 'Do I really want to take this product made from trees, use it once, and then throw it away?'"

He has also entered into co-marketing agreements with several large corporations. With every fifty moving boxes rented, Earth Friendly customers receive discounts on goods and services in their new neighborhood at venues such as Kinko's and Starbucks. "It's our way of saying thank you for your word-of-mouth support and welcoming you to your new neighborhood. We want to do everything we can to reduce the stress and aggravation so common with a typical move," Brown says.

All Earth Friendly customers also receive a "RecoRecognition certificate" e-mail after completing their move, which proclaims them to be
"stewards of the environment."

Keeping with the 4 R's of the environmental cycle (Reduce, Reuse,
Recycle, Replenish), Earth Friendly plants a tree for every hundred
RecoPacks rented per household. "That's another way to grow our busi-
ness — one tree at a time," Brown explains.

"People are blown away by moving with us," he continues. "They
have this euphoric sense of accomplishment. We've actually built a
certain hysteria with these boxes. People call, people e-mail, people ask,
'Is there anybody else like you?'" Earth Friendly is building customer
loyalty by overperforming and delivering a different experience. "We're
just out spreading the green love."

Constant tinkering produces a dynamic brand.

The Earth Friendly headquarters sits at the rear of a monotonous yet
somehow welcoming California-style office park in Costa Mesa; it's easy
to spot with the lime-green vehicles parked nearby. Spencer's office is a
very packed affair that obviously mirrors his mind, with bits and parts
of past experiments, drawings, specimen jars . . . in every corner. Spencer
wears a version of the same outfit every day: green shoes, green pants, a
green THE FUTURE IS GREEN T-shirt.

Of late, Brown is calling himself an eco-entrepreneur. He is determined to turn the concept of trash on its head all across the country. To
do so, he's instituting some changes, most importantly in the color of
the boxes.

"I couldn't look at that gray anymore. I couldn't feel good about the
color. The boxes had to be green. They had to be appealing and sexy
and attractive and cool," he explains. "If you ask people on the street
[about] ecology, they can't really tell you. They don't understand the
difference between ecology and the environment. But 'green' they
understand."

He has experimented to produce the right green color for the boxes,
crushing and melting and blending them together until he came up with
the same green he's been using with his marketing materials. Such are the
lengths he'll go to in order to tweak his brand's identity. Earth Friendly

has recently taken delivery on fifty thousand lime-green boxes, made out of two million pounds of resin from recycled containers removed from landfills.

"Ultimately, what we're delivering is environmental consciousness in a box," he says, employing another new slogan. "That's what makes people feel good, because it looks good — it's crisp, it's simple, it's green, it's not hoity-toity, it's real basic."

Spencer has also struggled with the company name. The *Moving* part of *Earth Friendly Moving* has created some market confusion. "It has made people think we're a moving company, when we're not," he explains. In response, Spencer has begun using a new company name to point to his services: www.rentagreenbox.com with the tagline, "It's cheaper than using cardboard." Says Spencer, "This works in the biggest way . . . total market understanding, as we have the word *green*, an illustration of the RecoPack, and the word *cardboard*, so our audience now gets that we have something that is better than cardboard. This is the final company name and tagline. This is the one that will go national."

He may have had second thoughts about his company name, but Brown is sure about what to do in terms of branding his trucks. He's in the process of replacing the smaller Earth Friendly delivery trucks with Dodge Sprinters — stand-up mobile delivery vans that will run on a biofuel/veggie-oil mix. "They look more like a delivery truck, less like a moving truck," he explains.

Finally, Brown is in the midst of enhancing his Web site to build a larger community. He will be posting a list of recycling centers and including a page to help with tax deduction issues. "We're going in a direction of selling ourselves as a moving concierge, providing the customer with all kinds of information," he says. This is entirely consistent with the current strategy of many low-margin companies. It's called servicing. Instead of selling a product, you sell a package of services that includes the product.

Creating credibility through positive customer stories.

Two years down the road, Brown still takes pride in small accomplishments, such as what happened recently at St. Joseph's Medical Center in Orange.

The hospital, run by nuns, was set to use a special moving firm that specializes in packing up and moving hospitals. The markup on the cardboard boxes for this move was estimated at eighty thousand dollars. When Spencer convinced the hospital to move green, "the mover began kicking and screaming because he wasn't going to see that money," Spencer explains. "So the hospital had to fire him."

"See, we're disruptive," he adds, determined to brand the company this way. "We're changing the world."

Growing without the pain.

Brown is now poised to spread Earth Moving across the country. "We have people from all over the planet asking for franchises," he explains. "But I don't like franchises." Instead, Earth Friendly will have operating partners — something Spencer long ago committed to having by his one thousandth day of business. The first partners will be in place soon in San Diego, Santa Monica, Ladera, Laguna Beach, West Los Angeles, and Pasadena.

Brown seems determined to keep sole proprietorship of his company, at least for now. "This is my craft," he continues. "I've studied it. I've studied ergonomics. I've studied human dimensions down to the way your chest and your arm reach . . . In terms of the average consumer, how much can you physically lift? I've had the experience in my life to bring us to this place," he says. "We're really innocent about it. We don't want to drive fancy cars. We're not into the showmanship. We're not into a *We're going public* kind of mentality, which frankly is a turn-off to most customers."

All of this, of course, reaffirms the notion that the eco-conscious are defined by more than just their greenness. The group Spencer represents also shares core values about responsibility to fellow riders on the planet.

By putting himself in the environmental space, Brown has been able to make money, make a difference, and feel good about all of it. He has become an unofficial spokesperson for vegetable-oil conversions and waste management issues. He fields inquiries from politicians and officials from all over the state asking his opinion on environmental issues. Earth Friendly was recently given an award for Best Use of Recycling in the state by the California Resource Recovery Association.

Brown believes he is putting his time and his energy where they need to be placed. "The '70s was about American pride in product, the '80s was technology, the '90s was about branding," he says. "This decade is about sustainability. And to be about sustainability, a company must have integrity, it must have a soul, and the leader of the company has to have a Zen-like approach. He or she must see past the needs of the company itself to deal with the needs of the planet. If companies don't re-craft themselves with this kind of image, they won't survive."

Concludes Brown: "Two years ago, the people selling me trash called me an idiot. Now the same people are calling me a genius."

SUMMARY: THE POWER OF AUDACITY

Never underestimate the power of an original idea, especially if it's powered by a strong personality. By virtue of the sheer audacity of Spencer Brown and his sustainable idea, he's managed to revolutionize an entrenched industry with profoundly unsustainable practices. Just as the Industrial Revolution uncorked new products and new markets, the Age of Sustainability can provide a green wave that resourceful ecopreneurs will ride.

Spencer has also been a pioneer in the use of the Gort Cloud. His intuitive understanding of its existence led him to many forms of outreach that resonate well in the green community. He did his homework and built a solid case for his product on his Web site. He then reached out to the first adopters and trendspotters, who eagerly picked up and telegraphed his story. Both green and conventional media echoed his brand messages. Once an audience was captured, he continued to engage them with videos, e-mail blasts, and his newsletter. He also shows up at green community events and trade shows with his signature green vehicles and boxes, and he partners with unrelated green businesses in the hope of sharing a common customer.

Unfuckers United
The Rise, Fall, and Resurrection of Nau Clothing

THE CHALLENGE

The founders of Nau Clothing presented themselves with an enormous challenge. They set out to fashion a technical apparel company on a new model of corporate responsibility that would benefit not only stakeholders but also the community and the world at large. In doing so, they would buck conventional wisdom on how and why to establish a new clothing line in a notoriously difficult market.

THE SOLUTION

Instead of hiring an ad agency to hype its brand, Nau Clothing built integrity into the product, the distribution system, and the corporate blueprint itself. The result was greater differentiation of product and brand, loads of free press, and an image of integrity that was appealing and spread virally among Nau's employees, investors, and core customers. How did it do this?

Nau differentiated itself in a crowded market by building a brand on the foundation of quality, profitability, and sustainability. By targeting key audiences with a message of integrity, Nau built a small but loyal following across multiple fashion segments: sports enthusiasts, fashionistas, and the eco-conscious.

Ahead of its time? Yes. Which may have contributed to the financing problems that forced Nau to close in spring 2008 — only to be resurrected by an angel investor just six weeks later. Innovation was both a risk and ultimately an asset that kept the firm going.

All members of the Nau team were aware of the power of the interconnected green community to help them develop product and get the word out to core customers. Nau was intertwined in the Gort Cloud in innumerable ways, including very direct outreach through its Web site; its blog, called the Thought Kitchen; a digital storytelling venue called the Collective; its monthly digital newsletter, *Off the Grid*; and its Partners for Change sponsorship program. In fact, it was the trendspotters, bloggers, and green news sites within the Gort Cloud that fairly rang with mourning in the days after Nau's thankfully brief closing.

The power of the company's brand image, goodwill, and loyal following proved to be a critical asset in riding out this rough patch.

Reinventing a fashion business, from the earth up.

Mark Galbraith, then a top product designer at Patagonia, remembers the autumn 2004 call from Eric Reynolds, a founder of the outdoor gear manufacturer Marmot, asking him to lunch. Galbraith knew Reynolds, but not well.

The sushi lunch lasted all afternoon and turned into a dinner of more sushi and sake. The men discussed Reynolds's view that the modern corporation, an entity with great opportunity to do good, was instead often doing great damage. A student of Robert Hinkley's writings on corporate social responsibility, Reynolds explained that he was determined to found a corporation on a business model that would be radically different, a corporation that would give back, that would be responsible not just to the shareholders but to the whole planet. Reynolds was betting on his knowledge of his customers, who were often outdoor sports enthusiasts with grave concerns for the health of the planet. He was betting that there was room for one more active sportswear maker, one with a mission to do it better.

He was planning to launch the new corporate model in one of the toughest industries of all — fashion. He was taking on this competitive and margin-driven business with a new set of rules, rules that he believed would attract customers who love style and performance as much as they love the earth. Reynolds was doing what I recommend as a brand consultant: starting with a core audience and building an offer around that audience. With focus and clarity, a business can stand out and grow organically.

When Reynolds asked Galbraith to review the business plan, dropping it on the table as he rose to go to the restroom, Galbraith saw that the heading stated the company's name, UTW, but gave no indication of what the acronym represented. He had his answer when Reynolds returned to the table wearing a Michael Franti T-shirt that boldly declared UNFUCK THE WORLD.

"He was telling me what the business was about," says Galbraith, who was to become UTW's vice president of product design. "He was saying, 'I'd like you to be a fellow unfucker.'"

UTW's name eventually changed to Nau, pronounced *now*, which is Maori for "welcome, come in." Nau hoped to unfuck the world in general, and the fashion business in particular. The firm broke considerable new ground before it died and was subsequently resurrected in 2008, and that is why there is much to learn in Nau's story.

Building an earth-friendly brand experience.

Entering the Nau store in Bridgeport Village, south of Portland, you immediately sensed that there was something different going on. The design was sparse, the clothing racks uncluttered. Unique aluminum forms functioned as display tables, and the checkout island dominated the center of the space. Like the kitchen counter in a designer loft, this is where everyone congregated.

Here, at one of the nine stores Nau had opened by July 2008, almost everything was produced from recycled materials, from the hip and styled garments to the graphics made out of recycled cardboard to the display hangers created from recycled plastic. Even the mannequins, traditionally made out of nonrecyclable fiberglass, were resin-based and could be recycled.

"We went through every single element of the store from a sustainability point of view," explains Ian Yolles, Nau's vice president of brand communications. "We needed to function as a retail environment, but we also needed a design sensibility that would reflect the [differentiating attributes of the] brand." Working with local Portland architects Skylab Design, Nau also brought in Green Building Services to help it conform to LEED standards in building this retail showcase, which is arguably the most important touchpoint between an apparel brand and its customers.

The Nau stores turned out to be more than a retail experience. They functioned as an immersive tool that introduced first-time customers to the brand's philosophy, commitment, and sense of style. The stores, along with the Web site, provided copious information about mission, sourcing, manufacturing, care, and reuse, all of which instilled knowledge and brand loyalty. Many companies would love to cultivate this level of loyalty but can't because their attention is too focused on profits, at the expense of ideals.

"Our goal was not to have a sustainable aesthetic so much as a sustainable concept," says Jeff Kovel, the founding architect of Skylab, who views the world of retail rollouts as a throwaway culture. "Stores come into a vanilla shell, rip it out, and start over. They're constantly putting fixtures in, tearing them down, and throwing them away. We thought a lot about how we could change that whole process rather than just use some green materials."

The solution: a prefabricated, component-based environment with fully reusable fixtures that are built off-site, shipped in a flat pack, and assembled on-site in the existing store shell. "We want to be provocative, we want to catch people's attention," Galbraith explains. "You can be environmentally friendly, but you can also be high-performance. You can be all organic, but you're not some crunchy burlap bag all in undyed white heading out to the office. You can be styled and look great." All of this came through in the stores.

Differentiating with style, function, and sustainability in a saturated market.

"There's been very little growth in the outdoor apparel industry," explains Nau CEO Chris Van Dyke. "So there's really little room for somebody new. Even with a good product. Unless you're doing something really new." This warning comes despite the fact that the total value of US-made apparel is around $16 billion and US imports of clothing are around $72 billion, according to Plunkett Research in 2006. The demand for clothing in the United States is huge, but the market is hugely competitive.

Van Dyke worked for many years at Nike and Patagonia after his earlier career in the legal profession, during which he was elected district attorney in Salem, Oregon, at the age of twenty-nine. Bearing a striking resemblance in looks as well as charm to his father, actor Dick Van Dyke, he came out of a "sailing-and-surfing" retirement to work for Nau.

"We still want to appeal to the outdoor market customers, 'cause that's kind of our roots, so our performance focus is there," said Van Dyke when the company was still trying to make a go of it. But, he explained, Nau brings "this element of beauty into it, this design. We include pieces you could wear in New York City to go out to dinner, but are waterproof and breathable and stretch. So you combine this very urban fashion design aesthetic with high performance. And no one's done that in this way."

Indeed, Nau realized that sophisticated activewear customers also want high style. They'll go for that more fitted, slightly awkward look because it's cool and it works technically. Fashion pundits have compared Nau to a fusion of Patagonia and Prada. But the key point the Nau folks didn't miss is that branding and marketing clothing comes down to the clothes themselves. Cool and distinctive clothes are their own best promotion, garnering free media exposure in channels that are respected and trusted by customers — like the Internet trendspotters, among whom Nau is a favorite.

"A lot of customers out there have no idea that a sustainable clothing line could look this good or perform this well," Galbraith said of his line. "We want to totally exceed their expectations by introducing them to something that they don't even know exists." This comment contains a cloud of concern. Educating customers to a new category takes energy away from selling the goods.

"If somebody walks by and knows nothing about sustainability, they'd look at this stuff and go, wow, that's beautiful, they'd be quickly compelled to want the product," he continued. "And when you tell them, 'Hey, guess what?' And you went down the list of everything, from how we're set up, to our prices, to what it's made of, what happens to our product at the end of its life, what we are giving back as a company . . . all these things, [they'd] be like, 'You're kidding!'"

Even the design of the company logo was well thought out in terms of functionality. The simple Nau logo is an ambigram, a word that reads the same when rotated 180 degrees. It's a nice touch for clothing, which is often viewed from different angles.

So the driver of preference, the thing that causes a customer to buy this over that, was Nau's style; but the extra kicker was that it was eco-friendly and functional. It might not make a difference in an individual purchase, but it created goodwill and cemented customers to the brand once they chose Nau.

Apparel that multitasks, making it more attractive for more uses.

Van Dyke pointed to the simplicity of the European-style design of Nau's men's and women's lines: "American companies have a tendency to think they're done when they can't put anything else on. And we think we're done when we can't take anything else off. A certain look follows from that. I think that's what makes [our clothing] so versatile. [It can be used by] a skier, or a snowboarder, or a mountain biker." This is brilliant because the customer doesn't say, "Well, I already have a ski jacket, or a car coat, or a biking shell . . ." He or she can justify the purchase because each garment is multifunctional. In an industry so closely defined by categories, this was another way that Nau broadened appeal.

"We wanted to design a product that could follow you throughout your life," explains Yolles. "We don't live these compartmentalized lives. So I'll be up in the mountains, skiing during the day, and eat at a nice restaurant later, and I need clothes that can do that."

Reaching for what the company named the Courier Windshirt, Yolles says, "This is iconic. It's made from recycled polyester, designed to be recycled at the end of its useful life. It's inspired by bicycle couriers. It's completely functional. The front zipper is slightly shorter than a traditional zipper so if I'm leaning forward on my bike it doesn't bunch up around my waist. But if I'm going out in the evening, going to a restaurant or whatever, I simply close the snap below the zipper so it's appropriate for the change in environment."

In a way, this follows a style of dressing introduced in the women's market in the late 1990s called day-into-night dressing. My wife, Elaine Kim, was the designer behind the line of clothing known simply as Product, and a pioneer in this category. A woman could wear the same garment at work and later at dinner. She didn't look overdressed for work *or* underdressed for dinner, thanks to the simplicity of the design. Women saw value in the versatility of those clothes in the same way that Nau customers see value in the versatility of their streetwise activewear.

Cradle to closet to cradle . . . and back again.

"When we set out to design the line, we thought about the life strategy for a particular garment," Yolles says, adding that the Nau jackets made from recycled polyester were intended to be 100 percent recycled when their projected ten-year life was over.

Traditionally, outdoor products are made out of petroleum-based nylon or polyester. Early on, Nau made a commitment to "no new oil," as Yolles explains. "We worked with Teijin, a vendor in Japan who supplied us with really beautiful recycled polyester fabric. They developed a way to maintain the integrity of polyester through the recycling process for use in waterproof breathable fabrics."

"Recycled polyester comes from soda pop bottles," he continues. "It's been around the outdoor industry for a really long time, but it's only used in insulation-fleece-type garments. Nobody had really developed recycled polyester that could be used in two- and three-layered, shell-type garments."

"Even before you actually get to the right product, you have to have the actual tools." In Nau's case, that was fabric. "Most apparel companies just show up at the fabric vendor for any given season," Yolles explains. "They pull out a suite of fabrics that are commercialized by the fabric vendor. They say, 'This is kind of what we've got this season.' And you kind of shop the line."

"We not only didn't do that, we really couldn't," Yolles concludes. "Because if we were serious about sustainability and serious about creating product, the reality was the fabrics we required didn't really exist. So in our initial spring '07 line, there were thirty fabrics, and twenty-six involved very significant development efforts. We worked with partners and found the vendors to develop them from scratch."

Sourcing sustainable fabrics is no easy task. Organic cotton, which is far preferable to traditional chemical-dependent growing schemes, is in very short supply and commanding high prices. It's also not as sustainable as we might think because cotton is a thirsty crop. So is PLA (polylactic acid) fabric, which is made from biodegradable, corn-based resin. The hidden cost is in the water that is used in both growing and processing. The depletion and subsequent desertification of the Aral Sea was largely due to the cultivation of cotton in the former Soviet Union. As a result, fabric buyers at a recent Premier Vision international fabric show in Paris reported that sustainable fabrics, including organic cotton, were fetching premium, demand-driven prices, according to the industry trade bible, *Women's Wear Daily.*

In a margin-driven industry, it's difficult to purchase an ingredient that will automatically price you out of your category — unless you compensate in other ways, like increasing value, which Nau did.

Sustainability doesn't stop at the cash register.

Nau was as concerned about the *care* of its clothes as it was with the wearing of them, especially with regard to an item's carbon footprint. Explains Jamie Bainbridge, the firm's director of materials research, "A huge portion of the embedded energy in a piece of clothing comes after the person buys it."

To meet this challenge, none of the Nau product required dry cleaning. Not even the wool products, says Bainbridge, pointing to a peacoat that can be laundered in a washing machine in cold water on a delicate cycle and then hung up to dry.

"We purposely didn't want to produce a wool outer garment with a separate lining in it, because when you launder something like that you get differential shrinkage. If you've ever tried to launder a sport coat, it never looks the same again. So here we've bonded two fabrics together using a hot-melt, solvent-free bonding system. When they're stuck together, they're not going to behave so differently when they go through washing. And it also means that we do a very simple, clean construction. You're not going to put your hand in the sleeve and get all tangled up in the lining. It easily slides over clothing."

The company augmented its eco-advantage in this area by educating its consumers on energy-efficient laundering habits that will actually extend the life of the garment. All that lint in your dryer? That's your clothes dissolving away.

Did Nau's audience appreciate the eco-advantages the company offered? Many in the fashion business old guard still believe a green label is the kiss of death for the fashion buyer, and most kids going to Forever 21 may not give a hoot about sustainability. Nevertheless, there is a growing and quite visible sustainable fashion movement that is being awarded a special place in the fashion press, on runways, and in preferential areas of influential apparel shows. It's also bouncing around the Gort Cloud through trendspotters like Inhabitat.com and CoolHunting.com and the green blogosphere. Sitting at the very visible apex of this movement is Nau — because this company did it the hard way.

Built from scratch around a mission.

For Ian Yolles, previously a marketing director at Nike in Beaverton, Oregon, the excitement over founding a different kind of company began to build at the Urban Grind, a coffeehouse in Portland's Pearl District. He, Galbraith, Bainbridge, and Van Dyke were now four of the seven outdoor apparel professionals that Reynolds had gathered together to start the company he envisioned. All of the men and women came from a sustainability perspective, all knew one another from their work at Nike, Patagonia, or (like Yolles) both, and all were excited about working as a team. "We were saying to one another, 'Well, are you going to do this?' 'Well, I'll do it if you do it.'"

Galbraith explains that while some people may ask, " 'Should we wait for the government to make this change, should we wait for this or that to make this change?' . . . this was a group of people [who] don't wait and honestly probably never have waited for things to change." The seven "unfuckers" left their secure jobs behind, taking what Yolles describes as a pretty significant risk. They were drawn by a deeper sense of purpose, and by what they saw as tremendous potential in the business model.

"This entire effort has been an exercise in design in the fullest sense the word," Yolles explains. "We've had this real opportunity to design an entire enterprise strategy, informed not only by the goal to make a profit, but also by our commitment to sustainability and a responsibility to the community. From day one, we tried to be intentional and deliberate and conscientious about every decision we made with those bigger ideas in mind."

By that time, Eric Reynolds had taken himself out of the process. "He realized he was not the person to breathe life into his ideas," explains Yolles. But the seven-member "collective" was mandated to respect Reynolds's four main organizing principles.

Nau's Organizing Principles

1. The corporation recognizes an obligation not only to its shareholders and investors, but also to the earth.
2. Distribution of product will be through the company's own distribution system, rather than through other retailers. This not only ensures the integrity of the line and a close relationship with customers, but it also allows the company to keep the price point at a competitive level despite higher production costs.
3. The company will adapt itself to the Internet Age by bridging the gap between online sales and the more traditional bricks-and-mortar stores by combining the efficiencies of online commerce with the touchy-feely experience of shopping fashion.
4. The company will donate 5 percent of every sale to a nonprofit organization [unprecedented in corporate America] and will include direct customer participation in the giving process, purchase by purchase.

The collective's early brainstorming sessions at the Urban Grind centered on what Yolles describes as the flame model. "At the center of the flame is the little white core of the flame. It's what I would describe as identity," he explains. "This identity is expressed congruently through every single dimension of the organization." More traditional corporations alternatively refer to this core identity as the mission or the purpose. For Nau, it was the desire to make really cool, fun stuff that didn't, as the team liked to say, fuck up the world.

Next came a discussion of tone. Explains Ian, "We asked questions like, 'How would we react with one another? What's the atmosphere like? Is it creative? Is it safe? Can you speak your mind? How do you nurture or create this kind of atmosphere?' That started to inform the kind of structures we needed to put in place that supported this identity and tone, and that led us to generate results and activity in the action space. It was identity and tone before action. Not the other way around."

In doing so, Nau was establishing its corporate culture, where employees and partners were motivated and empowered by the higher ideals of the brand. This shining goodwill opened doors and a floodgate of free publicity.

A declaration of earth dependence.

When it came to making Nau a legal corporation, the collective didn't pass by any golden opportunities to make sure they were positioned the right way.

"The corporate bylaws, are, in some ways, the legal DNA of the company," explains Van Dyke. "So we said, 'If this is who we are, is there anything in these bylaws that should reflect who we are? And not only that, can we do something with the bylaws that would enable us to protect who we are over the long term?'"

According to a blog maintained by New York–based business attorney Stephen Filler, "Corporate attorney Robert Hinkley influenced Nau's founders. Hinkley incorporated the work of management expert W. Edwards Deming and systems theorist Peter Senge to develop new ideas pertaining to the notion of a corporation as citizen. Deming had written that 'most of the time it's the system that causes the problem, not the people in the system.' He combined this idea with the insight of Senge, who said that to change any system you should 'look to make the smallest change possible that will generate the biggest effect.'"[1]

From these theories, Hinkley created a code for corporate citizenship that contained a twenty-eight-word caveat (here in bold) to the traditional profit motive: "the duty of directors shall be to make money for shareholders, **but not at the expense of the environment, human rights, public health and safety, dignity of employees, and the welfare of the community in which a company operates**." Nau included a version of these twenty-eight words in its bylaws.

The founders also went a step farther and included a document called "Rules of Corporate Responsibility" that contained eight commitments. One stated that the highest-paid employee could not make more than twelve times the salary of the lowest-paid employee. Another stated that the company would never pay less than one and a half times the US minimum wage. A third promised that all spouses or partners would be guaranteed benefits regardless of sexual persuasion. "The kicker to all of this," says Yolles, "is that it says that none of these rules or commitments can ever be changed without a minimum of 75 percent shareholder agreement." What the collective didn't fully realize at the time was how much the new corporate bylaws would affect capital fund-raising.

"We had raised $2 million from friends and family to kind of get the thing going," says Yolles. "But then we needed to raise our next round of $5 million." Yolles and Van Dyke went to New York to meet with an anonymous investor who had $1.5 billion in a new hedge fund. After a grilling that lasted forty-five minutes, he agreed to invest $5 million in the company . . . but not without a snag.

The investor's attorney discovered the twenty-eight words and balked. The attorney pointed out that this language equated to a greater risk for the investor, because in the event of a liquidity situation, the company would be devalued — it was assuming more responsibility and therefore more risk than a traditional company.

Nau's defense came from the heart. Explains Yolles, "We told them that from a branding point of view, we thought this language would increase the value of the company because it's what enables us to build this congruency, which is what a strong brand is about. It's what enables us to differentiate ourselves in the marketplace. It enables us to establish much more loyal, stronger, deeper relationships with our customers who care about these things. That is what is going to make us a stronger brand and lead to a bigger-valuation kind of company."

The investor's attorneys sent the bylaws out for review, and the opinions that came back were consistent. Nau's proposed bylaws, without a doubt, represented greater risk. The investor wanted them out.

Recalls Van Dyke: "We sat down, and I told everybody where we were, and I said, 'If this money goes away, we're probably done before we ever get started. Here's what they want us to give up.' And we talked for about two and a half hours. One person at a time, we went around the room, and everyone essentially said the same thing: 'I'm here for doing business differently. These rules are really at the core of what we're doing and why we're doing it. No way.' And there were people in that group who had kids they had taken out of school . . . sold their homes, moved to Portland, taken a 40 percent cut in pay."

"So we went back to the investors and said, 'Sorry, this is who we are.'" They stood their ground, and eventually the investor recanted and funded. "It was amazing," Van Dyke continues. I mean I just get chills thinking about this. It was one of those moments where we said, 'We've gotta put our lives where our mouths are here.' And that kind of kicked off the next two years of raising funds."

The idea of a shared fate wedded to a common vision continued to drive the company through its initial fourteen-month life. "I think the brand really reflects the idea of a community and a collective. When we talk to our customers and audiences, there's a group of shared values. People who share experiences and beliefs about what they love and what makes the world go 'round and what needs to be done to make things better," reflects Van Dyke. "I think it's smarter capitalism. We can create more wealth by just being smarter as a group rather than relying on any one person to do it."

This single story is the theme that has driven dozens of articles on the company, including a particularly admiring piece in *Fast Company*. The payback in brand awareness was invaluable.

Make it. Sell it. No middlemen.

The outdoor apparel industry, like most clothing categories in the United States, is structured so that most of the product is distributed through a network of specialty and department stores. Companies such as Patagonia and North Face as well as the broader active sport industry brands, like Nike, Adidas, and Reebok, create the product, build the brand, and then sell it to consumers mostly through independent retailers.

Following Eric Reynolds's mandate, Nau created its products and sold them through its own distribution channels — not easy to do, given the difficulty in gaining access to America's large but broadly scattered market, and because it forced Nau to be both a maker and a seller, wearing two hats.

"The middleman — the retailer — has a tremendous amount of power and control," explains Yolles. Retailers employ buyers who determine what products show up in their stores. "And these people are typically very conservative," says Yolles, "just by the nature of the job. They need to annualize their numbers, so they say, 'This is what sold last season.' You know, change the pocket or change the color. And they tend to cherry-pick your line. If you have a line with a hundred styles, they might buy five or ten of them."

As Yolles explains it, if a manufacturer has a product that is not traditional or mainstream, it can be difficult to negotiate through this buying process. Traditional buying channels tend to filter their product selections to the lowest common denominator, so the customer cannot feel the full force of a collection statement. "Choosing to make our own distribution channels [through our stores and our Web site] means we're not subjected to that constraint," Ian says. "It allows us to build a much more intimate relationship with our customer."

"We can also design the customer experience ourselves," he continues. "We're able to present the product in the way it was meant to be presented and wrap an experience around it in the way it was meant to be wrapped."

The outdoor apparel business, like other businesses, has seen a tremendous consolidation in the past two decades. Many independent retailers have disappeared, which makes the problem all the worse. An example is the recent consolidation of Gart Sports, Oshman's, Sportmart, and Copeland Sports all under the Sports Authority big-box retail label. "The sole proprietors, the specialty outdoor shops, were owned by individuals, and they tended to be pretty serious users of the products," Yolles says. "They were very passionate, very knowledgeable, kind of really inside core to all the sports."

Nau harked back to these earlier days, when the consumer could access that kind of passion and knowledge. Nau also knew its customers — even if this insight was initially based on gut instinct and a strong feeling for the new market sector. Customers may have been relatively few, but Nau could identify with them and cater to them personally.

Ones and zeros with a few bricks.

Eric Reynolds's third tenet was to bridge the gap between online sales and brick-and-mortar stores.

Since the advent of online shopping, "people often start by researching or learning about a product online," says Ian Yolles. "They then often, particularly if you're talking about apparel products, go into a store to try it on to make sure it fits, make sure it looks good . . . [to] have a tactile experience of the fabric. But then they often turn around and go home to surf the Internet to find that item for the least possible cost."

To meet the demands of these Net-savvy shoppers, retailers have built an online experience to parallel the experience in their stores. But "nobody has really connected the two channels in a manner that actually adds value to the customer experience and that reflects how customers are shopping," Yolles explains.

To blend the traditional online shopping experience with the traditional storefront experience, Nau installed what it trademarked as webfronts in all nine of its stores.

Customers who entered Nau were able to purchase merchandise in a traditional manner, but they could either walk out with it or receive a credit for having it shipped. "What's never been done before, to our knowledge, is this kind of alternative purchasing methodology," explains Yolles. Shoppers who chose to have the product they had selected shipped to them within two or three days, similar to what would happen if they'd ordered it online, received a 10 percent discount on their total purchase price.

According to Van Dyke, Nau faced tremendous skepticism from potential investors over whether or not this concept would work, but those concerns were proven wrong. "We estimated that the ship-to-home percentage would begin at between 10 and 20 percent and, by the end of 2007, grow to 30 percent," says the CEO. "We came right out of the gate at 50 percent" — and held there.

This innovation has the potential to be a "much, much more productive retail model than that of any existing retail business," says Yolles. "It's a lot more efficient to manage inventory when it's sitting in one place versus having it distributed in multiple locations all over the country. So there's efficiency from a logistics management standpoint."

The company also benefited from holding more inventory in a warehouse facility at the cost of five to ten dollars per square foot than in a retail venue costing up to seventy dollars a square foot. Even more important, Nau could offer the same selection and service in a smaller retail space than it would otherwise, making for reduced rent, labor, and utility expenses, a smaller carbon footprint, and less capital outlay necessary to build stores.

"So all of a sudden you have a very efficient, very productive retail model," Yolles says. "And we've created a much more boutiquelike setting where the product can really be showcased the way it deserves to be showcased . . . where the customer can navigate the product in a much easier way."

According to Van Dyke, the reduction in carbon footprint from this model is significant. "The big inventory moves in a large retail business come at the end of the season, when you've run out of product in Seattle and you have some in Atlanta," he explains. "Stores are moving inventory between stores, and then eventually back to the warehouse for liquidations. So product gets moved two and three times. With a centralized warehouse, we move less of it out. And that really is where the carbon impact comes in, with transportation."

Another Nau innovation is called the product tree — interactive touch screens where customers could learn more about the company's products by simply using their fingertips. Also, a small card imprinted with the name, price, and image of the style was included with every piece of merchandise on the racks. On the back of the card was a retail bar code that could be taken to the product trees and scanned. Information about the product instantly appeared on the screen. The same card could also be used to initiate a self-service transaction within the store environment.

Yolles explains the concept: "In addition to the product trees, there were two additional interactive touch-screen devices that are integrated into the cash wrap adjacent to traditional POS [point-of-sale] machines. If you want to purchase a product, have it shipped to you, and receive a 10 percent discount on the purchase price along with free shipping, you can use the same card to initiate the purchasing process. Once again, you scan the card, and it immediately brings up the product detail page from our Web site associated with that particular style. It asks me what color I want. I want blue. What size do I want? I want small. How many do I want? I want three of them. Then it asks me if I want to check out, just as if I'm shopping online. And I say yes, and then it asks me if I'm a registered user. And I say yes. And it asks me for my password, I put in my password. Up pops my credit card information, my shipping information, my billing information, and I simply confirm the details of the order. I make sure it's all right and then I'm done."

"So," Yolles concludes, "we've literally taken the checkout experience from our Web site, repurposed it for an interactive environment, and enabled a self-service transaction."

Yolles credits much of the success they experienced with this model to a well-trained and knowledgeable store staff. That staff knew when customers wanted them to "hang with them" while in the store and when they wanted to be left alone. For customers who disliked being approached by sales associates, the Nau model worked well. "I can come into the store, I can browse the product," notes Yolles. "I can learn everything I need to know about the product, the availability, what sort of fabric it's made of, where it's made, the features and benefits of the product. I can try it on; I can make sure it fits. And I can go through a transaction, complete my purchase, and walk out the door having never talked to anybody."

Customer-directed corporate social responsibility.

In the rear of every Nau store was the Giving Wall. It was large and it had a graphic component that invited the customer to participate by interacting with one of two touch-screen devices. Each had a menu listing the ten nonprofit organizations to which the particular store would be funneling 5 percent of gross revenue, allowing the customer to see a short presentation on each of the choices. Some of the nonprofits are working on environmental issues, others on humanitarian issues. Some are international, some are national, and some are local. Later, when making his or her purchase, the customer would designate the preferred nonprofit. This is just another way that Nau made customers not just sources of revenue, but actual stakeholders in Nau's future and the future of the planet.

The partnerships with the local nonprofits were especially important because of the synergistic storytelling component, Yolles explains. The idea was that Nau could tell its growing community the stories of its nonprofit partners' work. In turn, those partners could share Nau's story with their constituents. The average level of corporate philanthropy in the United States is less than two-tenths of 1 percent of sales. The average benchmark for a company that gives significant contributions to charitable causes is 1 percent, pioneered by Patagonia.

"Five percent is, like, out of the stratosphere," says Yolles. Nau decided that it could afford to give away 5 percent based on its business model of distributing product directly to the customer in an industry structured on a wholesale model.

Getting the word out.

Because Nau had attempted such lofty goals — to build a company from scratch on an untested sustainable model, to approach manufacturing and distribution in such a unique and labor-intensive style, to involve customers in the process of sharing profits, and to make edgy clothing that multitasked — the company did not need sales agents, or advertising, or fashion shows, or a print catalog for that matter. It didn't need any of these promotional staples of the fashion business because free publicity was everywhere.

Fashion bloggers and the fashion press regularly featured Nau, as did members of the Gort Cloud. It was a favorite among the Internet's green trendspotters and environmental hubs, like TreeHugger.com and GreenLivingIdeas.com. Business publications of all types featured the company in their start-up profiles, including one very nice cover in *Fast Company*. For fashionable insiders, the fact that the company didn't pay for promotion gave it even greater credibility.

Adding fuel to the fire were the firm's own efforts to promote awareness and brand loyalty, including a robust blog on the Nau Web site. Called the Thought Kitchen, the blog was full of related sustainable information. Another area of the site hosted user-generated content that extended the spirit of the brand. Nau created one particularly clever video clip, called "Little House on the Trailer," in partnership with a videographer. The clip documented a young woman's life living in a very tiny house mounted to a trailer, with the message that living small was living sustainably. This represents the *push* side of the Gort Cloud.

Nau also encouraged local awareness through monthly Collective Commons events in stores. "Not only is Nau a great emerging apparel company, but they are bringing exciting speakers into their stores for small community gatherings on slideshow topics relating to the outdoors, adventure and sustainability," according to the HauteNature blog.

The companywide commitment to real sustainability protected it from charges of greenwashing. This created customer loyalty and trust, which is the cornerstone of any successful brand. Whenever I'm asked to define what a brand is, I say, "Brand equals Trust."

Challenging people to think.

In fact, Nau was branding itself as a company that challenged consumers, as well as other retailers and wholesalers, to reconsider their assumptions and change the way they think. "Our goal from the beginning was to raise the bar in terms of how the whole apparel industry thinks about sustainability," Yolles says. "I'd like nothing more than to have the rest of the industry follow us."

This plan to raise the bar seemed to be working. Much larger corporations, apparel and otherwise, were watching Nau and attempted to learn from it. Procter & Gamble invited Chris Van Dyke to speak to the company's product designers. PepsiCo sent three divisional senior VPs from its new healthy foods division to talk to Nau about building a sustainability-focused culture. Business schools including Harvard, Kellogg, Columbia, Stanford, and Haas called to talk about innovative corporate strategy. Van Dyke said of the attention, "The sub-part of our mission statement is to work to help influence other businesses."

"This is business activism," he continued. "It's social, it's environmental, it's political, it's all of those things, and it's for profit. We're challenging the nature of capitalism."

SUMMARY: HOW DIFFERENTIATION CREATED BOTH RISK AND BRAND EQUITY

There is no question that green has met fashion. The most recent holiday catalog from Barney's promoted a sustainable fashion theme. There are dozens of clothing lines featuring sustainable and/or organic materials, and many of them are featured in the Gort Cloud on such sites as the Sustainable Style Foundation (SustainableStyle.org) and StyleWillSaveUs .com. Nevertheless, just being eco-correct will not ensure popularity. In fashion, you must have a point of view. There must be a singular direction that will get the attention of early adopters and the critical fashion press.

Nau attempted to do this. There were no other products out there that looked quite like this. Layered atop was its deep commitment to social and environmental responsibility. It was a program so heavily ingrained in Nau's brand DNA that everyone from vendors to investors to customers couldn't escape the message. This set it apart and fueled its publicity engine.

So what went wrong?

Bloggers have offered different reasons. Carissa Wodehouse of EcoMetro wrote, "The outdoor industry, especially snowboard clothing, is trendy and seasonal, requiring frequent replacement. Away from [Nau's] drawing board went neon colors, away went blue camo prints, and good riddance. [Instead,] Nau came out with a line almost exclusively in forest green, mud brown and a dirty cream." Her point was that making durable, trend-resistant clothing didn't foster return sales. She went on to question the low-key nature of the clothes that emphasized the individual and not the brand: "There was nothing visually special about the clothes — at first glance. As outdoorsy as any of us may be, we walk mostly on urban streets. And what's the fun in a $250 sweater if no one is going to ask you about it, giving you the chance to talk about the organic fibers or recyclable clasps?" This is true. There was no obvious logo, nor were customers turned into walking billboards for the brand.

A post on the site Murketing.com posed the question, "I wasn't getting direct evidence of [the] actual Nau consumer. I totally got the concept, as [*Fast Company* described], 'The ultimate over-the-top, high-concept business. It makes striking, enviro-friendly clothing.' Okay. But my job is to write about why people buy things, so I was trying to figure out, 'Who is buying this, and why?'"

Well, I think Nau knew who its customers were and had done a fair job of defining them. After all, it was meeting sales targets and had an intensely loyal following. Ian Yolles puts it this way: "I think the reality of our product was that you could come to it in a variety of ways. The brand and the product were incredibly accessible and open because you could come to it through the lens of performance and function, or you could come to it through the lens of high design, style, and beauty, or you could come to it through the lens of sustainability. None of those things are mutually exclusive. I think there were multiple access points to the product. As a result, we were beginning to engage and grow a community in meaningful ways."

When I press Ian for a more traditional demographic profile of his customer, he responds, "From a customer point of view, we think in psychographic terms. We consider our core customer to be at the confluence point of three different but related communities: artists (in the broad sense of the word), athletes, and activists. That shorthand describes people who value the aesthetic realm of their experience and appreciate good design, live an active life and are drawn to the outdoors, and believe they can make a positive difference in their community and the world at large."

Nevertheless, these comments illuminate a possible failure to define product use clearly to a broader audience. As I mentioned earlier, Nau produced a hybrid clothing line, neither technical activewear, nor high fashion, nor casual sportswear, but maybe all three. Its core customers of fashion followers got this; however, the product represented a classification that the mainstream apparel industry had not yet wrapped its niche-making head around. Without a pressure wave of mainstream apparel industry education, the average consumer either wasn't aware of Nau or didn't understand it. Developing a niche takes time, something Nau ran out of — and the cost of opening its own showcase stores only compounded the need for large amounts of capital.

Yolles underscored the point: "We had a group of investors and work members that [had] been with us from early on that liked what they were seeing in terms of how the business was evolving on all fronts, and they were willing to continue investing money in the operations of the company, but there was a gap between their level of commitment and what we needed. And it was that gap that we weren't able to close." As a result, Nau was forced to close temporarily, but the uniqueness of the brand and the company's customer equity attracted new investor prospects. One of these bought Nau's assets and will relaunch the brand in fall 2008 with few substantive changes, except for the costly showcase stores. According to a TreeHugger post, Nau will pursue more traditional distribution through the independent retail system.

The team at Nau saw themselves as trailblazers, and I agree. Their efforts were bold enough to create a following and worthy enough to attract an investor committed to raising the firm from the dead. It reminds me of a tune in the Disney classic *Chitty Chitty Bang Bang* starring Chris's father, Dick Van Dyke: "From the ashes of disaster rise the roses of success."

Cleaning Up in a Crowded Marketplace
Seventh Generation

THE CHALLENGE

Seventh Generation, founded by Jeffrey Hollender in the early 1990s, has ridden to success on the green wave of eco-awareness. Today this family of products is the dominant brand in the much coveted and hotly contested green household cleaning and personal care market.

How does Seventh Generation maintain market share? How does it renew its message to established customers and reach out to new, less eco-aware consumers?

THE SOLUTION

Rather than compete directly with giants like Procter & Gamble with a huge advertising budget Seventh Generation doesn't have, Jeffrey Hollender has utilized connections within the green community — in other words, in the Gort Cloud.

His earliest marketing efforts targeted the green-aware, a then tiny group of people willing to listen to his message and pass it on to others.

He sought out technical partners and environmental experts, who helped him design a line of products that would be effective, eco-friendly alternatives to standard household cleaners and that would pass muster with the scientific community.

He has continued to update and refine his products and accompanying messages to counteract green fatigue among existing customers, while evolving product differentiations to outmaneuver green competitors.

And he is reaching out to an ever-widening circle of potential customers as the perils of global climate change and pollution become more widely acknowledged.

Thinking generations ahead.

Seventh Generation of Burlington, Vermont, was one of the first entries in the eco-friendly household cleaning and personal care categories.

Since its launch in the early 1990s, it has leveraged an astute brand and marketing strategy to maintain significant market share in a category that is hotly contested. Many competitors have been attracted to this market because of its high volume, rapid product turnover, and astonishing growth.

Not only are brands such as Planet, Ecover, Begley's Best, Method, Mrs. Meyer's, and Shaklee presenting a serious challenge, now mainstream players like SC Johnson and Clorox, with its Green Works line, have introduced more competition — not to mention all the private labels at reduced prices. Even Procter & Gamble's Tide comes in formulations meant to appeal to the green-conscious shopper. Nevertheless, Seventh Generation continues to thrive and grow as the total market for green household products grows.

Seventh Generation has its roots in Renew America, a small Vermont environmental organization with a mail-order catalog that promoted energy conservation products. When Jeffrey Hollender, the former president of Warner Audio Publishing in New York City, acquired Renew in 1988, he added nontoxic cleaning items to the offerings and began selling the products to natural food stores and co-ops.

The *Seventh Generation* name was suggested by a Native American employee. Rooted in the culture of the Iroquois, a tribe that once stretched across New England and much of the Northeast, it expressed the notion that "in our every deliberation we must consider the impact of our decisions on the next seven generations." It was and remains a bold declaration that this particular company stands for protecting the planet's children for centuries to come.

Jeffrey Hollender, a type A CEO for the Age of Sustainability.

Seventh Generation founder and CEO Jeffrey Hollender is passionate, driven, and uncompromising. He is the model of what you might call the type A version of an eco-business CEO. "You can't ever be complacent around here," says Seventh Generation's director of education, Susan Johnson. "Jeffrey pushes hard."

At the same time, "it's amazing when you have a president of a company who is just so one of the crowd," says Stephanie Lowe, director of human resources, noting that Hollender's office is housed in an open cubicle no different from all the others.

Hollender's egalitarianism is just part of his inspirational appeal. "You can tell when he's speaking from a place of real meaning for him," Lowe continues, explaining that Hollender is extremely adept at moving audiences, whether consumers or employees, and that this has had a lot to do with building the Seventh Generation name.

In the early days, Hollender "wanted to become an expert in all the [environmental] issues surrounding all these ingredients and what was wrong with the stuff that was in the mainstream, like dioxin and chlorine," says Jeff Phillips, executive vice president of operations, product R&D, and business development, who has worked with Hollender since 1994. "He did all the research. He's a voracious reader. Everything you read on our Web site about natural cleaning stems from all the early work he did."

By reaching out to academics, scientists, policy makers, and nonprofit organizations, Hollender was inadvertently using the power of the Gort Cloud to build his business from the get-go. The Cloud at that time was small, but growing. Nevertheless, Hollender instinctively knew that connecting with like-minded members of the green community would help him succeed.

The Gort Cloud connection only strengthened this CEO's passion for social responsibility, because others in the green community felt the same way. "Jeffrey was one of the early leaders in business with social responsibility," says Phillips. "They made him a public profile as a speaker and a writer. So you know, all that sort of tied together."

Early to market. Early to grow.

For years, Seventh Generation had the eco home products category pretty much to itself, at least in the northeastern United States. Planet, a Canadian brand, was introduced in the same period, but only on the West Coast. Ecover was growing in Europe, and Method was not established until 1999.

Back in the 1990s, Seventh Generation's marketing efforts were focused on educating the green-minded public. Hollender was peddling not just a new brand, but also a new idea and a new need, using the nascent Gort

Cloud as a base to get the message out. The company reached this community, and beyond it, through the Internet and through its packaging.

"When we put the name Seventh Generation on the box, we had done our homework," says Phillips. "We had lots of education on the package, on the Web site. It showed that we walked the walk, that we were really true."

The company's entry and growth in the marketplace roughly coincided with the ascendance of another cluster in the Gort Cloud, namely the green retailers, led most noticeably by Whole Foods and Wild Oats. With eighteen stores in the early 1990s, Whole Foods presented a major opportunity for Seventh Generation "to create a household products section in an environmental way and utilize this incredible concept of what Seventh Generation stood for as the engine," says Phillips. As a result of its connection with these markets, the company sustained a whopping 30 percent growth in sales per year for more than a decade.

"We brought up the quality and we brought down the cost so that all of a sudden it wasn't that much more expensive to buy our laundry detergent than to buy Tide," he continues. "It worked really well, and we became the leader in that category," taking a 45 percent market share of home cleaning products at Whole Foods and climbing onto the shelves at all natural food stores.

People began to "see us as the Procter & Gamble of natural products," Phillips continues. When it came to the nonfood products, "we were the choice. We had people really passionate about who we were and what we stood for. We had created the brand."

As a result of the partnership with Whole Foods and Wild Oats, as well as other relationships, Seventh Generation's growth spurt has been sustained. Now worth a hundred million dollars, the company is twice the size it was just three years ago.

Target audience: An ever-lighter green.

Seventh Generation estimates that it has saturated its hard-core green consumer base, with 70 to 80 percent of that segment regularly purchasing Seventh Generation products. To continue its rapid growth, the company must go after lighter green segments.

Although Seventh Generation owns just 4 percent of the total household cleanser market, "there's a huge opportunity [for growth] in the grocery world," says product development associate Reed Doyle, a former employee of Michael Braungart and William McDonough, authors of *Cradle to Cradle* and partners in the consulting firm MBDC, as well as of Amory Lovins, founder of the Rocky Mountain Institute. "But how do we bring the lighter green consumer into our brand and engage them and make them understand? What will really resonate?"

One marketing effort under way is to better understand consumers. "There's such an amazing movement in the Christian, [and] Jewish tradition, to really look at 'How do we make a difference in the world?' So faith-based buyers can be a huge demographic," he says. Doyle also talks about targeting positive contributors who don't necessarily see themselves as environmentalists but who do want to "find more and more ways to do good."

Targeting the nurturing sex, women.

Doyle points to young mothers as perhaps the most important target demographic. "Mothers with babies and/or small children naturally want to protect them," he explains. "They're very aware of the kinds of products they're using in and around their home."

Outside of this smaller target subset is the much larger consumer population of women in general. According to the marketing-to-women firm TrendSight Group, women are decision makers in purchasing home products 80 percent of the time, and they also control at least 50 percent of business-to-business purchasing.

One of the most compelling factors affecting a woman's purchasing decisions is her view of a particular company's "corporate halo," hence women are generally more green-product-conscious than men. Fifty-nine percent of women put "environment, ecology, and energy" at the top of their "good corporate citizen" checklist. As leading PR agency Golin Harris states on its Web site, "Give her green products, packaging and programs, and she'll hand her greenbacks to you instead of your competitors."

These trends are one reason the British grocery chain Tesco is relabeling seventy thousand products to detail carbon footprint, enabling consumers to comparison-shop with regard to carbon emissions as easily as they do with nutritional information.

Women can be tough customers who don't necessarily take advertising messages as gospel. They investigate the product options to make sure there's no greenwashing going on. Says Marti Barletta, CEO and founder of the TrendSight Group, "As the environmental movement continues to gain traction, eco-friendly initiatives will serve in the short run as an incremental point of difference, and in the long run as a loyalty insulator. But they will only work if they target the greenest consumers of all, women." This is just one more indication of the power of the Gort Cloud to confer credibility on aspiring green brands.

Jen Ganshirt of Frank About Women, a marketing-to-women communications firm based in North Carolina, says that with the firm's recent study, "not only did we discover that women definitely no longer see green brands and products as niche items; we learned that they are seeking them out and demanding that their favorite brands provide them with green alternatives."

Leveraging buying power: The Big Green Purse.

It is women who are leading the way when it comes to pushing the green cause. Diane MacEachern recently launched a national campaign and Web site, BigGreenPurse.com, urging women to shift at least a thousand dollars of their annual household spending to green products.

"We could be the most powerful force for economic and environmental change in the 21st century if we focused our money where it could make the biggest difference," MacEachern says on her Web site. "If a million people did that, it would have a $1 billion impact." Big Green Purse has done the research for busy women everywhere and has made it its business to recommend products that are really green at affordable prices.

Harnessing the power of moms: The EcoMom Alliance.

Another organization based in the San Francisco Bay Area is the EcoMom Alliance, founded by Kimberly Danek Pinkson "to leverage the power of mothers to help reduce global warming" and "to inspire and empower mothers to take first steps for a sustainable future by sustaining their homes, sustaining their planet and sustaining themselves," its Web site states.

From the perspective of the Gort Cloud, EcoMom belongs to a cluster I've labeled green parenting while Big Green Purse lies within the cluster of eco-bloggers, but the two organizations reach out to their constituent audiences in similar ways. They strive to educate and steer their communities toward sustainable products, like Seventh Generation.

According to Pinkson, the idea for EcoMom was born just after she co-produced an event for the United Nations World Environment Day in spring 2006. At a picnic with her children, Pinkson was asked by the other mothers for "information about things they could do at home to create a healthier environment for their families," she explains. "I was watching this conversation just completely take off. It was just this amazing moment — a wildfire of interest. And I thought, *I need to do something with the power of mothers as role models.*"

The alliance encourages its nine thousand members to become "EcoMom leaders" and host gatherings in their homes. Conversations range across many topics, from the pitfalls of antibacterial hand sanitizers to the nuances of composting to how to become a locavore — someone who seeks out locally, organically grown food.

Members follow a ten-step regimen toward using only nontoxic products for cleaning, bathing, and makeup; and, as might be expected, the best nontoxic products are widely discussed and vetted.

With regard to Clorox and its new green line, "people hear about that stuff and they want to know our opinion on it," Pinkson says. "They're very leery . . . They're not able to take the time to read the whole label and they don't know half the time what all the ingredients mean. They're asking about the authenticity and the integrity behind this — if it's as green as the company is saying it is."

"Conversely there's a lot of excitement when the big brands do start to offer ecologically friendly options because it makes it more accessible for them," she continues. "In order to make these changes happen on a global level, it's the big ships like Procter & Gamble that we have to turn around."

The EcoMom home gatherings are the perfect place for networks of consumers, voicing their content and discontent with green brands and product development, to create small bursts in the Gort Cloud. These bursts then echo through the Cloud, reaching other green consumer groups and, eventually, other businesses or the people who advise them.

Sometimes the EcoMom conversations center on the affordability of going green. "We recommend looking at the overall cost, so you're not just looking at the price tag but you're looking at it in terms of issues — how it's affecting your family and your own health . . . long-term, you may be saving thousands of dollars in doctor bills."

According to Pinkson, EcoMom tries to go easy on its members when it comes to laying on guilt. "If having all these choices is making you guilt-ridden and fearful and you're walking around like a basket case because you can't make the right choice, well then you certainly aren't bringing a more sustainable kind of living to yourself," she explains. "It's all about getting the people on board and taking that first step. Because once you're doing one thing, you're going to start doing another and another and another."

The EcoMom Alliance is preparing to launch EcoMom Approve, a section of the Web site where EcoMom-approved products will be promoted. Companies will pay a nominal fee on a sliding scale to be listed, but should they opt to use the EcoMom logo in marketing as a kind of Good Housekeeping Seal, "they would pay a fee for using our name," Pinkson explains.

In February 2008, the EcoMom Alliance was featured on the front page of the *New York Times*. Pinkson quickly found herself deluged by phone calls and e-mails from mothers as well as by requests for corporate partnerships. Such is the power of traditional media.

Priscilla Woolworth: Launching a green version of the venerable general store.

Priscilla Woolworth, a fourth-generation descendant of the original Woolworth store founder, will launch a new online, eco-friendly PriscillaWoolworth.com general store in fall 2008. It will be a "one-stop shop for everything you need for your household," she says, carrying "the best products I've come across that I think are of tremendous value and a very good investment." Woolworth is targeting women like herself who "want the best for themselves and their families, and therefore really are aware of what's going on."

"Women talk constantly about what they're eating, what they're cooking, what they're buying, so there's this shared information that's continuous," she says, explaining that she is relying on word of mouth, aided by blogs and Web sites, to spread awareness of her new venture. The Gort Cloud strikes again.

"I'm creating this business as a resource to educate people as well as to provide products," she says. "You feel a sense of pride in yourself using a cleaner product. You feel you're doing something as well as respecting the other people in your life."

Woolworth is considering minimizing the term *green* in her marketing, pointing to a recent post on the LOHAS Web site indicating that "eco-attributes test better with consumers when describing specific qualities such as 'recycled,' 'biodegradable,' 'cruelty-free,' and 'locally grown' — as opposed to the more general term 'green.'"

The competitive landscape: The good, the bad, the ugly.

Americans' longtime obsession with cleanliness, fueled in part by over-inflated advertising budgets for disinfectant products, can sometimes do more harm than good. Eradicating all bacteria in sight is not necessarily the best way to protect your family, and some have questioned whether we need *any* cleaning agent besides plain old baking soda and vinegar to keep a home clean and sanitary.

Indeed, many of the eighty thousand chemicals used in mainstream cleanser products are a big question mark in terms of their environmental effect, and some are notorious. The volatile organic compounds (VOCs) that are used to enhance product performance have been shown to impair neurological functions and can act as respiratory irritants, carcinogens, and reproductive toxins. Phosphates, often found in standard detergents, can lead to eutrophication of rivers and streams, depleting oxygen. Phthalates, which distribute dyes and fragrances and act as plasticizers, are thought to have adverse hormonal effects.

To date, there has been very little government regulation of cleaning chemicals, and virtually no labeling requirements. In fact, it is the least regulated chemically based industry. As a consequence, eco-conscious consumers have come to rely on brands such as Seventh Generation, Method, and Planet to provide products that are as environmentally safe as possible. Moreover, the modern green cleaners can get the job accomplished with maybe just a little more scrubbing.

This was not always the case. "There were people who tried our products ten years ago, and they didn't work very well." This comment reveals an early but persistent prejudice among average consumers that green cleaning products aren't as effective. After all, in ancient times people used urine or caustic soda to clean things. "Now when [these consumers] try [today's Seventh Generation products], they will repeat-purchase," says Director of Education Susan Johnson.

Seventh Generation began testing its products against mainstream and alternative brands approximately eight years ago. "The dish liquid has always been a phenomenal product. Laundry powder was always great. But the laundry liquid needed some help," Johnson explains. "Because of the testing and hearing from our consumers, we were able to really take a look at it" and begin improvements.

Differentiating through scent.

Seventh Generation has been searching for ways to differentiate its products in order to hold on to its market share in what has become a crowded marketplace. Reed Doyle admits, "Sometimes we haven't done a really good job of getting consumers to truly understand how we differentiate from the other stuff that's out there," as Method does through packaging design.

One recent Seventh Generation initiative has been to focus on improving the scent of the products. "Most people will buy a particular product because they gravitate toward a scent they like," Doyle explains. In coming up with improved scents, the company looked at the "ideal way for us to do this," from an environmental standpoint regardless of cost implications.

"People have a lot of allergic reactions to unnatural fragrances," he continues. "We're not interested in having your clothes smell synthetic. Seventh Generation is all about an all-natural clean smell." Researchers looked at what they labeled a "living home" or indoor ecosystem, where "every room is a *living* room, and we asked, 'How can we bring the outside in? How do we create micro environments?'"

The new scent blends were created based on the idea that every room in the house is a kind of "niche within that ecosystem," he says. "How do we develop a scent for the bathroom that gives the feeling of a spa?

How do we create scents for the kitchen that are very culinary and reminiscent of the Silk Road? How do we create scents that actually complement one another . . . so when the scents come together, they belong together, creating a whole perfume for the house?"

Although the new scents are more expensive to produce because some raw materials are quite costly compared with their synthetic counterparts, Doyle insists that it's worth it. "We said, 'Let's try to create blends that aren't going to be exorbitant in price, that aren't endangered, that don't come from a crisis area, where we can actually give producers of the oils and botanical extracts a fair price.'"

Connecting product to a social mission.

In creating the new scents, Seventh Generation set out to work with co-ops around the world to forge relationships that "emotionalize the whole experience — analogous to Aveda's Soil to Bottle campaign," says Reed Doyle. "We're making a connection between the earth and the consumer. We aimed to create a real story about what's inside our bottle." According to an entry on TreeHugger.com, the Soil to Bottle campaign is "a project which aims to follow step by step the journey of the essential oils used in Aveda products, from where they are farmed to the moment they get put in a bottle. The objective is also to set up sustainable business partnerships with the producers of these precious ingredients so that not only do they benefit the consumer, but most especially the partnership with Aveda benefits the farmers and harvesters who work in the fields."[1]

As an example, Doyle points to a scent that "comes from a wild orange grove on a plantation that's gone fallow in the Dominican Republic. And so that's a neat story to tell. It's not greenwashed . . . it's authentic. They're now growing orange trees without the use of pesticides and using the oranges for essential oil production."

"Seventh Generation was founded on the idea of how we create something that actually brings more value," he continues. "From a sourcing standpoint, it means that instead of going out and getting the next big scent at a fragrance house, where you have no idea what's in the product you're buying, we try to go directly to the source, creating relationships with the farmers, doing business in that way."

Differentiation by leading change.

Seventh Generation has consciously created a brand that represents societal change. If an Age of Sustainability is going to happen, Seventh Generation will be an emissary of that change.

"We've communicated to the customer that this company does what has to be done for the planet, and that we think outside the box," says Director of Corporate Consciousness Gregor Barnum, who originally met Jeffrey Hollender at Hampshire College in 1973 before moving on to earn a master's degree from Yale Divinity School with a focus on ethics. "It's about designing a whole new world. It's about our belief that we have to do more than just be green — that we actually have to redesign our lifestyle."

Barnum believes that focusing on the negatives — on what not to do when it comes to the environment — is a "behavioral change format that doesn't work." Instead, marketing needs to focus a dialogue on "how we're going to make change happen . . . not only now, but for generations to come. It's about a changing of consciousness. Einstein said this a long time ago. You can't change the problems of the system using the same head that created the system. You've gotta actually think outside that framework."

Manufacturers need to consider where they take something from and where they put it back. "You're thinking about how it impacts the people along the way. How is the grower taken care of? How is the manufacturer taken care of? You're looking at the whole system as you go through this design process."

This consideration of the total cycle, he asserts, is lacking in 99 percent of the products that we buy. "We don't think end of life," Barnum laments. "We don't ask ourselves, 'Do we really need this?'" In short, says Barnum, if you looked at every consumer choice you make day to day and imagined the impact it would have seven generations out, you would see the world totally differently.

Promoting healthy homing.

The Seventh Generation marketing department is trying to raise the awareness of the home as a living organism. Barnum wants consumers to *think*. "So when you walk into your house, do you know what chemicals you're bringing into the house? If you're going to do construction in the house, do you know what's being packed in?"

"How do we begin to educate in this new framework?" he asks. "How we get more and more people talking about what it means to really do healthy homing?"

"Consumers have to be taught to look at product ingredients when they walk into a store," Barnum continues, saying that he's attempting to push Seventh Generation in the direction of Body Shop, the company founded by the late Anita Roddick. Very transparent in its practices, Body Shop informs customers of the origin of every single product.

Marketing as an interactive exchange.

According to Barnum, once people adopt the mind-set of looking at product ingredients, "they will buy our product," and then "they'll see all of the places that we haven't looked into yet. And then we get them to question us on it."

In this way, the customers are engaged in the design process. "We're trying to really get this thing flowing. We can be in a dynamic design process with our consumers. They can be in an interactive place of getting what they want. That's a lot of what the open-source world is actually asking us to do. No more hierarchy. No more white-man rule."

In fact, this is precisely what the Gort Cloud does — it's an undefined, boundless community that sieves, measures, and exchanges information on green products and services.

This all ties in with Seventh Generation's desire to move toward 100 percent sustainability by transitioning from doing less bad to doing good. "We're asking our customers to tell us what they want us to do better. We're asking them for suggestions on how to do better environmentally," says Doyle. "We're the first to say, 'Hey, we screwed up.' And I don't think a whole lot of other companies are really willing to do that." This, of course, underscores the proposition that the Gort Cloud is driven by truth.

Bringing consumers into the design process will no doubt help them form an emotional connection to the brand, a marketing goal that Seventh Generation has had much success with in the past. "You can tell by the way they call, the way they write, that they have a relationship with us."

The company's transparency is what creates an emotional connection to a brand, Doyle continues. "It's that people really believe what we're saying. This is what Seventh Gen has done over the last twenty years. We've created that emotional connection with our consumers where they really believe in what we're doing and they feel good about it. And when we do make mistakes, I think they're willing to forgive us because we're honest about it."

Honing that message on a bottle.

Seventh Generation is conscious of reaching out to what it calls "first-time greenies." One method the company has successfully used is "the savings statements, which you'll find pretty much on the back of every bottle that we have," Doyle explains. These statements, also found on the company's home page, pose a provocative what-if: "If every household in the US replaced just one 32 ounce bottle of shower cleaner containing chlorine beach with our hydrogen peroxide–based shower cleaner, we could prevent 1 million pounds of chlorine from entering our environment."

When designing new labels, the Seventh Generation teams asks itself how it can create a package and label that really speak to what's on the inside. "Because right now," says Doyle, "a lot of [our] stuff is in stock bottles that looks just like Fantastik or Formula 409. How do we create a package that isn't too disruptive, something people are gonna grab and say, 'I wanna try this'?"

"It's about trying to understand our buyers and really trying to see what resonates," Doyle continues. "Does 'nontoxic' really mean anything to anyone? Does 'chlorine-free'? If someone says 'chlorine-free,' is that really the right positioning? And is that enough? Because today, Whole Foods has private-label chlorine-free baby wipes, using the same pulp that we have. So do a couple other stores. They found the source that we're getting it from."

To that end, Seventh Generation is looking past labeling itself green. "It's more about labeling yourself as quality," Doyle says.

This speaks to the developing phenomenon of green fatigue. In a September 2007 article for *The Independent*, Hugh Wilson wrote, "Fifteen years ago, the term 'compassion fatigue' indicated a general disillusionment with fund-raising concerts and famine appeals. The cause was too hopeless, governments too apathetic, and individuals too impotent. Slowly, and for similar reasons, the term 'green fatigue' has started to creep into the dinner-party conversations of the composting classes."[2] Seventh Generation is mindful of this trend and does not want to confine its product discussion solely to the subject of doing right by the environment.

"What we're really trying to do here at Seventh Gen is to really walk the talk as best we can," continues Doyle. "I'm not a fan of the word *green*. To me, it's really about quality, and it's redefining [the meaning of] a quality brand . . . a trust mark that people can really believe in and say, 'I feel good about that.'"

Getting attention from the Gort Cloud and beyond.

Seventh Generation connects with its audience in the Gort Cloud by linking itself with causes found within this community. It is promoting itself by helping to get the country off its foreign oil dependency, for example. It is also pushing an agenda when it comes to the need for industry regulation.

"We're saying we're going to list our ingredients per certain nomenclature, and we're asking other companies to sign on to this compact and move the industry toward transparency," says Reed Doyle. This parallels the efforts of Dr. Bronner's in the skin care market.

At Seventh Generation, all employees are encouraged to participate on the company's widely read blog, the Inspired Protagonist. Containing a whole lot of Jeffrey Hollender's wisdom in addition to news about the company, it "seeks to cut the cords of negativity that bind us and replace them with hopeful strands of thought and deed that weave new worlds of possibility," the site reads. "This is the home of the voice of Seventh Generation and of all our friends and kindred spirits. It's the place for different thinking, dynamic action, deeper traction, and daring dialogue that move people to move our culture forward."

The firm has furthered its agenda to create an emotional connection between company and customer by developing a program where consumers tell personal stories about their experience with the product. "We've really been focusing in on the stories of one's home, the story that one's home tells, and how these products actually interact with that story." The tales are sometimes dramatic, such as "Gabriella's Story," from a mother who *didn't* have to rush her daughter to the hospital when the child consumed household products by Seventh Generation.

No P&G ad budget, just GIVE.

As an outgrowth of its branding-by-storytelling effort, Seventh Generation recently launched GIVE, short for "Generate Inspiration Via Education." The company's product brokers are taught how to "pass on good stories about Seventh Generation as they market the product to retailers," says Johnson, who runs the program. "It's about making sure these brokers — the first line of defense — are armed with everything they can possibly know about our product."

"The whole idea behind it is that we have tremendous opportunities through these wonderful stories that we get from our consumers. We can pass them onto people at the store level working with our product, giving them a means to explain things better when someone comes up to them on the floor at [green grocers such as] a Whole Foods or a Fred Meyer or at New Frontiers or Lazy Acres and says, 'Tell me about this. I've never used this product.'" In a way, "this is our form of advertising," Johnson continues. "We don't have a full advertising program. We can't compete on that level."

The brokers Johnson refers to have a sales force of their own whose members go into every retail location to make sure "that the product is on the shelf and set up correctly and priced correctly. We want to be able to get more of their time and energy," Johnson says of this sales force. "We want them to know more about Seventh Generation and be excited about it."

In the process of educating themselves, sales force members "reminded us that what people are most interested in is their children. Our products really resonate with new parents. It's one of those times [when] people make changes in their lives." As a result, the education program includes a focus on taking care of the next generation, and the series is now titled the Seven Truths About Seventh Generation. The particular truths were "pulled out of discussions we had with our brokers and with the consumers."

So far, Seventh Gen has trained over three thousand brokers and retailers. The trainees are asked to participate in a follow-up survey on the company's Web site and are rewarded with a three-dollar Seventh Generation coupon for doing so. "This is where we're able to measure how we're doing with the program," explains Susan, the company taking note of how participants have felt about the training and whether it has impacted their ability to sell Seventh Generation products. A second portal on the site gives the brokers and retailers an opportunity to pass on the information, as well as the gift certificate reward, to their friends and family. "We can see how many people they tell," explains Johnson. "We want to be able to connect these dots on who's telling who about what."

"By the time all of this is over, we'll have a speakers' bureau," she continues. "Now everybody who calls in wants Jeffrey, but nine times out of ten he can't do it, or it's too small a group. But it may be that there are a hundred people who are part of a PTA association, say of Greater Boston. Of course we should be there. We'd send somebody from this speakers' bureau to go down and talk to them and find out what they're most interested in."

Johnson believes this is far better than traditional advertising when it comes to reaching the Seventh Generation customer. "How many people go out and say, 'I saw this commercial'? But if they hear a story, they'll repeat it. And it will be repeated and repeated and repeated. It becomes a viral campaign."

SUMMARY: USING A FIRST-TO-MARKET ADVANTAGE

To underscore a previous comment, no one knew about a thing called the Gort Cloud as I began these interviews — including me. But many intuitively understood that an eco-conscious green community existed and that it traded ideas and information via the Internet. Seventh Generation is among them. But then there were a few of my subjects who actually went about seeding the clouds in the hope of increasing awareness and market share. Seventh Generation is a pioneer among this group. Through its Web site, blog, user stories, digital newsletters, and appearances, Jeffrey Hollender and his team have created an impressive outreach program, a program that reaches deep into various corners of the Gort Cloud.

So, despite considerable competition in their green cleaning products niche, they have been able to leverage their first-to-market advantage, resulting in maintenance of a sizable market share in a growth category. This is often difficult to do, as many companies that pioneer new product categories will exhaust themselves in the launch phase and are unprepared to take on the competition that results from their initial success. Witness Netscapes' collapse in the wake of the Microsoft Internet Explorer entry into the browser market.

Seventh Generation is also living up to its name. Through innovative product development and clever marketing strategies, it is attempting to shape a consumer who will think seven generations out. It's a very tall order, but given what this company has already accomplished in creating a new category and a new corporate model, it could very well get us there.

Building Green

Michelle Kaufmann Designs and Green Key Real Estate

THE CHALLENGE

The building industry and the residential, commercial, institutional, and industrial structures it produces are the largest emitters of global warming pollutants. Two companies in the San Francisco Bay Area are trying to change that. Michelle Kaufmann Designs creates prefab housing that is more efficient to produce than traditional site-built homes and is green by design. Chris Bartle has created Green Key Real Estate to help market and sell green real estate in the Bay Area and, soon, across the United States.

How do these green pioneers raise awareness and develop customers in a market segment dominated by traditional, not-so-green competitors?

THE SOLUTION

Both Michelle Kaufmann and Chris Bartle have exploited first-to-market advantages as pioneers within their respective industries. MKD is among a small group of architects designing relatively low-cost, high-efficiency homes for the prefab market, while Green Key Real Estate is the nation's first real estate resource for greener homes.

The principals in both businesses have dedicated themselves to green building initiatives. As spokespersons for more earth-friendly building alternatives, they have attracted tremendous publicity and positive exposure. They attend and are often speakers at green building expos and forums.

Both companies cast as wide a net as possible but share a target market of young, affluent buyers who are interested in green housing and are naturally receptive to their product offer. Green buyers and green sellers often connect via the Gort Cloud to find one another, and this is especially true in the case of MK Designs and Green Key Real Estate.

In September 2007, I attended the West Coast Green Residential Building Conference and Expo in downtown San Francisco with my writing partner, Scott Fields. It's one of many green building conferences that have popped up around the country and that join a growing category of exhibitions, competitions, product conventions, and conferences all designed to showcase and promote the green technology of tomorrow. For the marketers of green building products, West Coast Green is one of the best ways to meet their otherwise invisible customers.

Visitors browse past booths promoting straw bale homes, cabinetry certified by the Forest Stewardship Council (FSC), the newest technology in solar energy installation, recycled drywall, denim insulation, and something called "the durable alternative to modern plasters." The US Green Building Council has a presence here, offering the latest developments in its LEED certification program.

Two of the exhibitors — Michelle Kaufmann Designs and Green Key Real Estate — are Bay Area enterprises that have created awareness by positioning themselves as first-to-market in their specialties: MK Designs in green prefab homes and Green Key Real Estate in green real estate brokering.

Michelle Kaufmann Designs: Redefining Prefab

Outside the Graham Auditorium, in the middle of Civic Center Plaza, is a house that wasn't here yesterday. It was trucked in last night, along with the well-manicured garden that's surrounding it. Right now it is crowded with casually dressed businesspeople taking tours, glancing over everything inside.

The mkLotus house is sustainable, and so is the garden. Both were created by Michelle Kaufmann Designs of Oakland, one of several architects making their names known in the world of high-touch, sustainable prefab home building.

Yes, the mkLotus house is a "mobile home" in that it was wheeled in on a flatbed. But it's not a "mobile home" in that it bears no resemblance to the image of what that term generally conjures up in this country.

"In America, because we have trailer homes, when people think prefab, people think trailer," says Kaufmann. "In other countries that don't have trailer homes, this image issue doesn't exist." In Japan, for instance, "they are way in front with prefab housing because they don't have trailer homes. They don't have this misconception that prefab is substandard. There, if you're doing a high-end home, you want it done with precision cutting, you want it done in a controlled environment. You want it built in a factory."

"It's crazy that in the US, in almost every other industry, we have used automation and mass production to help bring good design to the masses. But with the building industry, it's so antiquated and so broken," she continues. "I heard a great analogy — to think the best way to build the nicest house is to build from scratch is like asking for your car to be built in your driveway. It's just a silly idea."

I have to agree with this assessment. Take the simple example of the two-by-four. Cut to eight-, ten-, or twelve-foot lengths, it is delivered to the construction site, where it is almost always cut to a shorter length. The result is that about 20 percent becomes waste and is relegated to a Dumpster, and ultimately to a landfill. You can multiply that by just about everything else that goes into building a house. In a factory environment, those wasted materials are seen as lost profits and are quickly designed out of the process.

"The quality of product that can be produced building in a factory is no different [from], if not better than, what you would get for a site-built home," Kaufmann says.

Buildings turn out to be the biggest polluter.

The American Institute of Architects (AIA) Government Advocacy team has pointed out, "In our quest to dramatically cut greenhouse gas emissions and lessen our dependence on fossil fuels, we have overlooked the biggest source of emissions and energy consumption both in this country and around the globe. Buildings and their construction account for nearly half (48%) of all the greenhouse emissions and energy consumed in this country each year. This includes energy used in the production and transportation of materials to building construction sites, as well as the energy used to operate buildings."

Until this and earlier reports came out, architects and builders were living in a bubble of denial, believing the majority of the climate change problem was linked to transportation and energy. But once the bubble burst, it didn't take long for the industry to organize in the form of the US Green Building Council (USGBC). This nonprofit association aims to shift the building industry toward sustainability, changing the way buildings are designed, built, and operated. Indeed, it ushered in the Leadership in Energy and Environmental Design (LEED) rating system and also initiated Greenbuild, a green building conference.

The LEED silver, gold, and platinum rating system, along with the certifications of other organizations such as the FSC, has gone a long way to bring positive action in the building construction industry. Compounding these organized actions are technology advances that are providing the means to incrementally reduce the environmental impact and CO_2 emissions of commercial and residential buildings.

One block of building technology advances has come with the building materials themselves: high-efficiency insulation, high-strength alternatives to traditional wood framing, low-VOC paints and coatings, light-regulating glass, residential wind and solar, water capture and reclamation systems, and so forth. Another block of advances has come from the factory-built home industry, an industry born out of the necessities of World War II to reduce waste and increase efficiencies. But something new is happening here. It's the debut of the *fabulous prefab*.

Turning yesterday's missed opportunity into a viable product today.

Of course, prefab or kit homes have been around a long time. In the early 1900s, Sears & Roebuck sold more than seventy-five thousand kit homes in America. They were ordered by catalog and shipped by rail to hundreds of communities that were growing and in desperate need of housing. A seven-room bungalow cost less than twenty-five hundred dollars at the time. The purchaser had to put it together.

R. Buckminster Fuller's Dymaxion House, a factory-built geodesic dome originally conceived in 1927, was remarkable for its use of lightweight aircraft tubing and an aluminum skin. It weighed 3,000 pounds, versus the 150 tons of an average home. According to the Buckminster Fuller Institute, it "was heated and cooled by natural means, made its own power, was earthquake and storm-proof, and made of permanent, engineered materials that required no periodic painting, reroofing, or other maintenance."[1] It was truly ahead of its time, and might have earned a LEED rating in today's market.

And just as prefab designers market their homes today, Buckminster

Fuller teamed up with Chicago retailer Marshall Field & Company to demonstrate his home in a department store display in 1929. An advertising consultant was also hired to come up with an attention-getting name. He strung together Fuller's favorite words, *dynamic, maximum,* and *tension,* which produced the word *Dymaxion.* Fuller's now famous Dymaxion House was born.

Another important advance in prefab design came at the close of World War II with the Lustron Home, a factory-built steel prefab with a porcelain-coated exterior. The Lustron Corporation built 2,498 of these units in Columbus, Ohio, before going bankrupt in 1950.[2]

Coincidentally, my Tokyo business partner, Sy Chen, bought the exclusive rights to sell a Buckminster Fuller–inspired modular dome system for distribution in Japan. He sold forty of them from 1997 to 1999. The system, called OmniSphere, was designed by Craig Chamberlain and was used in a well-known homeless shelter demonstration in downtown Los Angeles that closed in 2006. This temporary village stood on a large swath of vacant land in the shadow of skyscrapers. It looked like a collection of igloos, but the units were actually made of interlocking white fiberglass shells.

Despite these technological advances in manufactured housing and the lower cost, these early ideas just didn't catch on. The homes were a little too cookie-cutter and one-size-fits-all for the average American. They lacked the customization needed to adapt to specific site requirements. They were seen to clash with local building traditions. And, as mentioned before, because *factory-built* conjured up images of mobile homes and trailer parks, the industry became associated with transients and marginal income. It wasn't seen as an equity building investment.

Now a new wave of modern, eco-efficient prefab dwellings has gained attention. The tipping point may have been the endorsement and promotion of prefabs by the influential style magazine *Dwell,* along with a plethora of recent books and blogs on the subject. They have created a critical mass of public interest that has buoyed support for the work of Michelle Kaufmann and her contemporaries.

The advantages of modular.

"Our mission is to make green affordable and green accessible and easy," Kaufmann says. "And prefabrication is a way for us to achieve that goal. It's a means to an end."

Indeed, prefabs have caught the attention of young, hip family types. And because prefabs are efficiently built in a factory setting, they're green by design. Including green materials makes them all the more so.

Kaufmann customers are often homeowners who are looking to move into their second home. "They want something well designed, and they want something designed by an architect, but they want it to be easier than a typical [home commissioning] process," she says. Often, potential buyers contact the company after having seen one of the Kaufmann homes in print and or in person. Frequently, those customers have been working with an architect on something similar. When they realize they could get what they want with the ease of prefab, they've got to have it, Kaufmann notes. "That's really what we're after — the client that says, 'Oh my God, I love that. That is perfect for me.' Most of the clients come to us because we're green, too. I think that the sustainability and the design and materials really resonate with people."

Indeed, the new trophy home for the environmentally aware is now the small and ecological, according to a *New York Times* article.[3] "There's kind of a green pride, like driving a Prius," said Brenden McEneaney, a green building adviser to the city of Santa Monica, adding, "It's spreading all over the place." We may not have seen the end of the McMansion, but a growing number of people are discovering that they really don't need so much space to live comfortably and efficiently. This would be the first time in decades that there has been any resistance to the steady increase in the average size of homes in America — which has more than doubled since the 1950s.[4]

The competition.

Of course, there are many ways to build a home. There's custom-built, generally designed by an architect. There's spec-built, usually designed by a developer who is attempting to build quickly and cheaply to a mass-market standard. And then there are tract homes in large, planned communities. Prefab fills a spot between custom-built and tract. It's not quite custom, but it's certainly more custom and hip than a tract home.

Michelle Kaufmann doesn't seem to think she has much competition in the prefab market but rather sees her competitors as the large tract homebuilders with their so-called planned communities.

"Our competitors are more like KB Home," she says. "That's who I see as being our competitor. That's who I want to be up against. I want to go toe-to-toe with those guys. We're thinking at that scale. And building toward that."

Kaufmann doesn't have too many kind words for the KB developers. "They're just going out where the land is cheap and filling the landscape with crap, and it's kind of surprising, too, that even when they build in these beautiful places, they just have the little windows sprinkled throughout. When you're in the house, you're just focused inside. It's just nuts."

"There's an inherent conflict with the way these homes are built," she continues. "The developers want to build, and build it for the least amount, and sell it for the most amount. And the way that they do that is to build it as cheaply as they can with cheaper materials, cheaper insulations, cheaper mechanical systems." At the same time, what buyers want "is something that's going to last a long time. They want healthy environments for their family, they want lower energy bills, they want houses that are the right size that fit their family. Developers don't care about healthy environments. They don't care what the energy bills are going be."

These developers "miss so many opportunities." As MK Designs studies building communities of homes, it's looking at community "in a holistic way," Kaufmann says. "If we start to imagine alternative energy sources for a community, how we can use those energy savings to help maybe with proactive health care? Can we use that money to provide physical fitness or to teach people how to cook with organic food?"

"I guarantee you, people are becoming more savvy, and they're going to start requiring this shift in the marketplace, and real estate agents are going to have to start listing homes not as a four-thousand-square-foot four-bedroom, but [as] four thousand square feet and here is your energy bill," she asserts. "And it's been interesting that the big boys are [just recently] starting to pay attention."

"They [the KB-type developers] have been resistant to this idea about green," Kaufmann continues. "They have been in complete denial because it doesn't fit how they currently work, and I think it's only been recently where they're realizing they have to change, and now they're trying to play catch-up, which is good." At the time of this writing, KB Home announced that it will "build new homes exclusively with Energy Star–qualified refrigerators, dishwashers, and laundry appliances from Whirlpool Corporation" as part of its effort to protect the environment. This is a small step, but hopefully it's the first of more profound ones.

The top five builders, including KB, have lately been "sniffing around us," according to Michelle. "It's a tricky thing because they're so big that any kind of change is so difficult. In some ways, it's easier for us because we're smaller, we are scrappy, we can move fast."

MK Designs is "providing a model that is demonstrating a market. And that's really what it is about for us. It's not just creating a market for ourselves, but it's showing these big guys, Hey, you've got to change. There is a market here."

Creating a solution to meet her own needs.

In 2001, Michelle Kaufmann and her husband, Kevin, were looking for a place to live in the Bay Area. "We couldn't find anything that we liked that we could afford. We couldn't find anything that was green. I realized through that really painful experience [that] there's a problem. And it was visceral pain, right? We were wondering what we'd done wrong in our lives that we can't find a place to live."

"So we decided to build something for ourselves," Michelle says on the MKD Web site. "We found some land and started building our simple, sustainable home. As we were building, we had friends and colleagues ask if we could do something like this for them as well. What a great question! Could we make this house in mass-production?"

Kaufmann was intrigued. Searching for an answer, she found a whole world of modular factories out there, offering technologies that architects had for the most part not yet embraced. The result was that while Kevin built their on-site home, Michelle copied it in modular fashion for her first clients. The two homes were almost identical.

Michelle Kaufmann's homes are modern in the sense that they flow from the postmodern design spirit established in postwar California with the Case Study home project. The pioneers of this movement were the architects Richard Neutra, Raphael Soriano, Craig Ellwood, Charles and Ray Eames, Pierre Koenig, and Eero Saarinen. Their home designs, which are reflected in the MK Designs homes, were clean, somewhat minimalist, and devoid of the then popular Mannerist styles. *Airy, low-slung, lightweight in appearance* are terms I'd use to describe Kaufmann's homes and Case Study homes.

In 2002, Kaufmann founded Michelle Kaufmann Designs. Her first order of business was to find a factory to produce her modular designs. "When Michelle first started five years ago, she was calling factories just dying for someone to build a house for her," says Rebecca Woelke, an MKD spokesperson. "She got so many doors closed in her face — she jokes that she became a stalker. She finally found a factory to build the Glidehouse for her."

The new homes attracted attention, and the company was able to gradually expand its business from the Bay Area to the rest of California, and then to Oregon, Washington, Hawaii, and Colorado. It began working with other factories to meet the production demands but eventually came to the point "where our production needs were higher than what we could find the factories to fill," says Woelke.

As a result, MK Designs purchased a factory in western Washington last year and has so far produced twenty-eight homes with twenty-five employees. By the end of 2008, MKD plans to have completed a hundred homes; by the end of 2009, two hundred will be built. Kaufmann is pleased with the outcome. "We found that in doing business with other factories, we essentially lost control, to a degree, of not only the production, but [also] the quality," says Kaufmann. "You are what you produce."

The company is planning to expand to the Midwest and East Coast over the next twelve to eighteen months. In fact, MKD has given Midwesterners a chance to experience the first mkSolaire home ever built as part of the Smart Home: Green + Wired exhibit at Chicago's Museum of Science and Industry. "We want families and children to see firsthand how they can make their own living spaces healthier and more sustainable," says Kaufmann. "Plus, I'm from Iowa, and I still remember how inspired I was by my first school field trip to the Museum of Science and Industry. It's a real honor to help educate this new market on the benefits of sustainable modular design." Because of the heightened demand from these emerging prefab markets, MKD will most likely be looking for factory partners in the Midwest and mid-Atlantic areas.

Product differentiation through instant gratification.

There are many reasons to go prefab, if you listen to the Kaufmann people. First of all, there's speed. Prospective customers can first check out the MKD Web site to look over possible home options. They can then go to Google SketchUp, where they are able to take "a preconfigured Kaufmann home design and actually put it into their home site," says Kaufmann. "They have the [entire] material palette, so they can change materials. They can put it in the landscape and dream."

Once they've contacted MKD, prospective clients will get a quick assessment of whether or not the site they have purchased is appropriate for a Kaufmann home. For instance, can a large truck carrying the home sections get to the site? If the site will work, the customers will meet with MKD representatives to settle on various architectural and interior design options. Within a week after this meeting, the clients will receive a price quote.

That estimate will generally be very close to the final price. Ask anyone who's built a custom home, and 99 percent of them will say that it cost far more than they anticipated when they got started. With modular, it's right there on the spec sheets. When it comes to building, the typical fourteen-month time frame to build a custom home is reduced to four months with modular (another name for prefab).

To take delivery of an MKD home is "an emotional experience" for customers, according to Kaufmann. "Especially when you have this huge truckload of home coming down the street. It's just unfathomable to them."

"It's a turnkey solution," she continues. "Once it's fastened to the foundation, you open the front door, the flooring is there, the counter-tops are there, the cupboards, all the windows . . . everything. You feel like you should be able to just move your bed in and just sleep in the room that night. And it might take an extra month for the electrical to get through [the local utility] and just get it all worked out, but it's that instant gratification that's priceless."

A whole lot of solutions in one very cool package.

Michelle Kaufmann Designs offers preconfigured blueprints as well as custom options. All homes are solar-ready. Countertops are manufactured out of recycled paper and porcelain, and tiles from recycled glass and porcelain. Decks are made from composite materials, and soft floor covering comes from recycled carpet tiles made by InterfaceFLOR. Wood certified by the Forest Stewardship Council is a requisite, and green, living walls are used where possible. Bamboo takes the place of hardwood for flooring because it is a quickly renewable resource and costs no more than hardwood — provided it is not grown at the expense of native forests.[5] Paints contain no volatile organic compounds, and Kaufmann often partners with YOLO Colorhouse (a company that's featured later in this book). The top-of-the-line insulation in the homes *does* cost more than conventional systems — three times as much, in fact — but according to Michelle Kaufmann, the homeowner will earn it back in energy savings in three years.

"The homes I design create a clean, healthy living environment for residents, which I believe is an essential element in any home," Kaufmann states on the company's Web site. "With so many health hazards out there these days, your home should be as healthful as possible."

Moving through the mkLotus house here in San Francisco, I'm impressed with the finer points — the door handles, the kitchen cabinets — which are all very tasteful and contemporary. But more than that, I'm impressed with the thought that has gone into the design of this structure. The large and numerous windows minimize the need for artificial lighting during the day. Many features of the home serve more than one purpose, and there's a certain spaciousness to the interior that belies its actual square footage.

"We design big rather than build big, meaning we design to make a space feel larger than it is," according to the Web site. "We design outdoor rooms as much as we design indoor rooms, so that both become a part of the house."

Kaufmann's product line includes a selection of designs and floor plans, with customers making choices based on the size as well as the terrain of the site they have purchased, and on the home size they desire. Preconfigured homes include the Glidehouse, the original MKD design; the mkSolaire, designed specifically for urban in-fill lots; the mkLoft, which offers an open feel in an urban setting; the Sunset Breezehouse, distinguished by a central BreezeSpace situated under a slanting, butterfly-shaped roof; and the mkLotus, which is the firm's latest design and continues the MKD tradition of creating homes that have a direct connection to nature and landscape.

In a market downturn, green offers value.

So far, the company has not been negatively affected by the recent downturn in the real estate market, according to Kaufmann. "We're still crazy busy," she says. "It's the appropriate pace for us right now because we're still finalizing the refinement of the model. As the market starts to come back in the next year or two, we're going to be fully set up to really scale with it."

"What's interesting is that the developers are the ones that are the most nervous and the most concerned about [this downturn] . . . it's risky for them. So what they're seeing now is that they need to pay greater attention to what the buyers want to make sure they can sell [their homes], and they're starting to see, 'Hey, wait a second, green is marketable?' It adds value. So that's great," she adds.

"So in some ways I think [this housing crisis] actually makes positive things happen. That's when businesses actually can spend the time to create better value and improve their products and systems."

Advertising. What's that?

"We have never had an advertisement anywhere," says Michelle Kaufmann. "Up until about six months ago, we didn't even have our number listed. We're really not thinking about marketing per se, but more about education, about really trying to just demonstrate ideals and materials and strategies and systems that people can implement into their own lives and their own homes. It's also about sharing ideas."

The firm has benefited by a slew of articles in the press, and the fact that the homes are so photogenic doesn't hurt, either. Very favorable articles have run in the *Chicago Sun-Times*, *Sunset* magazine, *Discover*, *USA Today*, the *San Francisco Chronicle*, and many others.

Michelle Kaufman primes the Gort Cloud through her personal blog on her Web site, which emphasizes green action and hosts handsomely produced videos featuring her customers' "green story" experiences with her homes. These videos are then picked up and echoed around the Gort Cloud via trendspotters, like JetsonGreen.com. Who needs advertising when you have this fantastic resource at your disposal?

MKD has also been invited to participate in a number of museum exhibits, putting homes on display at the National Building Museum, the Vancouver Art Center, and MOCA in Los Angeles in addition to the Chicago Musem of Science and Industry. MKD was listed as one of "The Green 50" by *Inc.* magazine, and Michelle Kaufmann was listed as one of the "100 People Who Matter Now" by *Business 2.0* magazine.

Expanding market potential from homes to multiunit communities.

Kaufmann has expanded from single-family homes to multiunit projects, such as a townhouse development in Denver and a twenty-four-unit multifamily complex in San Leandro that includes communal and private gardens as well as private garages. The company is also looking into building communities of single-family structures, which is "what I'm most interested in right now because that's where we can really make a huge difference," Michelle Kaufmann says.

She is now doing a complete remodel of a monastery in Big Sur and is in the design stage with prefab hotels, spas, and educational facilities. As the Web site states, "mkResorts will encourage guests to connect with your beautiful landscape and escape from their hectic schedules and stress. Ample fresh air, natural light, and healthy finishes will leave your guests feeling relaxed and refreshed."

Michelle Kaufmann is certainly not the only architect designing for the prefab (or modular) market. There are many others. What distinguishes her work is the commitment to prefab as a means for providing a greener, more sustainable alternative for the housing market. Her homes set an example for others to follow.

Green Key Real Estate: Creating a Market Channel for Sustainable Housing

Chris Bartle, founder and owner of Green Key Real Estate, would like to "make the San Francisco Bay Area and other cities with a similar focus on green building and remodeling the most sustainable regions on the planet — one green building sale at a time," he says. In that, he is appealing to others who, like himself, are proud to live in cities that set trends.

This is the second year in a row that Bartle has attended West Coast Green. Last year he was here to network, looking to expand his business from San Francisco to the East Bay, Marin, and the Peninsula. This year he is networking again, his sights set even higher. He is planning to take Green Key Real Estate national.

In creating a real estate brokerage specializing in green properties, Bartle is a first-to-market innovator, which isn't always an easy thing to be. It requires creating a niche and then filling it. As is the case with Green Key, this often involves connecting with like-minded people in related fields and selling them on the advantages of what the new niche offers.

At West Coast Green, "we're recruiting not only clients but also agents who want to join our company and potential franchisees who want to open an affiliated office," Bartle says. "The other groups we're here to meet are the builders and developers. If we can make connections with these guys, when they do green development we would be the logical company to come in and help them sell those units."

Bartle points to a connection he made yesterday with a developer building a multiunit LEED-certified building in Sonoma County. "Those kinds of situations are perfect for us."

Finding his BHAG.

Chris Bartle learned his start-up ways in the tech industry. As with other Bay Area eco-entrepreneurs who were part of the Silicon Valley boom, the burst of the Internet bubble presented him an "opportunity to figure out how to align my environmental values and beliefs with my livelihood."

Searching for something that would be good for the earth as well as the bottom line, Bartle founded the Evergreen Group in 2001 as a business brokerage that sells green businesses, among them Sun Dog Hemp Body Care, which was purchased by none other than Dr. Bronner's Magic Soap. Following the sale of Sun Dog, Bartle launched his Green Key venture.

BHAG, or Big Hairy Audacious Goal, is a term coined by James Collins and Jerry Porras in their 1996 book *Building Your Company's Vision.* "A true BHAG is clear and compelling, serves as a unifying focal point of effort, and acts as a clear catalyst for team spirit," Collins and Porras wrote. "It has a clear finish line, so the organization can know when it has achieved the goal; people like to shoot for finish lines." It is a form of vision statement — an audacious ten- to thirty-year goal.

Chris Bartle's BHAG is to create a green standard for selling real estate that will eventually become the preferred, premium standard for all buildings sold.

A lack of inventory.

San Francisco is one of the greenest cities in the country, yet the present stock of green homes available to buy and sell is not substantial enough to sustain a company like Green Key. Until those inventories increase, Bartle is linking prospective buyers with homes that can be remodeled green, as well as with the resources they need to make it happen. He is able to do so because real estate agents often get involved with advice on financing, remodeling, furnishing, and decorating that home. "We attract green-minded buyers and we educate and enable them to buy a property that is not green and green it," he explains.

Green Key is poised to ride a wave that has not quite yet arrived. According to publishing giant McGraw-Hill, which puts out many building-industry-related books, green building makes up just 2 percent of all US construction, but by 2010 that number will grow to between 5 and 10 percent. This would bring what is today a $7.2 billion green residential market up to $38 billion in just a few years. As the CNET Web site states, "For the near term, at least, most homeowners hoping to go green must settle on renovation nips and tucks utilizing both high and low technologies."

A young middle- to upper-middle-class target audience.

Green Key Real Estate attracts clients who are middle to upper middle class. The typical clients are in their early thirties to late forties, and they are often first-time homebuyers.

Whatever their age, most Green Key clients typically fall into one of two categories. Either they are energy-conscious and hoping to save money on their utility bills, or they are looking for healthy indoor air quality. Some of the clients are hard-core green and others are lighter — "consumers who would do something green if they were told how," Bartle explains.

"Some clients may be worried about indoor air quality for the health of their kids," he adds. "We sometimes get some very specific needs — an allergy or sensitivity to a certain chemical, like formaldehyde or a specific type of pesticide. Searching for homes to meet these clients' needs is a challenge, but we've become expert at working with clients with such issues." This underscores a point about crafting effective sales messages — it is almost never just about green. It's almost always about a tangible benefit that is *also* green.

A multichannel outreach program.

Green Key has been fortunate in attracting the attention of the Bay Area media and has been featured in national media such as CNN, the *New York Times*, the *Wall Street Journal*, and *Newsweek*. "We've had a lot of great exposure," Bartle says. "We've had links to this media coverage on our Web site, and it's generated a lot of great Web traffic. We get a dozen or more leads every month just from the Web."

In addition, he makes sure to attend industry events, from West Coast Green — where a symposium he gave this year was well received — to the Green Festival and others. For the past several years, Bartle has hosted the monthly San Francisco Sustainable Business happy hour, which means that "more than six hundred people get my e-mails each month," he says. "E-mail marketing like this and through Green Key's monthly newsletter *Green Key Notes* has been a critical part of raising awareness of our new company." In a sense, Chris is playing the Gort Cloud.

Bartle is reaching the audience through the associates he has carefully hired. "All our fifteen agents and employees are involved with their own spheres of influence, with little overlap between them," he explains. Among these agents is an East Bay "teacher/guru in the permaculture world. She looks at how we live and how we interact with nature — a holistic approach to sustainability." Other agents include an astrologist, a concert violinist with the Philharmonia Baroque, a feng shui expert, a green MBA graduate, and "a couple of snowboarders," he says.

Company culture that reflects sustainable values.

The company's diversity makes for a great corporate culture. All of the agents are sustainability-minded, but their approaches to it are different. That's called synergy.

Green Key strengthens its company culture further by positioning itself as part of the fabric of San Francisco, such as with its certification as a green business by the Bay Area Green Business. What's also helped, according to Bartle, is that "we walk our talk as much as possible." Several Green Key agents ride bicycles to an office where many recycling and waste reduction measures have been instituted.

Using a web-front when there's no storefront.

With the launch of Green Key Real Estate's Web site in January 2006, "the goal was search engine optimization," says Bartle. "We wanted to get eyeballs to the site. Because we didn't have a storefront, we didn't have any kind of retail visibility in San Francisco, so we were going for Internet visibility instead. And most real estate companies aren't very good at that."

By maximizing search engine optimization, the company quickly amassed hits from consumers who Googled "green real estate San Francisco." Once landing on the site, customers are posed with a question and then given an answer: "How do you find a Realtor that understands your unique needs for buying or selling real estate, provides top quality service and shares your values on environmental and social responsibility? The truth is, you couldn't . . . until now."

A boutique brand in a very crowded marketplace.

Green Key is going up against a long list of competitors, from national giants such as Coldwell Banker and Prudential to well-established local companies like Zephyr Real Estate. Where Green Key has fifteen agents, the bigger companies can have up to a thousand in the Bay Area.

The boutique differentiates itself from its larger competitors primarily by educating its agents, who "all have a deep and broad knowledge of green building and green remodeling," Bartle explains. All fifteen are EcoBrokers who have completed an online training and education program with EcoBroker.com. In addition, they are certified as Green Building Professionals by Build It Green, a nonprofit that, according to its Web site, promotes "healthy, energy- and resource-efficient building practices in California." This certification requires each agent to fulfill two full days of classroom training. "You're in there with architects and city inspectors and builders, so you learn from the dialogue as much as from the professor," notes Bartle, who was recently elected to Build It Green's board of directors.

As evidence that this education process is working in the marketplace, he points out that many of the city's real estate agents are "looking to our company as an opportunity to really differentiate themselves and stand out from the competition." He continues, "Real estate agents are dying for a differentiator right now because the [transaction] volume is slowing down."

The firm also differentiates itself by offering to connect clients with "green real estate and green business circles not only in San Francisco, but nationally," according to the company's Web site. That includes its listing as an EcoBroker on EcoBroker.com. These circles comprise not only green builders but also green mortgage companies, green interior design companies, and more. "This gives your home exposure to people who value sustainability," Bartle says. They may very well send the information on to others who are moving to San Francisco, or perhaps just live there.

With all this exposure, "what's happened is green-minded real estate agents around the country have been calling" to learn more about Green Key so they "don't have to reinvent the wheel," Bartle says. When and if these agents have a client moving to San Francisco, Green Key will more than likely get the referral.

Although Green Key Real Estate has not spent much in the way of advertising, it does buy space in the *Green Pages* and *San Francisco Natural Pages*.

Green property value.

When it comes to evaluating the added value of a green living space in the Bay Area, Chris Bartle believes that, all other things being equal, a green home will sell faster than a non-green home. Nevertheless, he has nothing to prove the point because "the data isn't there yet. It's too new."

All real estate data come from the MLS (Multiple Listing Service), and there are different services in different counties and sometimes cities, and "each MLS has ownership of their own data," he explains. From his position on the real estate council of Build It Green, Bartle is assisting in the task of "going from one MLS to another to get them to add green rating criteria" in the listings.

"Once we capture the sales data, we'll be able to see, in any given block or neighborhood, that a two-bedroom non-green house sold for this much, and the two-bedroom green house sold for this much more and that much faster," he explains. "But right now, it's more subjective."

In San Francisco itself, the green rating system has started, but "it's a long process because houses don't sell that fast," Bartle explains. "Every time a house that's rated sells, we'll get that green rating in the MLS."

Reaching the trendspotters.

Bartle maintains an active Green Key Real Estate blog covering green building issues and real estate issues, a combination usually unseen in the real estate world, updating it two or three times a week. He also began e-mailing a monthly newsletter, "kind of a best of the blog," which is the "best thing the company has done in terms of marketing," he says. "The readership [of the blog] is going up, the subscription rate is going up, and our unsubscribe rate is almost nil."

By becoming part of a like-minded blogging community, Green Key gains credibility and readership within this community. Invariably, trendspotters come along, hopefully talking up the business and increasing general awareness. Although Bartle says the company has not actively sought out media exposure and blogging coverage, that will change in '08 "when we go national and our audience gets a whole lot bigger," he says, explaining that he plans to bring in a PR company to "make inroads in both online and offline media."

Bartle believes that the blogging has been crucial for an increased presence on the Web generally and in the Gort Cloud specifically. "We started to get coverage — free PR — in places like TreeHugger.com, Inhabitat. com, and JetsonGreen.com," he explains. These articles spawned coverage in the mainstream press like CNN, *U.S. News and World Report*, the *New York Times*, and the *Wall Street Journal*.

Green McMansions?

Green Key will represent any home of any size, regardless of whether it has green features. The question comes up, of course, as to how big a house can be and still be considered green, no matter what features it has. Bartle stays away from the "oft-mentioned notion that people need to be living in smaller spaces to be sustainable," he says. "I think that's kind of a forced minimalization that . . . kind of makes people think, *Oh, the green movement means I'm going to live in a cave and eat berries.*"

As to what would happen if he were asked to represent the seller of a green ten-thousand-square-foot home in Marin, "I guess it's better than a ten-thousand-square-foot non-green home," Bartle responds. "It's like a green Wal-Mart. Is that a good thing? Well it's better than a not-green Wal-Mart."

"I don't think we should push that [minimalization] so much," he continues. "I think it's important to communicate the concept of an ecological footprint to people and let them resonate with that for a while and draw their own conclusions."

"The bottom line is that we would rather sell a not-green home to a green-minded buyer and help that buyer green their new home. Then we've added to the inventory of green homes," he concludes.

The green rental market.

Bartle is hopeful that Green Key can eventually crack San Francisco's rental market, especially because two-thirds of city residents live in rental properties, as opposed to a national average of closer to one-third.

"As more and more green properties are created, we would love to be a property management company for green [living spaces]," Bartle says, pointing to the slower green growth in this market due to the fact that landlords are not as concerned as homeowners about such issues as healthy air quality. In addition, the rental market is so competitive in San Francisco that apartment owners don't need to go green as a differentiator.

As for helping clients find apartments, Bartle says, "It's just all about Craigslist. And really the only people we can help are out-of-town people who don't have the opportunity to come look at a place every day. We can be their eyes and ears to an extent, and we have agents who do just that."

Looking forward to a fruitful marketplace.

Things seem to be going Green Key's way in the Bay Area. San Francisco mayor Gavin Newsom and the San Francisco City Council have announced initiatives to green the city's building codes, as well as to require green minimum standards when applying for building permits for large-scale residential and commercial construction.

On a state level, the California Building Industry Association recently endorsed Build It Green's rating system, GreenPoint Rated. "They're saying this green building thing is coming, that it's not a fad, that we'd better get on board with it," Bartle explains.

Bartle also points to a new initiative by the US Green Building Council to rate residential structures for Leadership in Energy and Environmental Design (LEED) certification.

As this book goes to press, Green Key has a presence in eight of the San Francisco Bay regions. As for expansion nationally, Bartle says, "We've registered to franchise in California, and we're in talks with brokers in several other states as well."

SUMMARY: FINDING ECONOMIC SHELTER IN GREEN BUILDING

"By the year 2035, three quarters of the built environment in the U.S. will be either new or renovated," according to the AIA's report *Architects and Climate Change*. This presents enormous opportunity for Michelle Kaufmann and Chris Bartle.

The MKD and Green Key green experiments are too new to document success, but both principals are innovators who have created new categories in the residential building market. While the market is still small for green homes, both companies expect the demand to grow — especially as the high cost of energy drives more people to more efficient housing solutions.

Both companies are also participants in the Gort Cloud's exchange of information. Both recognize that eco-conscious consumers are their core customers, and these customers receive much of their information from bloggers, trendspotters, and social networks within the Gort Cloud. Of course, they also rely on conventional media and PR, but the two are not mutually exclusive. They work off each other. Nevertheless, the unpaid, and therefore more credible, endorsements from the Gort Cloud pundits are typically more valued for truth and objectivity. There's also a sense that the Gort Cloud provides insider or early knowledge — something particularly attractive to first adopters always on the hunt for what's new.

Creating Green Street

Ecotrust, Portfolio 21 Investments, and ShoreBank Pacific

THE CHALLENGE

Out in the Pacific Northwest, a band of financial entrepreneurs has set out to create a new Wall Street. As with the older East Coast model, they seek opportunities for return on investment; but in this new version, the earth, as well as investors, is factored into the calculation of risk. They call their community Salmon Nation and have evolved a new financial nexus to both serve and conserve it.

With the market demanding high returns at the expense of long-term objectives, how can this band of eco-capitalists, each an independent business, win the hearts and wallets of investors?

THE SOLUTION

The three Salmon Nation citizen-businesses profiled here all create stakeholder buy-in by living, not just stating, a common mission. These people walk the walk on sustainability and concentrate their business in the backyards of their constituents. They target a common core audience, share expertise, and then build loyalty through performance.

All three use a rigorous vetting process to ensure that all investment choices abide by their collective brand promise, and they follow through to ensure that their investment portfolios maintain sustainable standards.

To counter the power of the large Wall Street financial institutions, each of these businesses has become a big fish in a small pond by focusing brand development on local markets and/or highly targeted markets.

In a world of hype and unrealistic promises, they also differentiate by being humble and low-key. Instead of hollow promises or empty taglines, this financial collective has become a networking hub for customers.

New York's Wall Street was born in the early days of the Industrial Revolution. It was to become the new order's financial center, where profits and returns to investors trump all. Now comes the next evolution in financial networks — a new eco financial center burgeoning in the

Pearl District of Portland, Oregon, where profits aren't necessarily everything, because protecting the health of the planet is just as important.

The companies joining in this Portland financial venture are thinking big. They are attempting to build not only their own individual financial brands, but also a whole new conservation-based economy stretching over a thousand miles of the Northwest Pacific Coast. They've labeled their community Salmon Nation, after the area where Pacific salmon run.

Three of the financial organizations involved in building and branding Salmon Nation are Ecotrust, a self-described conservation organization promoting natural capital objectives in the Pacific Northwest and the creator of the Salmon Nation concept; Portfolio 21, an investment company that works in partnership with Ecotrust objectives; and ShoreBank Pacific, a full-service bank formed by a partnership between Ecotrust and Chicago's ShoreBank Corporation. All three are neighbors at the Ecotrust Building in Portland, and all share in the vision of Salmon Nation.

I can relate to their objectives because I grew up in the Northwest — in Bellevue, just outside Seattle. People here are close to nature. The fog, the rain on our faces, and the occasional but magnificent sunny day connect us to the planet in a visceral way. I miss the place. But back in my youth, I would never, ever have thought that our little stepsister, Portland, would amount to much. I would never have suspected it would become the epicenter of an eco-economic insurgency.

Ecotrust: Building a Trust Brand

Spencer Beebe founded the nonprofit Ecotrust in 1991 to preserve the temperate rain forests of his Northwest home and to spread the economic rewards from sustainable development among all the region's citizens, including Native Americans. He's a fourth-generation Portlander who had previously spent fourteen years with the Nature Conservancy, serving as the organization's West Coast director. He also helped to found Conservation International.

In 1998, he purchased a Pearl District warehouse that was once the hub of a frontier economy at the time of westward expansion, and he turned it into an incubation lab for businesses entering the green space that would "push the bounds of twenty-first-century technology and ideas."

Ecotrust's underlying principle is that sustainability is best achieved through the development of localized economies. To that end, it funds local and sustainable projects that fall roughly under the headings of food and farms, Native American, fisheries, and forestry. But when it comes to marketing its purpose and cause, Ecotrust has struggled to brand itself in a way that is clear to stakeholders and the public.

"What do you call an organization working on sustainability?" questions Howard Silverman, director of public information. "You can call it an environmental organization, but it's not."

At first, Ecotrust positioned itself as an organization concerned with "ecosystem economics." Later, it moved on to "conservation-based development," and then "a conservation economy." But none of these rang the bell. Part of the problem lies with the word *sustainability*. "It has too much stasis," explains Silverman. Adds Beebe: "When you ask, 'How's your marriage?' no one answers, 'Sustainable.' It doesn't sound like a goal for something you'd be working toward." It sounds like the status quo, the way things are now, and not the way things should be."

"The sustainable development model wasn't energetic enough . . . it wasn't fun and cool, [it was] too ho-hum and academic sounding," explains Beebe. "That's why we went to the term *conservation economy*." According to Ecotrust's Web site, the conservation economy is "predicated on the notion, gaining an ever wider currency, that economic and ecological systems are mutually interdependent. To this relationship Ecotrust and others have sought to add a third 'e' — social equity — to ensure that economic development awards benefits to all the region's citizens. Economy, ecology, equity equal the triple bottom line." *Triple bottom line*, or 3BL, is a phrase coined by John Elkington, whom *BusinessWeek* has described as the "dean of the corporate-responsibility movement for three decades." The term was expanded on and made famous in his book *Cannibals with Forks: The Triple Bottom Line of 21st Century Business*.

Birth of Salmon Nation.

The conservation economy message needed some added impetus, so in 2004 Ecotrust repurposed the phrase *Salmon Nation* from a book Ecotrust had published in 1999. It became a goal-defining phrase linking Ecotrust to the conservation economy theme. Since then, the organization's Web site explains, its primary mission has been "to build Salmon Nation." The genius in this seemingly layered set of brand names is that you create a brand around a goal that everyone in the Northwest can take ownership in. Even those who aren't investors or account holders can take pride in the vision. Try that with Citibank, or Merrill Lynch, or Oppenheimer Funds.

"We've tried to capture a bigger idea with more enthusiasm and energy, and use it to brand more effectively," says Beebe. Nearly every corporation has a mission statement, often a set of hollow platitudes that rarely have meaning for stakeholders, but this goes farther. It's a mission that has been transformed into a living program of local activism. It's a mission writ large.

The Salmon Nation concept turns its staff, investors, donors, and recipients into citizens, or coinhabitants, of this financial community. "If you live in this place where the salmon run, you're a citizen of this place," Beebe says. "If we reorganize our society around the natural lines of the environment, it will be more enduring and more prosperous."

Of course, the citizens of Salmon Nation are expected to be committed to sustainable goals. "It comes down to whether you walk or you drive, what you drive, what you wear, what you eat, how you relate to your neighbors, the choices that you make," says Beebe. This further binds his audience to his brand because both vendor and customer are expected to make changes and sacrifices together. They're joined to the same cause.

"You have to have a whole new set of governance. A whole new set of flags. A new constitution. Figure out what the myths are about this place," Beebe continues. This produces a wellhead of communication themes that are rooted in the uniqueness of the Pacific Northwest, including the native habitat, the food, the Native culture, local building techniques and styles, and the seasons and the pulses of nature. In this sense, Ecotrust is like a venture capital company, but one that invests capital in the local, sustainable economy. "The line between for- and nonprofit is getting blurry," wrote environmentalist and author Paul Hawken in 2007.[1] Ecotrust has created a unique hybrid of for- and nonprofit entities that work to develop natural, social, and economic capital.

"Salmon Nation is an idea, a place, a gift . . . you could call it a kind of meme," says Silverman. "We've tried to invest those two words with a set of values, a set of ideas about regional economies. To the extent that people look at that brand and they are intrigued by it, perhaps one need not even go to the Web site to learn anything more. We hope there's something that's inherently simple and understandable about it."

"It's a self-replicator," he adds with a nod to viral marketing. "[It's] something we've tossed out there. If it's attractive, then the ideas behind it will replicate." The natural attractiveness that Silverman is referring to is a notion that people in the Pacific Northwest buy into by virtue of their shared values. It's not like talking someone into buying the corporate values of an East Coast financial group that's investing all over the world. This Salmon Nation idea is different. It's about a regional population buying into something that actually reflects and affects the place where they live.

For Ecotrust and its partners, a local and united brand platform with broad stakeholder buy-in insulates them against aggressive outside competition. Without the Salmon Nation idea, Ecotrust, Portfolio 21, and ShoreBank Pacific would be left to fight their own battles against large outside banks with their deeply funded marketing programs. This explains the steady loss around the country of local banks to mergers and acquisitions: they can't compete against the juggernaut. Add in the Salmon Nation concept, however, and local loyalty is cultivated. Customers relate to these smaller, local institutions because they reflect their own ideals and goals, especially when it comes to sustainability — or beyond sustainability.

A home for adventurous eco-capitalists.

The Ecotrust Building, officially known as the Jean Vollum Natural Capital Center, is a seventy-thousand-square-foot turn-of-the-twentieth-century warehouse with the vibe of a university student center but the look of a cutting-edge office complex. There's a spacious coffeehouse and an inviting outside deck. There's open architecture and engaging design. Bending over to take a sip of water at the water fountain, you come face-to-face with a painting of Mount Hood and the Bull Run Reservoir, source of the city's drinking water. The bulletin board has notices about things like a symposium on the fundamentals of contaminant chemistry, the schedule for a bike ride to visit local organic farmers leaving from the parking lot, and an invitation from the City of Portland for a wine-and-cheese reception to promote solar energy incentives around the fireplace on the roof.

In addition to World Cup Coffee, the other retail outlets on the first floor are Patagonia and Hotlips Pizza. There's also an ATM in the middle of the lobby that advertises a Salmon Nation Visa card offered by ShoreBank Pacific, whose lending and banking office is also here. According to TreeHugger.com, the Salmon Nation card offers "the biggest eco-bang for your buck" of any eco-friendly credit card in the United States.

What's most impressive of all is to hear glimpses of the conversations taking place — in the lobby, in the upstairs public areas, in the expansive kitchen and dining hall. They are invariably conversations about new ideas.

"We built a place where people could work, where people could shop, where there'd be open space," explains Spencer Beebe. "On Thursdays, we have the local farmers' market in the parking lot. On the weekends, old ladies come in to play chess and have a slice of pizza. So far, we've had sixty-five weddings here . . . and we didn't think of weddings at all in the design stage."

At the time of the Capital Building's restoration, "everyone thought it should be about LEED certification," Beebe remembers. "But you could either be a demonstration project of all the latest green technology — solar cells on the roof, all that stuff — or you could be a lab that encourages change and innovation and creativity. And those are two different kinds of things. Demonstration is rigid, it's a structure, out of date in a few years. We chose to go in the social direction."

"It's much more interesting to be a lab. I didn't want to do this to follow someone else's checklist to find out what's righteous. We used natural models of development — models from nature, from ecology," he says. When it came to a tenant pool, diversity was emphasized, from both the for-profit and the nonprofit worlds.

Bettina von Hagen, Ecotrust's vice president — who has worked beside Beebe for fourteen years — explains that although the tenants are diverse, they do share values about the way to work in the world. In this way, Salmon Nation fosters a common culture. On Wall Street, it may be the quest for profit, but here it's the quest for a quality of life. "There has been a strong emphasis on creativity and imagination, as well as on conservation. But it isn't the conservation of deprivation, it's the conservation of plenty," she explains.

The nexus spreads.

Another important trait shared by all tenants is openness to collaboration. "We want the tenants to work together," von Hagen says. "We think up ways to advance each other's missions . . . There's a power created among the network. It all comes from the same source . . . the goal to create a world."

Indeed, collaboration seems to be all over the place here. Hotlips Pizza participates with the Ecotrust Food and Farm Program. ShoreBank Pacific funded Hotlips, as well as Sustainable Harvest, the well-known and highly respected organization that began the notion of Fair Trade coffee twenty years ago. Half of the income generated by the bank's Salmon Nation credit card goes to Ecotrust to help build Salmon Nation.

Ecotrust's works include support for the Wild Salmon Center to restore critical salmon watershed and for Trout Mountain Forestry in an effort to develop landscape-scale examples of ecological forest management.

The City of Portland's Office of Sustainable Development, on the third floor, interacts with just about every other organization here in some capacity. And it's no surprise that the city is represented, because Portland is quickly becoming recognized as the most eco-conscious metropolitan area in the country. Much of what the city government does reflects a sustainable perspective.

Portfolio 21, on the second floor, has collaborated with both Ecotrust and ShoreBank Pacific in transforming itself into the top-performing green investment firm in the country. Of the collaboration between Ecotrust and Portfolio 21, von Hagen says, "We have to capture the interest of entrepreneurs and private capital. They should want to participate actively and willingly in creating this new economy."

Portfolio 21 Investments: The Clustering Effect

"Spencer Beebe called us and said, 'I've got this wild idea. I just bought this old dilapidated warehouse, and I'm thinking about doing this. You want to sign up?'"

Carsten Henningsen, chairman of Progressive Investment Management, the parent of Portfolio 21 Investments, sits in a conference room on the second floor of the Ecotrust Building.

"When we first came here, we thought, *Okay, we're going to be in a green building*," he continues. "But we didn't really grasp the gravity of what it meant to be in a sustainable community, a think tank really." Which helps explain why an earlier era, the Industrial Revolution, started in a little village off in the hinterlands of England. There is something about a critical mass of like-minded people that creates a movement. We see this in all sorts of products and services: they tend to be born out of and cluster around specific geographic areas.

"From a branding, retail standpoint, it's much better for us to be here on the second floor [of the Ecotrust Building] than on the street corner with a big sign. This is our target market. People, tourists . . . come through here from all over the world. This building is a big draw."

"Portland becomes a very small place when we walk in here," he continues. "People see folks they know in the coffeehouse. Deals are made in the hallways, so it really has become a wonderful synergy for sustainability in our community."

Carsten didn't know it at the time, but he was about to become a tribal leader in Salmon Nation.

The natural.

Carsten Henningsen became fascinated with the stock market at the age of ten, when his parents bought him two shares of Mattel. By twelve, he had branched out to Disney, riding his bike to the Dean Witter six blocks from his home in the Bay Area to tend to his account and check the numbers on the screens, standing next to a lineup of retired folks.

In college, Henningsen traveled around the world for class credit as often as he could. He saw the impact of multinational corporations on developing countries in small, remote towns with no electricity. No matter where he was, he'd be offered a warm Fanta or some other Coca-Cola product.

"The power that multinationals exert on cultures around the world cannot be exaggerated," Henningsen says. "You know, marketing and brands are very powerful things — more powerful than nation-states." And then, "it sort of dawned on me that maybe there was a way to influence corporate behavior through the investment process."

Upon graduating from the University of Puget Sound, "I asked myself the question that I hope a lot of young people ask themselves, which is, *What am I going to do with my life, how can I make the world a better place?* I put two and two together and thought, *All right, I'll start an investment company that tries to influence corporate behavior.*"

At the time, American and European investors were divesting in companies that supported apartheid in South Africa, but no one was thinking about companies that were supporting the degradation of the environment, at least not until Carsten came along. "The original tagline when I started the company in 1982 was 'Socially and environmentally responsible investing,'" he explains. Of course, there were lots of socially responsible investment firms. But "at that time, nobody was sticking the environment in there."

When Henningsen looks back to the early 1980s, he realizes that he must have had "a lot of tenacity and some ignorance and naïveté to just open up a shop at the age of twenty-two."

"Everybody told me to go to work for Merrill Lynch or Dean Witter and make your mistakes, get trained by them, and then go off on your own. And I didn't have the patience for that. So I just said, 'Forget it, I'm just going to put my own shingle up,' and here I go."

Henningsen attributes his fierce entrepreneurial spirit to his father, an industrial engineer who grew tired of drafting work and opened a pizzeria — complete with a theater pipe organ — in 1959, because he believed pizza was going to be big. The younger Carsten was so stubborn that he didn't do any feasibility studies for his new venture. If he'd done them, he says, "I never would have started this company because there was no market."

The entrepreneur's wife, Betsy, took a job in newspaper editing. The couple was now living on her twelve-thousand-dollars-per-year salary and on the even paltrier sum Carsten earned at his day jobs as a DJ, news director, and airtime salesman at a local radio station. "That was the best marketing sales training you could ever have," he explains. "If you can sell air, you can sell anything, right?" Including, it seems, a mutual fund.

To meet like-minded individuals and kick-start his venture, Henningsen joined the Social Investment Forum, now an industry trade association of six hundred companies that meets at what's called SRI in the Rockies, an annual summer conference in Colorado. Back then, "it was just a small group of us getting together in a room," Henningsen says. "We all knew there was something afoot. We just didn't know how long it was going to take."

By the way, Spencer Beebe sits on the advisory board of Portfolio 21 Investments and Henningsen sits on the Ecotrust Council, which all links back to the Salmon Nation idea.

Small player. Big voice.

Portfolio 21 took a progressive approach to investing and, some would say, a provocative approach to promotion. If you're a little bird, then you need to flap your wings to get attention. In the beginning, Carsten Henningsen adopted an unconventional strategy for targeted buzz marketing. The message: Here is a company that goes for the jugular, here's a company that will affect where companies obtain funding.

The word-of-mouth campaign was directed solely at the early adopters, "folks who already understand the environmental crisis," Henningsen explains. "You don't need to educate them, you don't need to prove it to them. All you have to do is put the fund in front of them. They're just saying, 'I don't care if it makes sense or not, I'm just doing it 'cause it just feels right to me.'"

This tactic, which is often overlooked by even the most experienced marketing advisers, targets the innermost circle of a target customer base. These are the folks who want something the market doesn't offer yet, and they can and do influence others. Many of these customers inhabit the Gort Cloud. In Carsten's case, this was just enough to get him started, and then it was on to step two.

Henningsen and his associates went to all the appropriate conferences and talked things up. They were fortunate to start the fund in 1999, when the SEC began allowing the offering of a prospectus online. The money began to roll in, and eventually there was enough to budget an advertising campaign. "As you begin to mainstream, now you're into education," he says.

"We didn't have the money to use outside creative, so we did it ourselves," he continues. "And we figured, 'We're spending this much money on a full-page color ad, it better stop people in their tracks.'"

The first ad campaign featured the image of a dog peeing on a Hummer. The tagline read, "He's Taking a Stand Against Big Oil." The second, after the Bush reelection, showed a small Bush doll clenched between the teeth of the same dog. The tagline read, "Four more years is a lot to chew on." The company went straight to the core audience, attempting to buy space in the left-leaning press, but even some of these publications refused to print the ads. The *Sierra Club Magazine*, after agreeing to do so, refused a second printing because of the reaction from the readership following the first.

More recently, Carsten has hired egg, a Seattle brand communications agency specializing in "creating powerful relationships between consumers and sustainable brands," according to its Web site. Under egg's guidance, the most recent Portfolio 21 campaign features the unsettling image of a wedding where everyone in attendance is wearing a hazmat suit. It's one in a series. The copy reads, "What kind of future are you investing in?"

"We felt like there was a tighter message that would be more effective," says Marty McDonald, creative director at egg. The Hummer and Bush doll ads were fun, but came off "more as a political statement than a message about an investment fund."

A unique selling proposition.

"Portfolio 21 didn't seem to be coming from their true brand character, which is all about assessing positive growth based around the idea of ecological risk," continues egg's McDonald. "It's similar to the concept of health maintenance in insurance — if we can plan for a better or healthier future in our behavior today, which necessitates consideration for the future, we should be able to benefit from that in both the near term and long term. And it obviates the need to clean up the damage later on. That is the essence of sustainability. And it's more inspiring. We developed a campaign that captured this idea in a fun way to stay in brand character, as opposed to the typical sermonizing approach." With the hazmat ads, "It's not the doom and gloom that you think, it's the doom and gloom with a wink."

Portfolio 21's target audience is cynical about marketing, McDonald believes. "They're educated, and smart . . . The more you can wink with them, and share a common understanding of the seriousness of the issues, the better."

"Advertising is so hard to make effective. It's so tough to first break through, and then emotionally connect to people. It's important to be likable, trustworthy, and authentic. You want people to feel invited into and included in your world, and to have a conversation with the brand on the issues that matter to them." The takeaway is that because of its diligent and rigorous research and analysis, Portfolio 21 has "figured out the secret formula in terms of criteria for an investment mix that balances earnings and growth potential within this concept of sustainability."

"It's amazing that they've generated the numbers they have," McDonald says, "and so satisfying for the mission. Ultimately, it shouldn't be surprising, and the approach will only prove stronger in time."

Progressive Investment Management is reaping the benefit of egg's considerable research on the rapidly emerging and broadly interspersed values-oriented consumer, which in turn helps direct brand strategies.

"There's this sense of lack of control due to environmental and globalization issues. Joe or Jane Consumer feels out of balance and, frankly, anxious," McDonald explains, citing a survey that suggests that consumers have a better chance of regaining the feeling of control by shopping in the green marketplace than they do by going to the polls. Shopping green becomes "their way of making a little difference . . . And they feel that's the only thing they *can* do."

Yet for the vast majority of American consumers, the bottom line is still immediate self-interest. "The consideration set must be framed in the context of self-interest," McDonald explains. "The mainstream is about 'What's in it for me?' . . . That's why organic food is doing so well . . . 'It's good for me and my kids. I'll do it.'"

With egg's guidance, Portfolio 21 stays away from tying the fund to a traditional green label. "We frame it around innovation, inspiration . . . a better way to do things," explains McDonald. "It's a differentiator and an advantage."

Nevertheless, as the environmental crisis has come to the fore, Portfolio 21 has similarly brought it front and center in its marketing material. Because of this approach, which has yielded strong returns, it's taking advantage of the connection between doing good and doing good for profit. For instance, on the firm's home page, the headline reads, WHAT IS YOUR IDEA OF A HEALTHY RETURN? — which prompts viewers to think through the double entendre. The site goes on to explain, "Portfolio 21 companies seek to prosper in the 21st Century by recognizing environmental sustainability as a fundamental human challenge and a tremendous business opportunity."

Says Marty McDonald, "When you can put a strategic point of view like that into a brand — when you can say, 'We focus specifically on companies that are strategically managing ecological risks, and therefore we can deliver a strong performance with our fund' — then you get the goodwill and the good feeling about where you're investing, but you're also getting those returns that socially responsible investing hasn't been able to deliver in the past."

"You want to push the envelope in this business," he continues. "Most advertising is such drivel . . . it speaks down to people, common-denominator-izes itself . . . frankly I was going to do something else if I couldn't work on accounts like this."

About Carsten Henningsen and others like him around the country, McDonald says, "There's something attractive about the idea that these people are thought leaders. Their success in its own right will be an indicator of where we're all going. If they can be successful, that's where people will put their money."

Progressive begets Portfolio 21.

Portfolio 21 Investments, hatched by Progressive in 1999, describes itself as "a global equity mutual fund investing in companies designing ecologically superior products, using renewable energy, and developing efficient production methods." Its goal, emphasizes the company, is to prosper in the twenty-first century by recognizing environmental sustainability as a fundamental human challenge and a tremendous business opportunity.

Of late, Progressive Investment has made quite a name for itself in the financial community with its Portfolio 21–branded fund. Fund asset revenue has doubled from $125 million in 2006 to $250 million in 2007. Once waiting in the wings for the green wave to build, Portfolio 21 is now riding right on top of it. The fund has done so well, in fact, that Progressive is in the process of rebranding itself under the Portfolio 21 Investments Advisors name. This is not unusual. A product brand will sometimes eclipse the parent brand. If there is only one primary product, it may make sense to retire the parent brand in the interest of consistency and recognition. It's a process of simplifying the brand architecture.

"First, we have to communicate to ourselves, and we've just kind of come around to that," says Henningsen. "And now we have to come up with a language because we're going to completely redo the Progressive Web site as Portfolio 21 Investment Advisors."

"It's like Progressive was the parent and Portfolio 21 is the child trying to grow up, embarrassing its parent with radical ads of a dog and a Hummer and Bush, and all of a sudden the child is now the adult."

"Portfolio 21 is where the revenue comes from . . . that's the brand," Henningsen emphasizes.

Building trust, performance, and reliability.

As president and chief investment officer, Leslie Christian is in charge of Portfolio 21's investment strategy. A former Wall Street professional banker, she reached "that point where you just can't take it anymore" and moved back to her native Northwest. Interested in sustainable economies, she joined the SRI community and attended a conference where she met Henningsen. Five years later, he asked her to run Portfolio 21.

Leslie understood that an investment fund is only as good as the companies it invests in. Under her leadership, the vetting of potential investment vehicles begins with the immediate exclusion of companies with negative performance in the areas of employee relations, human rights, community involvement, and product safety, as well as those with significant business activities in nuclear energy, tobacco, gambling, or weapons. The driver for inclusion in the Portfolio 21 selection criteria is the environment.

"It's a real challenge," says Christian. "We've looked at over 2,000 companies around the world, and we've invested in only 106 . . . so it's a very strict criteria selection process." Some of the companies that you might think would be appropriate have failed to pass the test, Toyota among them.

"Toyota didn't make it, despite its hugely successful Prius, because its business model is still pushing gas-guzzling SUVs," Henningsen explains.

Other companies have fallen off the investment list, such as Nike because of its labor and social issues, and Toshiba when it acquired Westinghouse, a corporation with significant nuclear holdings. Church and Dwight, an early sponsor of Earth Day, was originally included because of its environmentally friendly cleansers but ultimately dropped due to its acquisition of companies that were well below the sustainability parameters.

By enforcing its strict rules and leaving such generally profitable companies as Toyota and Nike out of its world, Portfolio 21 is building a brand that its investors and the citizens of Salmon Nation can trust. For any company, the most prized attribute is trust.

The medium is the message.

Carsten Henningsen attributes much of the company's current success to the Internet. "It's the reason our brand recognition has increased so radically every month," he says. "We have the power of the Internet to do the work for us. So it's really not what we're doing from the branding standpoint, it's more about how we're being passed around in the public, and by the media" — a reference to the number of articles written about the company on the Web. The various online investor forums, like SocialFunds.com, Kiplinger.com, Morningstar.com, CSRwire.com, and GreenBiz.com, also spread the fame of Portfolio 21.

The latest advertising strategy seems to be going in the digital direction as well. "We are decreasing our print advertising," says Christian. "The advertising we're doing on Google, the advertising we're doing on the Web, seems to be just as effective" with less cost and better metrics.

The original radical ads got the fund off the ground with the original core audience, who simply trusted them with no proof or track record. Now that it's established, Portfolio 21 has entered a maintenance and awareness-building phase, and its financial performance has outperformed the MSCI World Equity Index and the S & P 500 Index since the fund's inception in 1999.

Sustainable Economics 101.

If Carsten Henningsen's not thinking of teaching a college class in Sustainable Economics 101, he really should be. He likes to get out paper and pencil to draw diagrams of the financial landscape over time. "So the earth goes along for billions and billions of years . . . and this line represents the world economy's ecological footprint," he says, drawing an ascending line across the paper.

"Now Wall Street is living in neoclassical economic 1960s terms," he continues. "They believe that this line can just keep growing, can just go on forever, right? Unlimited growth. That's the corporate model if you look at the stock market today."

"But that's not the reality. The reality is that we have a ticking point here," he says, drawing a second, descending line on his graph. "We have loss of species, loss of natural resources, loss of biocapacity."

The space between the two lines on Henningsen's graph grows ever smaller over time, eventually forming a narrow opening, which he refers to as a funnel. Any company today that hopes to survive tomorrow's world, he maintains, must travel through this funnel, preferably by positioning itself to move through as soon as possible. Many companies, Carsten believes, "will hit the walls of the funnel before figuring it out. And that's happening already."

The funnel theory applies to any natural resource, and oil makes a great example. "As oil prices have gone up in the last few years, the companies that have been positioning themselves to become less dependent on petroleum products all of a sudden have a competitive advantage to make it through the narrow part of this funnel."

Dinosaurs versus smarter dinosaurs.

Portfolio 21 Investments divides its holdings into three categories: the dinosaurs, the smarter dinosaurs, and those companies that are building themselves on a local-economy model.

Vestas Wind Systems in Denmark is an example of a smarter dinosaur, says Henningsen. "They're figuring they're going to have more demand for their product as the resource funnel narrows and things get more unstable and oil prices go up."

"We used to say, 'How much do you want in bonds, how much do you want in stocks, how much do you want in real estate, how much do you want in gold and precious metals?' Now it's 'What do you want in dinosaurs, how much do you want in smarter dinosaurs, and how much do you want in sustainable local economies?'" The truth is, he notes, "we don't know the timing of this, so the weight that you put on each one of these categories is the variable, it's the guess that you have to make. The folks who optimize are going to do the best."

Henningsen advises clients to hold some of all three investment types — while being prepared to lessen the weight in dinosaurs in favor of smarter dinosaurs and local sustainable companies as time goes on. "Right now most people are beginning to weight mostly in the smarter dinosaur mode."

For the long term, higher returns will come from the local-economy models, according to Carsten; he's convinced that most of his clients will eventually weight toward that sector. "The pendulum is swinging from Wall Street to Main Street. Main Street will have a competitive advantage because of local distribution, local marketing, local manufacturing, less transportation costs."

"It's the pendulum swinging back," he continues. "The Wal-Marts and the Costcos and the Home Depots are not going to make it through this funnel unless they morph into something else along the way."

As a matter of fact, Wal-Mart is making smarter-dinosaur moves toward support for local economies. "In a bid to offset the rising cost of fuel," notes GreenBiz.com, "Wal-Mart plans to expand its offerings of fresh fruits and vegetables grown and shipped from local farms across the US. During the last two years, partnerships between local farms and the world's largest retailer have jumped 50 percent, and the company anticipates it will source about $400 million in local produce this year, making it the country's largest buyer of produce that is grown and sold within a state's borders. The move will allow Wal-Mart to save millions in fuel costs."[2]

A corporate culture of small, fun, and accountable.

Henningsen conforms his own companies to the local-economy standard. He lives the motto that bigger is not necessarily better. "Quality of life in here, in this office, is most important," he insists. Accordingly, the company often turns down business from large institutional, corporate, and nonprofit clients.

For these very large clients, "you really have to jump through a lot of hoops," he says. "You have to get on a plane and go visit those important clients and you have to fill out complicated questionnaires on a regular basis for all the consultants. And normally in the growth of a fund we would hire institutional wholesalers who would do that. They would get on planes and fly around the country."

"So we're now at $250 million [in assets] and I know we're going to be at $500 million and I know we're going to be at $1 billion," Henningsen continues. "It's just a question of how long it will take. We can get there faster if we go jump on planes and go to green festivals, but to what end? That's part of our ethos."

"We choose not to go in that direction," he stresses. "We want to maintain the quality of life here, which for us means keeping employees at about fifteen total. And we have something here called the fun factor . . . sort of our index for 'Are you having fun?'"

According to Christian, Henningsen's in-house title at the company is "the Minister of Joy." At company retreats, he often dons a cape for "ceremonial duties," she says. "It's really fun to work here and anybody here would say that," says Amanda Plyley, communications manager. "I mean we're laughing all the time, just having a great time joking and enjoying each other."

The company is horizontally structured, with Henningsen, Christian, Plyley, and the other twelve employees making decisions around the conference table. "Everybody knows how much everybody makes, all the financials are passed out every month," Christian explains. "It's a completely open-book, transparent organization."

Developing goodwill.

Carsten Henningsen's daughters are sixteen and twelve. When he took them to see *An Inconvenient Truth*, his older daughter fell asleep because none of it was new to her. She'd heard it all during the drives to school in her father's 2005 VW biodiesel, powered by waste oil from Kettle Chips of Salem, Oregon. Henningsen likes to share those kinds of things with his children.

He also likes his daughters to become involved in the nonprofit organization he founded, Community Friends, which assists economies damaged by natural disaster. Currently, the organization is assisting communities in Sri Lanka ravaged by the 2004 tsunami.

Carston posed a question to these villagers, "Where is the money leaking out of the village?' Because if we can keep the money circulating in the village instead of leaking out, you'll get a multiplier effect, and it will help bring people out of poverty and create more jobs."

"So [the villagers] just took that idea and ran with it and they said, 'Well, we grow chilies here,' and I said, 'Well, what do you do with the chilies?' 'We sell them to the chili factory that's out in the city,' they said. 'And then what happens?' I asked them. 'Well, they grind it up into flakes and powder, and they sell it back to us in little packages.'"

"So we gave them a social venture capital infusion of four hundred dollars that enabled them to buy the grinding machine, and then we started a collective of six teenage girls, 'cause they're the most vulnerable part of the community, they don't have any options. So the six girls and two parents and one teacher make up the chili collective . . . and now they grind the chili and put it in the packages and sell it in the community."

Projects like this are the fund's form of corporate social responsibility, and just one more thing it does to invoke goodwill.

ShoreBank Pacific: Channeling the Wave

Dave Williams, CEO of ShoreBank Pacific, sitting behind his desk on the first floor of the Ecotrust Building, describes his first meeting with Carsten Henningsen back in 1990.

"I thought he was one of these environmental nutcases, and he thought I was one of those guys way off to the right, and I was," Williams explains. "My children remember the time when I used to say recycling was a conspiracy to move garbage out of the landfills and into our garage." And now imagine Dave, this fiscal conservative, running a green bank in the People's Republic of Portland.

"Here we are, Carsten and I, working together and enjoying each other a lot, because I understood the business reasons" for going green, Williams continues. "It's the right thing to do. Secondly, you can't have a business if you're going to go out and cut down all the trees and then you have to shut down the mill because now you've harvested all the trees and have to wait forty years to start again. It doesn't work. Doesn't work to harvest all the fish so that you have to shut down all the canneries. So if you're looking for sustainability, and you're looking for sustainable communities, you've gotta have sustainable business, which means you've gotta do things in an environmentally sensitive way." Not surprisingly, ShoreBank Pacific is the banking partner behind Carsten's Community Friends microfinance fund.

Williams proudly describes a wooden frame around the main entrance of the bank's Ilwaco, Washington, headquarters. "That's a one-hundred-year-old Douglas fir that was in a pickle vat down in the redwoods," he says. "Came from one of our clients that bought a pickle factory."

A bank with a commitment.

ShoreBank Pacific's origins date back to 1991, when Spencer Beebe, on a rafting trip down the Salmon River, met Mary Houghton, a founder of Chicago's ShoreBank Corporation, a pioneer in developing inner-city community projects. The two began discussions about fostering businesses that would bring environmental and social returns while creating economic opportunity. As a result, ShoreBank Enterprise Cascadia, a nonprofit community development financial institution, was formed in 1994 (first as ShoreTrust Trading Group, then ShoreBank Enterprise Pacific, and finally ShoreBank Enterprise Cascadia).

In 1997, Ecotrust and ShoreBank Corporation formed ShoreBank Pacific, opening its doors in a double-wide trailer on the docks of Ilwaco as "the first commercial bank in the United States with a commitment to environmentally sustainable community development." This is one of the unique selling propositions the bank proclaims on its Web site. It's a perfect example of what Ecotrust likes to do — start and/or support unique businesses with a sustainable framework and brand them as such. It's all part of the expansion of Salmon Nation.

When Beebe found Dave Williams to run the company, he found a long-termer. A high-school-teacher-turned-businessman, Williams had worked in the oil and gas industries before taking the helm of the largest car wash company in the world in order to take it out of bankruptcy.

As more of his story came out, I realized that Dave had been a teacher at Newport High, my high school's crosstown rival in Bellevue, Washington. We both had our hair cut at the same barbershop on Main Street, next to Al Johnston's Grocery, where my pals and I tried to sneak peeks of the men's magazines piled up in the corner. That barbershop is where all the business news of the town was exchanged. The richest man in town, Kemper Freeman, sat side by side with the local high school teacher swapping stories and sharing experiences.

Williams came from a background of practicality, and in all the places that he'd worked in his sixty-odd years, he'd always asked the same question: "How can we be more practical?" And part of that question was, "Why is there always so much waste of resources?" He wasn't, he emphasizes, asking this question from an environmental perspective, but rather from a bottom-line business perspective.

On the first day on the job in Ilwaco as CEO of ShoreBank Pacific, Williams had to "crawl under the trailer and evict a guy who'd been sleeping there," he says. "You can't sleep under a bank." To put this in perspective, Ilwaco is a little summer holiday and fishing town on the southern Washington coast. According to the 2000 census, it has a population of about a thousand people.

After several years in the trailer, new quarters were found for the headquarters in Ilwaco; in 1999 it opened an office in Portland, and in October 2001 it moved to the Natural Capital Center.

Connecting its clients.

A majority of ShoreBank Pacific's loans have been made in Oregon, perhaps because "it has always been a state full of small businesses, all depending upon each other, which sort of live and die together," according to Dave Williams.

"If you think about the communities here and how you're going to have a vital state, you've got to have these communities that have vibrant businesses that are going to last a long time . . . And so when you focus on the community, it drives you in the direction we're talking about . . . it drives how you run the businesses overall."

ShoreBank Pacific attempts to develop a web among its clients, connecting sustainable businesses with one another. In fact, the bank actually lists its loan recipients on its Web site for all to see. The network of businesses is right there, out in the open. It'll even run stories about clients' products on the home page, such as the recent cover of Celilo Group, a sustainable news publisher.

"Historically, who was the best businessman in town? It was the banker, because he knew all the businesses, he knew how they operated, and he was putting people together." As Williams says this, it reminds me of the tight-knit business community in Bellevue when I was young. My dad knew his banker throughout his working life.

"The other banks aren't doing it . . . They're out chasing the next deal and you either make your payments or, if you don't, you go away. It's a different kind of relationship." Dave Williams is explaining that the fortunes of his bank lie with the fortunes of his bank's customers. If they do well and if he can help them do well, then he does well. It isn't simply about cutting losses and playing a margin game.

Scoring sustainability.

In taking on clients, ShoreBank Pacific has developed a screening process that involves a sustainability scoring system. "With every borrower, we go out and assess them when we first engage them. Then we go out every year thereafter to meet with them and give them a bunch of suggestions on how they can be better, and measure their improvement over time, because where we are is not where we need to be," Williams says.

In addition to loan officers, the bank has a sustainability group that holds these meetings. The group includes a scientist and an ecologist. "The goal is to meet everybody annually," Williams explains.

"We all need to get a lot better at what we need to do, so we have those conversations and most businesses are interested in hearing what you have to say. And then they say, 'I'm not an environmentalist, in fact I hate those guys, but what do you suggest that I do?' After a while, they come back, 'Yeah, I can do that. I can make money doing that . . . that works.'"

ShoreBank Pacific does not maintain the same stiff qualifications imposed by Portfolio 21 in looking for investment opportunities. It will take on companies that are less than sustainable as long as those companies are committed to moving in a sustainable direction. Officers tell potential borrowers, "We expect you to improve. If you don't want to hear that conversation, go down the street." If they go down the street, "that's fine," explains Williams.

ShoreBank Pacific's loan portfolio is approximately 60 percent real estate, half of that owner-occupied and the other half investor real estate. When a client requests funding for a multiuse building, he or she is asked to consider various environmental options, such as the use of bioswales for drainage, waterless urinals, green roof treatments, and solar energy.

The bank also investigates how the particular client treats employees. "All of our customers are starting to deal with that issue and think about health care and pay and living conditions," Williams says. So in its measure, ShoreBank weighs social as well as environmental improvement goals.

Let's change the world.

The bank has only recently begun to market itself as green. Up until two years ago, "we were very careful not to call ourselves green, not to call ourselves sustainable, but just to be a bank that had a conscience," Williams explains.

Two years ago, he continues, "it became acceptable to say you can be sustainable and you can think about things in an environmental way. That's when we sort of changed our pitch," with the bank beginning to sponsor environmental programs in the community. This collective message can be found in its tagline, "Let's change the world."

One of the ways the bank brings this message to life is through its credit and debit card offers. Cards have become a primary touchpoint for banks in recent years, because it's the one brand experience that customers carry around in their wallets or purses all day. ShoreBank Pacific's EcoCash debit card replaces paper check writing and, of course, there's the Salmon Nation credit card mentioned earlier. Fifty percent of the interchange income goes to Salmon Nation causes. The bank also offers a joint-venture card with Redirect Guide, a Visa credit card that contributes a portion of purchase commissions to a carbon offset program. The tag is, "Make change with every dollar." I can imagine that the bank's customers feel a certain pride in choice when they whip out these cards to make a purchase. It doesn't eliminate the guilt of consumption, but it probably helps ease it. That is a positive brand experience.

"The amount of money we spend on advertising is zip," Williams continues. "The bank relies heavily on word of mouth," so a major benefit of getting to know the customer is that the customer then refers the bank to others in the community. "Instead of spending our time out cold-calling, we're dependent on our customers to bring us the next customer . . . and it's a high probability that this guy's okay because the other guy just vouched for him," Williams explains.

This is a good example of how the Salmon Nation concept links businesses at the local level and makes one firm's issues the concern of the other. It's a matrix uniting needs under a shared experience.

Within the financial community, ShoreBank Pacific's primary message is that it is possible for a bank to work with its clients toward sustainability and still be profitable. Its success has been so unique that it recently attracted the attention of the World Bank. Dave Williams was asked to speak to staff as well as to bankers from the giant international finance institutions about local, sustainable business banking practices. Imagine. This little bank, recently grown out of a trailer, is now teaching the world about local sustainability.

SUMMARY: COMBINING FORCES TO CREATE
A GREEN FINANCIAL ALTERNATIVE TO WALL STREET

Three financial institutions have been able to make names for themselves and buck the trend of national and international financial consolidation. They've done this by aligning around a common mission that has support from local stakeholders. While Ecotrust, Portfolio 21 Investments, and ShoreBank Pacific each has different objectives with different business models, each is committed to the others and to their collective community via the notion of Salmon Nation.

This Salmon Nation can be viewed as a geographic element within the Gort Cloud. Like a social network, it comprises a community of interdependent, like-minded community members who share a common ideal and have common needs. The interactions among Ecotrust, Portfolio 21, ShoreBank Pacific, and the citizens of Salmon Nation are facilitated by connections within the Gort Cloud as well as by their more traditional use of marketing and communications. In this way, the Northwest Native American tradition of potlatch, or redistribution and reciprocity of wealth, is facilitated by these financial organizations.

Driving Fast in the Green Lane

Tesla Motors, CalCars.org, Hymotion,
and Southern California Edison

THE CHALLENGE

According to the Department of Energy, 95 percent of all transportation in the United States runs on petroleum, and transportation accounts for 67 percent of petroleum consumption. Since the early 1980s, oil use for transportation purposes has grown at an average of 2 percent per year. This is despite the increasing price of oil, the uncertain dependence on totalitarian regimes from which most oil originates, and the growing concerns about global warming and pollution.

The auto industry has been very slow to respond, with some notable exceptions like the Nano, a twenty-five-hundred-dollar four-seater with a tiny engine introduced recently in India; the Norwegian-made Think City car, with a reported range of 110 miles per charge; and Mitsubishi's iMiEV, exhibited for the first time at the 2007 Tokyo Motor Show. Of course, add to this Toyota, Ford, and Honda with their hybrid innovations. But today's hybrid is already a vehicle of the past when we look to the near future. All-electric high-performance sports cars from Tesla Motors of San Carlos, California, are now in production.

This very high-profile automaker is the primary subject of this chapter. However, the earth-friendly automotive story is a complex one. There are parts makers, advocacy groups, and energy providers who also play an important role. Companies such as Hymotion, an advanced battery maker in Canada, and Southern California Edison are also involved in plug-in vehicle programs. Vehicles more fuel-efficient than the Prius will evolve as companies, prodded by energy-efficiency advocacy groups such as CalCars.org, begin to introduce plug-in vehicles (both battery EVs and hybrid EVs) in addition to the development others are doing with hydrogen technologies.

These auto industry pioneers face various branding challenges. Telsa has had to figure out how an automaker with no product yet for sale can make a name for itself. CalCars.org has had to mobilize consumers to demand a product that car manufacturers don't even offer. Hymotion, with its partner

A123, is in a highly competitive battle to be the primary "ingredient" brand for future electric cars, while SEC, one of the country's largest utilities, is augmenting its mission with sustainable objectives.

THE SOLUTION

Each of the companies profiled in this chapter has addressed its brand and communications goals differently.

Tesla Motors has banked on instant awareness by introducing a flamboyant product in the otherwise demure eco-transportation category, and then enlisted the support of celebrities and trendsetters in promoting the brand.

CalCars.org revs up publicity through high-profile and very exclusive events that auto industry reporters and bloggers feel privileged to attend. This creates a powerful echo effect that resonates in the news-hungry Gort Cloud.

For Hymotion, it's the "Intel Inside" idea — an ingredient brand that is all but invisible, yet critical to the performance and reliability of the vehicle that uses its batteries.

Southern California Edison, as a mature brand, has a different set of issues. It must protect its reputation as a reasonably priced and reliable source of power, while acknowledging that electricity must be conserved and energy sources made more diverse and sustainable.

As the world looks for transportation alternatives powered by something other than the infernal internal combustion engine, we need only look to the past. Before gasoline-powered cars were the norm, clean and reliable electric cars were the preferred form of transportation because, unlike gasoline cars, they did not vibrate or emit noxious fumes and noise, and they did not require gear changing, often a struggle in those days, or a hand-cranked start-up. Although steam-powered cars also needed no hand crank or gear changing, they had a shorter overall range than the electrics, and required a start-up time of up to forty-five minutes in cold weather.

The electric car, then, had a clear product advantage in the early days. The consumer had a wide range of makes and models from which to choose. Beginning in 1887, New York City had a fleet of electric taxis, and in 1899, the La Jamais Contente, an electric race car built in Belgium, set a world speed record of sixty-eight miles per hour.

Nevertheless, the electric car was virtually abandoned by the end of the 1920s, largely due to its Achilles' heel — a battery with limited life — and to the arrival of the electric starter that eliminated the onerous hand cranking of gas engines. As highways improved, the demand for long-distance performance outstripped the range of the electric vehicles, or EVs, as they have come to be known. Concurrently, the discovery of the West Texas oilfields, along with improved refining techniques and a national distribution system, made gasoline a relatively cheap fuel. And then along came Henry Ford, who mass-produced Model T's cheaply enough that they became affordable for the average American. The glamour of the gasoline-powered car was further enhanced by the popularity of automobile racing, with amazing speeds made possible by internal combustion.[1]

Thus, despite past failures, the electric car continues to spark the imagination of enterprising eco-capitalists — especially as demand increases for a realistic alternative to gas-powered vehicles.

Tesla Motors: Selling without Product

All-electric cars no longer have to look and drive like oversized golf carts. Tesla Motors is positioning its sleek new all-electric sports car as a better drive than most Porsches and Ferraris and with twice the efficiency of a Prius. Attracted by the promise of a guilt-free, zero-emissions vehicle, that accelerates from zero to sixty in four seconds yet costs two cents per mile to run, six hundred early adopters and environmentalists, many of them celebrities such as George Clooney, Arnold Schwarzenegger, Kelsey Grammer, and Flea, paid the full price of ninety-eight thousand dollars to be on a list for delivery at least a year before the car was ready.

Yes, you read that correctly. Six hundred people, most of them men, paid full price without having seen the car in person or driven it, when not a single Tesla was on the road (at least not officially), when it wasn't advertised, and when no critics had reviewed it. Somehow Tesla hit its target audience at the bull's-eye without much more than a concept and a design. How did this happen?

Some people like to drive fast. Some of these people have money to burn on a high-performance sports car but feel embarrassed to own one.

Maybe it's too ostentatious, not PC. Others might balk at spending two hundred thousand dollars or more on a trophy car.

The Tesla folks have turned these negatives around by developing a stunning, smoking-ass car that gives the owner a goodwill shine from driving an eco-friendly vehicle at far less than half the price of a Ferrari.

At the time of this writing, in May 2008, three Tesla vehicles have been delivered, the first to company chairman and chief fund-raiser Elon Musk, the founder of PayPal. All 2008-model vehicles are scheduled for delivery by March of next year, and customers are now able to order 2009 vehicles, of which fifteen hundred will be produced.

Building a perception changer.

The sleek lines and high performance of the Tesla shatter the perception that electric cars are either small, poky things you drive around retirement communities or decidedly unsexy family cars of the current hybrid variety. Trendwatching.com refers to highly visible green products, like Tesla, as "eco-iconic": "Eco-iconic is not about *all* green products, it's about those products that through their distinct appearance or stories actually *show* that they're green, or at least invoke some curiosity from onlookers, and thus help their owners/users attract recognition from their peers."[2]

"Nobody else realized what was needed was an EV that's sexy, that's desirable, that people want to own," explains Darryl Siry, Tesla's vice president of sales, marketing, and service. "It's no longer [about saying], 'I'm a pariah.' [Instead,] it screams out, 'You're cool.' I think that was one of the fundamental, founding principles of Tesla."

Fueling a word-of-mouth firestorm.

Awareness of the Tesla has spread mostly via word of mouth, especially in and around Silicon Valley and Hollywood. The company has helped to spread this chatter by offering test drives to those wait-listed for the vehicle. Afterward, the future owners are invited to submit a blog entry on the Tesla Web site to share the experience.

Writes Michael "Flea" Balzary of the Red Hot Chili Peppers, "It drove like nothing I have ever been in before. Made my Porsche feel like a golf cart! It took off like a rocket ship, handled so sensitively. I am so happy I went with my gut and bought that car. Yeah it is a long wait, but man, the thing is awesome."

The word-of-mouth firestorm has been fanned by trendspotters and green transportation bloggers in the Gort Cloud and in the mainstream media, with articles on the car's development appearing in the *New York Times*, the *Wall Street Journal*, *BusinessWeek*, and *Newsweek*, among others. Most of the stories have not been solicited by Tesla. The phone simply rings. But in some cases, the company is absolutely brilliant at planting the seeds of interest in just the right places. At a recent Burning Man festival, a hedonistic art fest where no branded products are allowed, an unbranded electric sports car on display turned out to be a Tesla wax model the company had used for wind tunnel testing. The wax display had no logo or identity, but the silhouette was an unmistakable touch of stealthy branding.[3]

In fact, citizens of the Gort Cloud seem to be following the company's every move, with a particularly intense buzz generated in April 2008 by the opening of Tesla's first showroom in West Los Angeles. Among celebrities in attendance were Quincy Jones, Jenny McCarthy, and Jenna Elfman. No doubt, the planned summer opening of a showroom near Tesla headquarters in San Carlos, as well as future openings in Chicago, New York, and elsewhere, will generate further attention.

Yet another intense media blitz followed the announcement that the Tesla sedan, called Model S, would be manufactured in the San Francisco Bay Area.

A brand name that harks back to the future.

Nikola Tesla was the other Edison, the one most people don't know about. Considered one of America's greatest electrical engineers, his work led to modern alternating current (AC) power systems, including the AC motor. He is sometimes called "the man who invented the twentieth century"[4] and "the patron saint of modern electricity." His most famous quote: "I have harnessed the cosmic rays and caused them to operate a motive device." Motive is right.

By resurrecting the Tesla name, well known at the time of the first electric cars, the Tesla Motors founders gave the company a brand name with a story and a nice sound, something that is critical in a market absolutely packed with competing car names.

Becoming an object of lust and desire.

Tesla's first product, the Roadster, is clearly meant to be the halo product, the brand's primary perception changer.

Early on, Tesla "identified a modular way of building the business where you could enter the market with a halo product, and then transition into lower-priced, larger-[volume] products, more mainstream cars as you go," says Siry. "That's fundamentally no different than when cell phones were introduced or plasma TVs or VCRs. The technology doesn't have to be immediately attainable. In fact, it should be an object of lust and desire."

The Tesla will remain "a premium brand, even as we go into more mainstream cars," according to Siry. The company may eventually produce an SUV along the lines of a BMW or Porsche, but "it's not our goal to ever become an economy car manufacturer, because that's just not the space that we see ourselves in." As mentioned earlier, the company plans to introduce a luxury sedan to compete with Lexus and BMW in 2010. It will sell for less than the Roadster[5] but run off a drivetrain that is an evolution of the Roadster's version.

Creating differentiation around product assets.

When it comes to building the brand around Tesla's assets, the company is quick to the take. Tesla differentiatiors are its extreme good looks, superb acceleration and handling, minimal upkeep, and environmental benefits. Indeed, images boasting the car's sleek style pepper TeslaMotors.com, where potential customers are encouraged to copy them onto their desktops as wallpapers. The site also uses a light, converstional style to tell stories like this one: "A favorite trick here at Tesla Motors is to invite a passenger along and ask him to turn on the radio. At the precise moment we ask, we accelerate. Our passenger simply can't sit forward enough to reach the dials. But who needs music when you're experiencing such a symphony of motion?"

When it comes to touting the simplicity of the car, the focus is on the one-part engine. A conventional engine has four cylinders and, the company explains, more than a hundred moving parts. This, of course, leads to the claim that servicing and upkeep on the Tesla will be minimal. Says the site: "The engine in a conventional car also needs lubricating oils, filters, coolant, clutches, spark plugs and wires, a PCV valve, oxygen sensors, a timing belt, a fan belt, a water pump and hoses, a catalytic converter, and a muffler — all items requiring service, and all items that aren't needed in an electric car."

Where beauty and function meet.

Speaking of the car's environmental credentials, mainstream adoption will occur "where design intersects functionality," Siry explains. "Products that make it will be either well designed, so that people like them, or well positioned, so that people think they're cool."

"At the end of the day, as human beings, we are pleasure seekers, and a big part of the green thrust now is about [adapting to that]," he continues. "If somebody makes a windmill that works, that's great. Somebody makes a windmill that works and looks good, it's better. We're going to get more adoption." Which is precisely the strategy that Southwest Windpower, another subject in this book, has taken in the design of its beautifully sculpted wind turbines.

Turning engineering features into marketing advantages.

At Tesla's San Carlos headquarters, two engineering-prototype Roadsters are housed in the rear warehouse. One is red and one is green, and it's difficult to say which is more beautiful. They look like two of the sleekest race cars on the planet, but when they are put into motion, all that can be heard is the low whine of the electric engine and the tires rolling on the pavement. Imagine a fleet of these silently rounding the NASCAR racetrack at Daytona. Pretty strange.

On opening the trunk of the Tesla, you find an orange bin housing the motor and the transmission. The motor has just one moving part, and at less than seventy pounds, it generates horsepower equivalent to a much heavier combustion engine. The total curb weight of the Roadster is 2,690 pounds, just a bit heavier than a Mazda Miata at 2,500 and substantially less than a Porsche 911 at approximately 3,300. Weight considerations are one important differentiator between the all-electric and hybrid technologies. With hybrids, two engines are required, as well as a gas tank.

The Roadster's ESS (energy storage system) battery comprises 6,831 consumer-grade lithium-ion cells, the same used in a conventional laptop. The system comes with adapters for adjustment to any voltage and can be plugged into a standard wall outlet. Each charge will last approximately 220 miles, an important claim for Tesla's marketing purposes because it is a significant improvement over the range of previous electric vehicles.

Transitioning an upstart brand to mainstream.

The mainstream auto manufacturers have been hovering around Tesla, watching. It's not about worries over competition, but more about scoping out the future of auto technology. The company has been in conversations with some of these manufacturers about possible future partnerships. To emphasize Tesla's impact on the auto industry, Felix Kramer of CalCars.org mentioned, "GM's Bob Lutz has publicly said that watching Tesla helped convince him to start the Chevy Volt plug-in hybrid program."

"As you grow from the little rebel company, the revolutionary upstart where people are cheering for you because you are the little guy, and you start to grow your business, you start to have big-guy problems. You have to start to make real decisions," Siry explains. "There's a tension between that grassroots thing of keeping it real and then trying to make real change happen."

"So if we come to the conclusion that the best way for us to get the maximum number of electric vehicles on the road is to partner with a major [auto company], there's a good chunk of the fans of Tesla that would see that as a sellout. But I personally say, if that's the route to getting a hundred thousand EVs on the road, if that's how you make real change on a global scale happen, [then the answer is obvious]."

"In a perfect world, continues Siru, "if you have unlimited capital, [a startup company would make] a pure EV for people who want those [as well as making] a range-extended EV, which is better than a Prius but it still has a small gas motor on it that runs the generator. Do them both. But the problem is, going out and getting somebody to write a check for $500 million is not easy. It's also not easy to go out and say, 'We're going to do a couple of things.' In that case the VC [venture capitalist] will say, 'Which is the best one, and I'll give you the money to do that one.'"

So the grand experiment continues. We'll be looking for the echo of the Tesla coming in new EVs from Ford, Chrysler, and Toyota — or whoever survives the ongoing automaker shake up.

CalCars.org: Creating Demand for a Product That Doesn't Exist

There's a prediction on the Tesla Motors Web site: "We foresee a day when all cars run on electric power, and when people will struggle to remember a time when a love of driving came with a side order of guilt." While society waits for this day to come, those who can't afford a hundred grand for a Tesla or who don't fancy themselves driving a sports car are able to look to other alternatives that could be here right now and cost a lot less.

The business of promoting efficiency.

We're at the Santa Monica airport in autumn 2007. An eclectic mix of vehicles line the Alt Car Expo in the old Barker Hangar, everything from electric skateboards and scooters to full-sized propane and biofuel pickups. There are three-wheeled Neighborhood Electric Vehicles that travel at up to twenty-five miles per hour, flex-fuel vehicles designed to run on a blend of ethanol and gasoline, and cars fueled by compressed natural gas.

All the exhibitors at this event have something in common — they are proud of the product they're exhibiting, and they're here to hype it. All of them truly believe that they can reach the masses and transform a nation. In that, we've come a long way since the introduction of the

Prius. Toyota saw the car more as an experiment than as the best seller or green product leader it turned out to be. I saw it firsthand. I was working with Toyota as a consultant at the time.

A post at CalCars.org explains just how successful that "experiment" was: "When it was first launched, Prius benefited from the halo effect of the Toyota brand reputation . . . Now, the Toyota brand is benefiting from the halo effect of the Prius." There has even been talk of creating an entirely new Prius brand with a family of different body styles and an identity separate from Toyota, not unlike the Lexus.[6]

Related to this are numerous posts including one on Inhabitat.com that describes Toyota's move into non-auto markets — more specifically, into the Japanese prefab housing market using auto-assembly techniques: "The steel-framed Toyota prefabs leave the assembly factory 85 percent complete; in half a day, the modules get stacked into place with a crane, and it's nearly done. The company offers various sizes and designs, with an average family home comprising twelve modules and coming in at just under $225,000."[7] So is a Prius home for your Prius car loaded with Prius appliances on the way?

At the CalCars.org booth, founder Felix Kramer gives tours of a prototype Prius converted into a hybrid plug-in. CalCars explains itself as "a nonprofit startup formed by entrepreneurs, engineers, environmentalists, and consumers" to promote "projects that tackle national security, jobs, and global warming at the same time." CalCars' primary goal, at least at the moment, is to get carmakers to build plug-in hybrid vehicles (PHEVs) — cars akin to the hybrids we are now familiar with, but with larger batteries and the ability to recharge from a standard outlet.

Felix Kramer: Human PR machine for a good cause.

The T-shirt Kramer wears at the expo displays the same message that is boldly etched across the car next to him: I GET 100 MPG.

Kramer likes to connect with people. By founding CalCars, he has built a platform to preach the message that, unlike all-electric technology, hybrid plug-ins can be made right now. He travels around the world preaching this mantra. "I'm the world's first consumer-owner of a plug-in hybrid," he says of this vehicle, which he drove down from his home in the Bay Area last night and which he uses as his primary mode of transportation.

Felix and a couple other partner organizations have become the unofficial marketing arm of the hybrid plug-in business. For reasons unknown, the major automakers have been dragging their feet on better fuel economy or switching from fossil fuels to electricity, but Felix and his friends are convinced that if they apply enough pressure and stimulate the appropriate incentives, the world will soon be rewarded with hybrid vehicles that will power commuting miles with electricity and bring us cars that average at least a hundred miles per gallon. This could dramatically reduce foreign oil dependency.

"This is my main prop," Kramer explains as he holds up an ordinary yellow extension cord. "Former CIA director James Woolsey, who gives speeches about plug-in hybrids, loves to say, 'Every household that gets a plug-in hybrid will have to invest in the infrastructure — they'll have to buy one of these.' And you know, that's a really powerful message."

Kramer explains that "there's always a footnote" to his hundred-plus-mile-per-gallon claim. "You have to add the cost of the electricity — about a penny a mile," he says. Of course, the electricity comes from the car owner's household electricity. Only some of the power from today's grid is renewable, but it's still lower in greenhouse gas emissions than gasoline. And the hope is that the grid will get dramatically cleaner over time.

When explaining the hybrid plug-in to consumers, Kramer says, "It's like you add a second, smaller fuel tank in your car that you fill with electricity. You charge at night, and you use it first. So that's your commuter tank. When you leave every morning, it's full. But if you want to go to the mountains, you've always got that bigger tank with you. So that's why it's the best of both worlds."

Marketing 101 for a nonprofit start-up.

"How often do you hear of a nonprofit organization that's described as a nonprofit start-up?" Kramer asks. "How often do you hear about a nonprofit that does technology *and* advocacy? You know, we're a hybrid ourselves."

"It's a difficult organization to brand," he continues. "We start off by saying to people, 'We're environmentalists and engineers and entrepreneurs and consumers.' You know, that's an unusual combination. And then they say, 'Where's your office?' We don't have an office. We don't use letterhead. Our biggest meetings are when we get together to convert cars." And then "once you do get people excited about the product, they can't even have it right now."

CalCars has had to struggle with what it's asking supporters to do. "We can ask them to support CalCars, we can ask them to tell their dealer that they won't buy a car until it's a plug-in hybrid . . . things like that," Kramer explains. He is mobilizing supporters to demonstrate demand for plug-in hybrid cars that the auto industry is not yet making. He uses the analogy of the "I want my MTV campaign" of the early 1980s when music fans were asked to badger their cable companies to add MTV to their service roster. I saw just how effective this can be as I was working at Warner Bros. when this happened.

Mobilizing the consumers.

Kramer moved to the Bay Area in the late 1990s to found eConstructors .com, an online marketplace for Web development. When he sold the company a few years later and was searching for his next venture, "I realized cars are just so important in so many ways — they're the fulcrum for everything that could change in society," he says.

After a year of "looking around at fuel cells and other things, I discovered plug-in hybrids and they were just completely off the radar," he explains. Studying this model, Kramer came to believe that the battery technology to power the car was "good enough to get started" on development. But no one in Detroit seemed to agree.

"Carmakers today don't understand what's needed," he explains. "They don't understand 'versioning.' They're waiting for the perfect car before they start." For instance, "GM says, 'We're gonna build Volt, but we're not gonna do it until it has a forty-mile range.' Why? Why not start with a twenty-mile range? Or they'll say, 'We're not gonna do it until we're sure the battery will last the lifetime of the car.' Why? You know people replace parts on cars. There's a community of hundreds of thousands of people who would buy the car knowing they needed to replace the battery. It's like a cell phone company saying, 'Our first cell phone would be the size of a brick and it would cost three thousand dollars so we're not gonna build it.' If they'd done that, we wouldn't have our cell phones today."

The auto manufacturers "still have the mind-set that only they know best," he continues. "Who decides what cars get built is this very narrow circle of people. It's just basically the carmakers and government. And that's it. Nobody else has a say." What CalCars is trying to do is to "give consumers a voice." Its mission is to "assemble a group of people and say to the auto companies, 'This is the car we want, and we want you to build it for us.'" Felix is working to rally green consumers who are fed up with the alternatives out there. And to prove his point, CalCars has "green-tuned" stock Prius cars to plug-in hybrid functionality with the help of his tech-savvy friends.

Mr. Kramer goes to Washington.

Soon after Kramer's first successful and unauthorized Prius conversion, CalCars flew his own by-then converted car to Capitol Hill in Washington DC, where representatives and others were impressed. After all, if CalCars could convert a car, why couldn't the American auto industry? Among those he won over was Senator Hillary Clinton, who later said in a speech, "The next step is hybrid plug-ins, enabling drivers to use household electricity to recharge car batteries at night. You can drive a hundred miles or more for every gallon of fuel you put in the tank." Even George W was impressed.

Perhaps due to CalCars' efforts, the attitude toward manufacturing hybrid plug-ins among major car companies has shifted. Both GM and Toyota have blogs in which they actively respond to the demands from the plug-in community (which is a very vocal component of the Gort Cloud). GM has announced that it hopes to get the PHEV Saturn Vue and the Chevy Volt on the road in 2010. Ford and Toyota are delivering a few converted Priuses and Escape Hybrids for evaluation to universities and utilities. Daimler has built a few prototypes of its fifteen-passenger Sprinter van, and Volkswagen/Audi recently showcased a Metro project Quattro Sub-Compact concept car with a sixty-two-mile all-electric range at the Tokyo Auto Show.

The automakers finally seem to be getting it. Hopefully, they will also keep their sights on what's ahead. The plug-in hybrid may prove to be a transitional solution until broad mass production of all-electric vehicles, perhaps using the Tesla model. But it's a stopgap that will work for now.

Hymotion: The Better the Battery, the Better the Car

Adjacent to Kramer's Prius plug-in at the Alt Expo show is another Prius, this one converted to run plug-in by Hymotion, a Canadian company based in Toronto. "It's a different implementation," Kramer explains, pointing to the placement of the battery in the rear of the car. Located next to the battery are Hymotion's batteries, which convert hybrid electric vehicles (HEVs) into plug-in hybrid vehicles (PHEVs).

Compared with a standard Prius, Hymotion's PHEV conversions provide better fuel economy, less pollution, and a significant all-electric drive range. The Hymotion Web site claims that the conversion multiplies the available electricity seven times.

A123Systems of Cambridge, Massachusetts, a company that manufactures the nanophosphate lithium-ion batteries used in the Plug-in Conversion Module, acquired Hymotion in May 2007. A123 is also one of two consortia vying to provide the batteries for the Chevrolet Volt. The other is a unit of the Korean company LG Chem. This would be a coveted prize that would significantly expand the market for the winner's products.

Ricardo Bazzarella, president and director of manufacturing of Hymotion at the Alt Expo, explained that the company was finishing up its testing phase and hoped to have sixty vehicles delivered to buyers by the end of 2008, followed by scaled-up production in 2009. In April 2008, Hymotion announced that it would start shipping crash-tested, federally certified ten-thousand-dollar conversions in volume starting in July. Initially, these will be for the Prius only. "Some people just want to have the car because they want to drive the world's cleanest extended-range vehicle," Felix Kramer says of the cars. "And that's what this gets you."

A vital ingredient brand.

Hymotion is positioning itself as a dependable, sought-after ingredient brand. An ingredient brand is a component of a product that has its own brand identity — such as PC computers with Intel Inside, diet soft drinks with NutraSweet, stereos with Dolby noise reduction, and Chevron gasoline with Techron. Although electric car buyers will not readily see the batteries, knowing that the best, most advanced technology is powering the vehicle adds trust — and value.

Tesla, on the other hand, is not saying what brand is under the hood. Perhaps it is waiting until a true winner emerges in the race for the next-generation high-performance battery. We'll see very shortly.

Southern California Edison: Seeking Respect from the Green Community

Across the way at the Alt Expo show is a booth maintained by Southern California Edison (SCE), a utility that is working to reinforce the green credentials of its parent company, Edison International. The Edison Web site boldly proclaims, "Edison International, through its subsidiary Southern California Edison, leads the nation in the use of renewable energy . . . enough to supply more than two million homes." According to Ed Kjaer, director of SCE's Electric Transportation Division, "SCE purchases, on behalf of its customers, one-sixth of the nation's wind and 90 percent of the nation's solar energy. Sixteen percent or more of the energy we provide to our customers comes from renewable sources, and this excludes our major hydro, which accounts for another 5 percent. If you look at this from a carbon perspective, about 40 percent of the energy we provide to our customers comes from low-carbon sources." Nevertheless, most American utility companies are highly dependent on nonrenewable resources, particularly coal, because of legacy facilities and inherent problems with the grid.

In addition to renewable energy sourcing, SCE's Electric Vehicle Technology Center in Pomona, California, is a nationally recognized testing facility for advanced energy storage systems. EVs, plug-in hybrids, and even electric forklifts are tested here. In partnership with the Ford Motor Company, SCE is evaluating and demonstrating the nation's first plug-in hybrid SUVs. SCE and Chevron Technology Ventures have launched a five-year hydrogen energy station demonstration program at the utility's Rosemead, California, headquarters. The utility is also studying how hydrogen is made, stored, and delivered to vehicles.

SCE is in the process of "electrifying" its fleet of company cars and trucks. It already has three hundred Toyota RAV4 EVs, the largest such fleet in the United States. They are driven primarily by meter readers.

"Our cars have traveled almost 16 million miles," the Web site says, "reducing green house gases by more than 8400 tons."

One other point of interest is the career path of the current SCE chairman and CEO, John Bryson. Mr. Bryson was a cofounder of the Natural Resources Defense Council (NRDC), one of five budding lawyers fresh out of Yale Law School with a passion for protecting the environment. The NRDC went on to become one of the most prolific sponsors of environmental action, including passage of the Clean Water Act, the phasing out of lead in gasoline, protecting the Arctic National Wildlife Refuge, and heading up legal action to protect polar bears under the Endangered Species Act. Back in California, his legal and environmental experience led to political appointments with the State Water Resources Control Board and later with the California Public Utilities Commission during Governor Jerry Brown's administration. According to author Robert Gottlieb, "Eventually, Bryson secured a position with Southern California Edison, becoming its chief executive officer in 1990. And he served on the Board of Directors of Boeing, where he met CEO Alan Mulally, who later became Ford's CEO. In the process, Bryson's career demonstrated how one industry had come to recognize that the professional wing of environmentalism also provided training for high-level industry jobs."[8] Bryson plans to retire in July 2008.

Expanding the market for electricity by promoting electric cars.

Converting its fleet of vehicles to all-electric or partial electric power is just part of SCE's strategy to push for the transition to plug-in vehicles on the nation's roads. This is not entirely altruism. More plug-in cars and trucks could help lower future customer rates by spreading the utility's fixed costs over more energy uses. According to Ed Kjaer, fifteen years ago the company began "to evaluate emerging transportation technologies and how they interact with the electrical grid."

"We are now doing a tremendous amount of advanced battery technology evaluation. We're generating industry-leading data in partnership with leading battery companies [like A123Systems], with automakers, and with the Department of Energy and the Electric Power Research Institute."

"Our thinking is that there's a natural convergence that's beginning to take place between the electrical grid and transportation," he continues. "It's been Edison's philosophy for the last twenty years that we have to work closely with the auto industry if we are going to connect transportation's wheels to the grid. With automobiles powered electrically, we start to share the same customer."

"We've been a leader in promoting energy efficiency with our customers. Energy efficiency is also a driving imperative with the auto industry. That's another reason why these two industries need to come together."

Well, I'm not sure it has been a driving imperative with the auto industry, but hopefully that record will improve.

Toward a smarter grid.

SCE is attempting to make the American public wake up to what Kjaer refers to as the "little-known fact" that "of all the alternative fuels that this country is pursuing, only one has a ubiquitous infrastructure," he says. "Only one has significant excess capacity. And that is the electricity industry." And that is true. The major problem with hydrogen is building the fueling stations. For electricity, the fueling station is any convenient AC outlet.

Given that the nation's electricity grid is designed for peak demand, there is indeed significant excess capacity at the majority of nonpeak periods. "You've built the power plants, you've got the generation online, and you've got significant excess off-peak capacity just sitting there," he says. "With appropriate control — and that's part of the smart grid of the future — we're going to be able to connect the transportation wheels to the grid, off-peak, and not have to build one new power plant."

In fact, federal studies have shown that there's enough excess off-peak capacity to charge about 73 percent of all the light-duty cars and trucks on the road today. "As this nation tries to get itself off its dependence on foreign oil, it has to view its national electricity grid as an energy security asset," Kjaer says.

The snag in this logic is that electricity cannot be stored on the grid. It's use it or lose it. As a result, electricity systems are built to meet the very highest demand, which may be only a few days a year. To utilize this otherwise wasted capacity, SCE is evaluating a system it calls the Smart Home of the Future. This idea, still in development, allows the battery in a plug-in vehicle or in a stand-alone garage unit to become an electricity storage center in the home, in essence making an energy storage reservoir for the home and eventually the grid.

With this system, the advanced battery is connected to a "home energy management system," which in turn "communicates" with Edison's new generation of advanced meters called Edison Smart Connect. Customers will know when to charge the car — say, at 2 AM, when demand is low and rates are lowest. The car battery or the stand-alone energy storage device may then "discharge" energy back to the home or eventually up to the grid when energy costs are high and the system is stressed.

This could translate into significant customer energy cost savings, Kjaer estimates.

Winning customer trust.

Let's face it, utilities have something of an image problem. They're perceived as monopolies, they use coal plants and nuclear facilities for power generation, they have often resisted calls for more renewable sourcing, and they're suspected of price gouging. It's no wonder there's been some damage control.

Perhaps that's why Kjaer explains that SCE sees its efforts in this area more as education and outreach, and less as advertising or PR. And this is smart, because it makes the utility less vulnerable to accusations of greenwashing. Adds Felix Kramer, "It helps that legislation in California has decoupled power generation and sales, so that utilities don't benefit by selling more electricity — rather, they're rewarded for improving the energy efficiency of their operations and of their residential and commercial customers."

"We are trying to get customers to be good consumers of energy," he adds. "We are looking to help them understand cause and effect. Today they don't understand why their utility bill is so high, especially given the fact they receive their bill thirty days after they've consumed the energy. We'd like to show them how they consume and why things cost what they cost and help them control their energy use and ultimately help them reduce their bills in the future."

"At the end of the day, we want customers to view Edison as their energy partner," he concludes. "Utilities are for all intents and purposes monopolies. That doesn't mean that you don't work hard to create trust. The Edison brand is a trust mark. When customers come home and they turn on the light switch, Edison's there." Trust translates into reliability. "They [also] look to Edison as their energy services adviser." Now that America is finally waking up, Edison wants its customers to trust it to be green.

On the verge of an electric revolution.

Kjaer, originally from New Zealand, previously spent fifteen years working in marketing advertising for Nissan, Acura, and Mazda. "I like to say I spent the first fifteen years of my career on the dark side. And then I found religion for the second fifteen years," he says, referring to his work at SCE.

"What floats my boat? I have the best job in the world. I get to drive next-generation clean technology. I have a seven-year-old kid who thinks this is the greatest thing since sliced bread. And this is what motivates me. This is the technology for the next hundred years. Connecting transportation to the grid is, in my opinion, as significant as the evolution from the horse and buggy to the iron horse."

SUMMARY: DIFFERENT STROKES, SAME COURSE

Creating demand and brand appeal for alternatively powered vehicles requires innovative strategies to overcome the inertia of buying tried-and-true gasoline-powered cars. They must perform at least as well as conventional choices and offer an eco-advantage. In the Tesla case, the vehicle appeals to sports car lovers while delivering awesome fuel efficiency. And as with the processor in a PC, the choice of an ingredient-brand battery provides the assurance of reliability and performance. Partners, like CalCars.org and SCE, also help promote the value of switching to electric or electric hybrid cars.

Together, these companies are creating an aura of desire for higher-efficiency transportation. Each is approaching the market from a different angle, but they are collectively moving in a new direction — and they are each using the power of the Gort Cloud to broadcast their messages. Because transportation and energy are such important issues among the eco-conscious, every statement and every move these companies make are widely reported and commented on.

Marketing Your Green Expertise

Mohawk Fine Papers and Time Inc.

THE CHALLENGE

The pulp and paper industry has been working hard to clean up its act. Mohawk Fine Papers, of Cohoes, New York, is doing its part in reducing carbon emissions and harvesting from sustainable forests.

Time Inc., with more than 125 magazine titles and headquartered in New York, purchases over 70 percent of its paper from sustainable forests and is leading the charge in recycling programs and other key environmental areas.

Both companies are branding themselves green, and in both cases, this push toward sustainability is being propelled by a new C-level manager, sometimes known as the CSO or chief sustainability officer.

How are CSOs guiding their businesses toward a green agenda?

THE SOLUTION

Just as businesses hire expert managers in finance, human resources, and information technology, responsible companies are turning to experts to lead environmental and social responsibility efforts. These experts are relied on to assess impacts and make decisions about difficult manufacturing and sourcing trade-offs.

Greening businesses are using their CSOs' work to differentiate among stakeholders. While green may not be the most important driver of choice, it can be a tiebreaker and a source of significant goodwill.

CSOs are often the chief environmental spokespersons for the brand, tirelessly educating key constituents about the benefits of doing the right thing.

Because CSOs often come from regulatory or scientific backgrounds, they can be important emissaries between their employers and NGOs or certifying organizations. This helps ensure brand message integrity and trust, which is yet another example of how the Gort Cloud provides partnerships and credibility.

Because it is impossible for existing companies to abandon bad habits overnight, CSOs can plot a long-term course and align promotional and marketing efforts around a work-in-progress green objective.

According to a recent report by the Environmental Paper Network, the paper industry is the fourth largest contributor to greenhouse gas emissions among US manufacturing industries. Accounting for 40 percent of the world's industrial wood harvest and 25 percent of all landfill waste, it is one of the planet's largest consumers and polluters of fresh water. The report states, "Paper production continues to come into conflict with indigenous and other communities around the world over land rights, culture, human health, and livelihoods." The good news, however, is that a shift within the American paper industry is well under way.

Two companies making great contributions to this shift are Mohawk and Time Inc., the magazine-publishing arm of Time Warner. They have done it by adding sustainability experts to upper management and tasking them with the responsibility to build effective environmental policies. For Time Inc., that person is David Refkin. For Mohawk, the environmental expert is George Milner. They are founding members of a new category of C-level managers, often called chief sustainability officers (CSOs). Rick Walker describes the role of the CSO in an article he recently wrote for GreenBiz.com:

> What's missing in most organizations today is the position of Chief Sustainability Officer: a person that wears many hats. A CSO is an advocate and educator, a visionary, a change manager and a cheerleader, and above all else, a results-driven manager.
>
> CSOs must serve at least three roles: They must look inward, end-to-end driving business opportunity; they must look outward, walking the talk and communicating with customers and other stakeholders; and, they must lead. A CSO must articulate, implement and sustain the organization's vision of sustainability and provide visibility and transparency of that vision both internally and externally.[1]

The companies profiled so far were launched with a sustainable mission, but the greatest environmental improvement will come from existing companies that must change. Mohawk and Time represent two examples. With their eco-friendly policies in place, CSOs like Refkin and

Milner ensure that the sustainability message is communicated to key audiences. To the extent that these messages honestly convey information about commitment and hard choices, the Gort Cloud provides an important conduit, as it thrives on truth and credibility. Now that climate change and other environmental issues have reached the forefront, the efforts of Refkin and Milner are right on target.

Mohawk Fine Papers: Raising the Green Flag

The managers at Mohawk Fine Papers, one of the two largest premium paper manufacturers in North America, have raised the green flag over their own industry. They became experts in sustainability, and they have done a remarkable job presenting themselves as experts to their target customers, who are primarily graphic designers, print houses, and corporate and institutional clients. They've done this by:

- Becoming the go-to resource for questions about sustainability within the pulp and paper industry and beyond,
- Sending emissaries to end users to explain why sustainability in paper is important for the environment as well as for the corporate bottom line, and
- Enabling customers to calculate exactly how much and in what way any particular order of Mohawk paper will benefit the environment.

Ink loves Mohawk.

Mohawk was founded seventy-five years ago in Cohoes, New York, where the Mohawk and Hudson rivers meet and the Erie Canal begins. The company's primary business has always been the manufacturing of premium paper — the kind of paper stock used in high-end brochures or annual reports, for instance. But it also produces nonpremium paper, and all of its product is suitable for both offset and digital printing.

"We grew up manufacturing well-formed paper that prints very well," explains Joe O'Connor, co-owner of Mohawk as well as its senior vice president of sales/corporate accounts and international sales. And this is what differentiates Mohawk from lesser-quality papers and marks its appeal to discerning paper buyers.

Sharing a smaller paper pie.

The worldwide premium paper business has consolidated in the past ten years from sixteen companies to four. Mohawk helped set this trend with its 2005 sixty-million-dollar purchase of International Paper's Fine Paper Division, increasing Mohawk's workforce from 370 to 800 and giving it the Strathmore, Becket, Via, and BriteHue brands. Strathmore is known among designers as the premium of the premiums; Becket is also highly respected in this category. In buying these labels, Mohawk strengthened its high-quality brand image.

The consolidation may be due in part to the shrinking of the premium paper business, a result of the growth of a paperless society as well as the advent of digital printing presses, an emerging technology that thrives on shorter run lengths and therefore less paper. According to Steve Dusek, a sales consultant at Imagine Print Solutions, the market shrinkage is also attributable to widespread corporate cost-cutting measures. "Less expensive, nonpremium commodity paper can also be FSC [Forest Stewardship Council] certified, and the customer is getting a bigger bang for his buck with it," he says.

Nevertheless, Mohawk has managed to remain financially robust. O'Connor maintains that the smaller number of companies in the field benefits the firms that are still standing, thanks to decreased competition. "Our environmental messaging helps, too," he adds, noting that the firm's competitors are now following Mohawk's lead with such products as Domtar's EarthChoice line.

Mohawk has also positioned itself as the number one go-to for the printing of corporate social responsibility reports. Customers include GE, IBM, American Express, JPMorgan, Chase, BP, General Electric, Johnson & Johnson, and Time Inc. "We have the premier product for social responsibility," says O'Connor. "If you are a company with an environmental vision, paper is a wonderful way to communicate your message."

George Milner: Mohawk's in-house mentor.

George Milner is Mohawk's sustainability officer and eco-revolutionary expert extraordinaire. Since joining the company in 1974 to help it conform to environmental regulations, he has pushed to transform not only Mohawk, but also the entire pulp and paper industry, through the power of his ideas and personal persuasion. He has become a company touchpoint by personally communicating the newfound mission of the brand.

Although Mohawk sells primarily through distributors, it spends a lot of time and energy marketing to end users, be they designers, printers, or large corporations and institutions. When Milner meets with these folks, he speaks as an environmentalist, starting out by detailing everything that's environmentally horrific about the paper industry. Executives from rival paper companies in the audience have often taken Milner aside to ask him what he thinks he's doing.

"In the consulting role, we talk about the global issues at hand, which most people are aware of if they pick up a newspaper once in a while," says Milner. "And then we specifically talk about our industry and what that footprint looks like. And then we zero in on what we do as a company." Finally, Milner explains that using an environmentally responsible paper product adds value to the environmental message that's printed on it.

"George is incredibly unique in his position in terms of his expertise in environmental management, how that relates to government affairs, how that relates to the purchase of energy," he continues. "But at the same time, he can make a message relevant to clients so they can understand it and see the value in it."

His actions toward sustainability "became a part of our culture," Joe emphasizes. "And in the last four years, we've really used it in terms of building the Mohawk brand a lot more than we ever did."

Doing so has increased Mohawk's sales, according to O'Connor. Although Mohawk sells through distributors, the company measures the success of its marketing strategies by maintaining representatives in the field who report back on where the paper is being used or sold and in what quantities.

As Milner's reputation has grown, so to have the requests for his appearance. In past years, Mohawk's salespeople would pitch Milner during sales calls, offering to send him to meet with the client regarding environmental and sustainability practices. "Now I just get the calls," Milner says.

An unlikely revolutionary.

As an environmental scientist originally hired by Mohawk to manage the implementation of the Clean Water Act, Milner was one of the first environmentalists to ever work inside a paper factory.

"We went through the Clean Air Act, the Resource Conservation and Recovery Act, the Toxic Substance Control Act — we got into a whole bunch of acts, and every one of those affected the mill to a certain extent," Milner explains. "We were managing by permit, managing by the need to have a form mailed into Washington or Albany once a week or once a month."

"I had fifteen feet of books behind my desk," he continues. "I could pull them and I could read things, and look very impressive, but it was a very poor way of managing an environmental program."

By the mid-1980s, Milner saw the need to have a "less reactive" comprehensive management policy "addressing all those things at once, rather than one little thing, letter of the law, at a time." Rather than doing the minimum to conform to conflicting law, he led Mohawk into adopting a policy of doing the right thing.

This led to an approach that integrates environmental strategies at all levels of business: in risk management, procurement, production, worker training, corporate policy development, and production design and marketing. Under Milner's leadership, Mohawk began doing environmental assessments on R&D proposals, always keeping in mind federal and state regulations. Sustainability was becoming part of Mohawk's corporate DNA, its corporate culture.

It wasn't long before the company began saving money. The $250,000 annual cost of eliminating waste dropped to $27,000. "Everything that in the past we may have thrown away, we pretty much found a home for, except soggy lunch bags," says Milner.

Milner began building bridges to environmental groups. "If issues came up or we needed help with something, or we needed to write a letter to a senator or a congressman, we had people in the environmental community that would back us up because they trusted us."

When Milner went back to school for a graduate degree in the early 1990s, studying public policy analysis with a concentration in environmental economics, Mohawk became his laboratory for experiments in environmental policy changes.

"It's been great," he says. "I've never told anybody I've been doing an experiment. That's why I'm a subversive."

Transitioning from a product to a mission message.

Four years ago, the company pumped up the volume on its mission message when it came to overall marketing strategy. It began to use its environmental policies and achievements as a differentiator.

"I recall a conversation I had with Joe in 2003 about the fact that we were doing a lot of good things, and that we had a lot of recognition among the merchant community and the designers, but we lacked recognition from the end users. I'd just done a couple of speaking engagements at companies like Merrill Lynch, a potential end user, where nobody knew about us," says Milner. "I felt we needed to raise our profile as a company, rather than to raise our product profile."

"That's when we started talking to our end users [as opposed to intermediary buyers and retailers]," he continues. "We began to see it as our role to educate them in environmental business development . . . to help them create value in their spot in the channel."

"We are still emphasizing quality print characteristics as the driver of preference," O'Connor adds, "but the deciding factor now is the environmental."

"Back when the company started to invest in wind-generated electricity, it was an intangible value that we were adding to our reputation as a premium brand," says Milner. "When talking to the end users, people would always ask, 'Why is that important for me?'" But over the years, the intangible value has become tangible.

"It's not that we haven't done end-user selling in the past seventy years — we have," says O'Connor. "But we've spent more time with end users in the past four years than we have in the previous twenty."

"There's been less emphasis on product, more emphasis on environmental, and we've been approaching it much more from a research-based angle," he goes on. "Our customers have responded in a very positive way."

Milner's stump presentation is wide ranging. He explains how climate change will impact agriculture — that the Midwest will be drier, and other parts of the world wetter. He talks about the change in forest composition, deciduous forests moving north, replacing evergreens. He challenges corporate end users "to think about how your business might be impacted twenty or thirty or forty years from now," he says. "If you're an insurance company, you've got to be worried about coastal flooding. If you're a coffee company, you've got to be concerned about what's going to happen in agriculture. A two-degree change can wipe out coffee production."

He goes on to explain that commercial logging can be done in a sustainable manner, but that too often it isn't. "Know where your paper is coming from," he tells his audience. Of late, this has fit in well with the growing awareness that the supply chain matters, something other corporations have learned the hard way. Consider what happened to Nike with its Asian sweatshops and Mattel with its lead-painted toys. It takes years to build a brand, and only few days of bad publicity to bring it down.

In terms of finding the right audience, "we look for companies that have green procurement policies," explains O'Connor. "We do a lot of research, George and I. When we do presentations, we're talking a lot more about them than we talk about us. In fact, sometimes we know more about them than they know about themselves."

Says Milner, "A lot of corporate decisions are made at the top level and aren't filtering down to the level we're dealing with. So part of our job is to connect the top of the company with the lower levels."

Milner tailors his PowerPoint presentations, which are often as long as fifty pages, to the particular audience. "If we have a customer that's very environmentally sophisticated, let's say a Starbucks, we might do a very in-depth presentation of science-based information, say with regard to climate change. They don't want the broad brushstrokes, they want the detail," he notes. Customized storytelling is critical to selling any product or service, but it can be especially critical in the green marketplace because the audiences have such differing degrees of knowledge.

All of Milner's presentations include information about other companies or institutions in the same field that are already using Mohawk paper, and about how those companies turn that into a marketing advantage by educating their clients and customers.

In stressing that Mohawk's environmental efforts are enough to really matter, Milner points out that the company's product carries not only the FSC seal but also the Green Seal and Green-e logo. In marketing terms, this is similar to a product having a good *Consumer Reports* review or a high UL rating; all are marks of integrity.

Milner often suggests that the companies he's visiting apply for certification as well. "It makes you much more credible [to consumers] when those seals are on your product," he explains, citing it as a differentiator. "We've been instrumental in getting a lot of FSC certifications for printers. We've probably done more for the FSC in that regard than anybody else in the industry." To maintain these certifications, companies undergo a rigorous annual audit.

"People in the know that buy paper, whether it's made with renewable energy or it's post-consumer fiber, feel a lot more comfortable about buying your product when you have that third-party oversight," he says.

The design community: Relying on the pull-through effect.

As noted above, Mohawk spends a great deal of time with the primary influencers among its core customers. These include professionals among the graphic design and printing communities. Although the drivers of preference for these communities are often quality and price (or value), an emerging differentiator is the environmental factor.

"Our first point of attack is often the graphic designer community," says O'Connor, describing the pull-through effect Mohawk experiences when these designers are hired by advertising agencies, corporations, universities, and other nonprofit institutions.

"Especially with high-end paper, we have to create the demand, and that takes an awful lot of promotion and advertising and pull-through. The right designers at the appropriate times can be very influential to paper decisions for that particular client," he continues. "What we try to do is to educate them and point out that they have a very strong position in influencing people to make the right choices."

Mohawk begins wooing designers when they are still in graphic design school. "They love to lock in graphic designers" early, explains Dusek about Mohawk. "When these designers get [corporate work], they're making requests that go up to the CEOs. And then the CEO says okay and the order goes down to the purchasing level." O'Connor points out that while in the past, "environmental attributes just weren't important" to customers, now it's "all over the press, and it's real in terms of global warming and climate change," and so "it becomes easy for them [the CEOs] to make that decision."

"We're adamant that none of our products bears any environmental premium [in pricing]," he continues, explaining that Mohawk absorbs all extra costs incurred to make its product green. "We're not going to promote the use of environmentally responsible paper if it costs more money. A little cost differential is okay, but if it's a lot, people are going to say, 'You know what, I'm not there yet, no one's jumping down my back to use this stuff, and I'm going to pick the sheet of paper that looks the best and prints the best.'"

"We're right in the middle of the evolution of this whole movement in the paper business," O'Connor says. "If you go back two years, it was important to 20 percent of the design group, whereas now it's important to almost 80 percent. The pendulum has swung significantly."

Getting out the touchpoints.

Mohawk emphasizes its move toward sustainability with multiple touchpoints: sponsorship of events in the design and print communities, a smartly designed Web site, and well-packaged promotional pieces and swatch books of samples. In the past four years, since Mohawk began to spread its environmental mission message in earnest, the company has become more involved in event marketing. It primarily sponsors conferences within the design and print communities, such as with the graphic arts organization AIGA, but it goes way beyond that as well, such as with its 2007 sponsorship of Chicago's Cool Globes, an innovative public art project of 124 extraordinary globes designed to create awareness and inspire practical solutions to global warming.

"I was recently on an expert panel at a climate conference," Milner says. "It was interesting that they invited somebody from the paper industry to talk about the carbon market from the perspective of a manufacturer."

O'Connor says that Mohawk is conscientious about studying the effect of its outreach activities. "We do a pretty good job of measuring it," he says. "We get a lot out of it. The promotion of the brand has just been big."

Premier swatch.

Promotional samples and swatch books are an absolute necessity in the premium paper business, "because the way you sell it is when you put ink on it," explains O'Connor. "With premium paper, 80 percent of it is white. If you look at white paper without ink on it, it's difficult to sell it."

"We're told that we have the very best promotions out there," he continues. "We think very hard about our marketing and how it looks. Paper with ink on it tells a story and creates a message, and you try to draw people into that. Our marketing department is the best of any mill in the country, if not the world."

Get in touch with George.

Mohawk has a well-designed and graphically smart Web site. One of the most impressive attributes is under "Contact Us," where the viewer is presented with a link to "Get in Touch with George Milner" to discuss sustainability issues. "Sometimes he gets bombarded," O'Connor explains. "But it's important for people to have the right accessibility. It's become the culture of our company."

In addition to the George Milner link, there are a plethora of references to environmental awareness issues. The home page includes a link to the Mohawk Environmental Savings Calculator, enabling prospective customers to estimate "the net impact your purchases are having on the environment." Farther into the site, the visitor is invited to browse through volumes of information about sustainability at Mohawk, including an environmental FAQ page a mile long.

Mohawk, the first paper manufacturer in the United States to offset carbon emissions, proclaims its goal of becoming carbon-neutral on its homepage. By offsetting half a ton of CO_2 annually for every ton of paper produced — seven thousand tons of verified emissions reductions purchased for fourteen thousand tons of paper — the company has become the fourth largest purchaser of wind-generated electricity in the United States.

The Web site also notes that Mohawk's recent purchase of one hundred million kilowatt hours of Green-e certified Renewable Energy Certificates from wind power projects covers 100 percent of the company's electricity and energy consumption.

"We like to put it in human terms," the site states. "It's the equivalent of not driving 198 million miles in a Ford Taurus" or of "not leaving a diesel truck idling for 122 years."

What today's paper customers want.

According to Milner, today's paper customers are specifying that product come from recycled sources and/or sustainable forest sources. "People are very interested in the preservation of forests. They're a lot more educated. They want to know where the paper's coming from," he remarks.

Mohawk's paper ranges from 10 to 100 percent post-consumer waste content. "When we talk about recycled fiber, we're talking about post-consumer recycled fiber," O'Connor explains. "The industry used to talk about pre-consumer waste, but that term isn't used anymore."

The difference between now and twenty years ago, when recycled paper was first produced, is that "you don't have a trade-off in quality anymore," he continues. "Now you could buy a sheet of 100 percent recycled paper and you'd be hard-pressed to find a fleck in it . . . You can have the good-looking paper but still have the story around the recycled content paper. The reality is we're dealing in garbage."

Nevertheless, "we don't look at it [post-consumer waste paper] as a be-all and end-all." O'Connor explains that the company is also very invested in producing paper using virgin fiber from sustainable forests. "Recycled fiber doesn't last forever," Milner cautions. "The fiber supply chain has to be constantly replenished with virgin fiber."

Experiencing a growing customer interest in alternative fibers, Mohawk is currently looking into production of "tree-free" paper products, possibly using hemp or the residue left when ethanol is made from corn. In that, the company would be going back to the paper production processes of sixty to seventy years ago, when the commodity was manufactured from the residue left over from sugar production, as well as from cotton . . . or back to ancient times when it was made from papyrus reeds or elephant dung.

No matter what happens in the paper business, Mohawk is committed to keeping its position as the industry educator. Indeed, more than 1,000 inquiries about paper and other environmental issues came into Milner's environmental department in 2007, well over the 230 inquiries received in 2006.

Says Milner, "We had a meeting yesterday because the department is now so overwhelmed with questions and requests, we have to figure out what to do."

Time Inc. Magazines: The Green Press

When it comes to influence in the magazine publishing world, there is nothing like Time Inc. With more than 125 publications and three hundred million readers worldwide, it accounts for 19 percent of the total advertising revenue of US consumer magazines. *People, Time,* and *Sports Illustrated,* all published by Time Inc., recently ranked one, three, and four in ad revenue respectively.

Time magazine and its sister publications have been largely ahead of the pack when it comes to reporting on environmental issues. As far back as 1989, a prominent *Time* cover story portrayed the earth as Planet of the Year, reporting on issues such as scarcity of resources, climate change, water problems, and population growth. "We just ran a forty-four-page cover story in *Time* about climate change," says David Refkin, director of sustainable development for Time Inc. "When did we ever run a forty-four-page cover story on anything?"

Refkin also points out that *Sports Illustrated* did a March 2007 cover story on climate change and its influence on sports. *Fortune* has explored efforts by corporations to make themselves greener and boost profits at the same time, and *InStyle* runs a monthly green style feature story. "You have letters coming in from people who say, 'You know, I read *Sports Illustrated* because I want to disappear from reality and just escape. Why are you bringing me back to this?' But it's important for all of our magazines to cover these [environmental issues] editorially . . . In a way, it is kind of our brand [pact] with our readers."

Nevertheless, Refkin says, Time Inc. is not consciously biasing its editorial toward green stories to support a green brand reputation. "We have pretty strict separation of church and state," Refkin says of the division between editorial and marketing. "Things like that don't happen here."

Where Time *has* been marketing its magazines as green is to its advertisers. Like Mohawk, it has done so by becoming an expert on sustainability and talking about it.

David Refkin, pounding the environmental beat at Time Inc.

Like George Milner at Mohawk, Refkin is an unlikely revolutionary. He is practical by nature and an accountant by training, and he has spent most of his twenty years at the company overseeing paper acquisition for all of its magazines. He commutes from suburban Rockland County, where the forty-nine-year-old and his wife are raising three children.

Environmentally conscious since the age of eleven, when his parents took the family on an unusually long nine-week trip to the nation's national parks, it didn't take too long for him to begin seeing his job differently. "Twenty percent of my time I was dealing with environmental issues," he says of his early years at Time, much of that spent working as part of an Environmental Defense Fund task force. "We were ten years before our time, but we did some good work [toward becoming more environmentally responsible] . . . And then the issues started getting bigger."

In 2000, Refkin's immediate superior, Barry Meinerth, senior vice president for production and fulfillment, asked him to be more aggressive in addressing issues related to forestry, recycling, and climate change. Meinerth, an avid fisherman and skier, had been concerned about the environment for some time. Refkin was more than happy to comply, a tiger unleashed."

"The fact that we had a new president [George W. Bush] who didn't care about these issues made it more important," Refkin explains. "Barry's always had a passion for the environment. He really cares. He champions these issues."

"Enough people are focused just on earnings today, not on earnings five years or twenty years from now. Barry's modus operandi is to be proactive. And with the environment in particular, if you play defense, wait for trouble, you lose."

Uniting the supply chain.

Refkin set off on a mission to transform Time Inc.'s upstream supply chain. He began meeting with the company's paper suppliers — tree farmers and pulp and paper mills — to convince them to join the Certified Sustainable Forestry (CSF) program. By 2002, 25 percent of paper used in the company's overall magazine production was made from certified wood; by 2004 it was 58 percent, and today it is more than 70 percent.

"You have to talk to people and talk to people and talk to people," Refkin explains, "and take them on one by one by one."

Refkin travels often to carry out his mission. "My job is not to just sit in my office on the thirty-eighth floor of the Time-Life Building and say do this and do that. You have to get out into the field," he explains. "If you go to your paper suppliers and tell them to go out and do this or that for you, that's all well and good. But they need to hear it from the end user. It's a two-way dialogue. We need to hear what they have to say also."

Refkin describes a breakfast he had with 375 loggers in Iron Mountain, Michigan. "They wanted to eat *me* for breakfast. Thank God I had a microphone in my hand."

"That was just after *An Inconvenient Truth* came out," he continues. "I was there about forestry certification, and they went after me on climate change. 'This is bogus. This isn't real,' they were saying. What I learned from that is the American public is so not prepared for what's coming down the road. It's really frightening."

"Since Vietnam and Watergate, people have been taught not to believe what they hear from authorities . . . And you go through Enron and Tyco, and you go through what the government is doing these days. People don't believe what we're saying, they don't want to believe it," he says.

"There's the guy in Maine who said to me, 'This land has been in my family for eleven generations . . . No one has ever come up here from Boston or New York since 1760 to tell us what to do with our trees. Why are you coming up here to tell me what to do?' If I can't answer that question, I can't do my job."

"With the lumber companies, you make it so that they're proud to be certified. They'll go to their neighbors and they'll say, 'I'm certified . . . I'm somebody special,'" Refkin continues. The certification, he concludes, will pay off at a time when the market is soft. "When there's a lot of competition, the buyer will go with the certified company."

Becoming solutions-oriented.

Tensie Whelan, executive director of the Rainforest Alliance organization, who has worked with Refkin on forestry certification projects, calls him "a problem solver."

"David's a New York City boy," Whelan says, seated in her office in downtown Manhattan. "When he's been out there dealing with loggers in the middle of nowhere, he's done a great job — New York accent and all — navigating and getting people interested in sustainability . . . he's very solutions-oriented, trying to figure out ways to deal with the issues when people have legitimate reasons why they can't."

As an example, Whelan points to Refkin's work with small tree farmers. "Part of the problem with the US is that you've got a lot of small landowners. And those guys can't afford to do forest management plans on their twenty-five acres of forest. How do you make sure there's sustainable practices when 60 percent of the forest in the country falls into that category?"

Time Inc., under Refkin's lead, has also been working with the Rainforest Alliance in the southeastern United States "to develop a logging program where we train loggers in sustainable practices," Whelan explains. He has caused "a real shift in terms of Time's suppliers" and has been an important reason why "the paper industry has changed dramatically in the last couple of years," she says. "So it just goes to show you what buying power can do."

Nudging the paper manufacturers.

Refkin has pushed Time Inc. in a sustainability direction when it comes to the purchase of paper manufactured in a way that minimizes environmental impact. He initiated Time Inc.'s commitment to the purchase of "paper manufactured with advanced pulping and bleaching techniques, using totally chlorine-free or enhanced elemental chlorine-free processes," the company Web site explains, stating emphatically that "we do not purchase paper made from pulps bleached with chlorine gas."

Aware that millions of copies of its magazines have ended up in landfills over the years, Time Inc. has also joined with International Paper and the nonprofit National Recycling Coalition in a series of pilot projects to promote magazine recycling. ReMix, which stands for "Recycling Magazines Is Excellent," has increased recycling as much as 19 percent in the communities where it's been introduced. As the Time Inc. site proclaims, "The ultimate goal is to develop a self-sustaining national program."

Refkin has also led the way among publishers when it comes to measuring and reducing the carbon footprint of its entire supply chain. States the Web site, "We actively encourage our suppliers to boost their [energy] efficiency, decrease their use of fossil fuels, and increase use of alternative energy." Since 1989, the total reduction in paper weight for Time Inc. magazines has been 18 percent. In 2005 alone, the weight of the paper used by *Time, People, Sports Illustrated,* and *Entertainment Weekly* was reduced by 8 percent. This means fewer trees are used, of course, but it has also resulted in significant savings in transportation and energy costs.

A landmark carbon footprint study.

Time Inc.'s participation in a study conducted by the Heinz Center for Science, Economics and the Environment has been of landmark significance. The document resulting from the study, *Following the Paper Trail: The Impact of Magazine and Dimensional Lumber Production on Greenhouse Gas Emissions*, calculates the carbon footprint of an issue of *Time,* as well as of its sister publication *InStyle,* from inception to delivery.

"This was a pathbreaking study, because the participating companies provided actual data from their own production chains," says Anthony

Janetos, vice president of the Heinz Center, on the foundation's Web site. "Few studies [in the past] have quantified the carbon content and emissions from wood and paper materials and none have had access to the industries' own data."

Paper production causes the bulk of the carbon emissions from the paper-chain process, the study found. Breaking down wood fiber to make paper consumes tremendous energy, which in many cases comes from coal plants. "It took five years to get [the study] done for a variety of reasons," says Refkin. "And the irony is that five years later, when it finally came out, people cared about it. I get asked about our carbon footprint a lot. And every company out there is saying we have to measure our carbon footprint. Again, we're ahead of our time."

Making green pay off.

Refkin admits that the average Time Inc. reader has no idea about the company's efforts in the green space, and at least at present, there are few marketing initiatives to change that.

"We are doing more in terms of publicly talking about what we've been doing," he explains. "And of course we're the only publishing company that has a sustainability report on our Web site. But as for writing about these efforts in one of our magazines, it's tricky. If you make a claim, who's to believe you and to what standard is it?" Management at Time Inc., it seems from what Refkin is saying, has been afraid of possible charges of greenwashing, particularly from environmental organizations and eco-bloggers like TreeHugger.com.

"Unfortunately, instead of recognizing who the leaders are, the NGOs tend to pick on the leaders who put themselves out there," Refkin explains, citing the Ford Motor Company as an example. "Bill Ford had his head in the right place, but the company didn't have the money to make the transition [to hybrids]. Instead of recognizing Ford's leadership and maybe finding ways to help them, [the NGOs] beat them up at a time when other car companies weren't even talking about these issues at all."

Targeting advertising clients with a green message.

In 2005, Refkin began to look downstream when it came to sustainability issues. It began when he heard that Aveda, the world's largest manufacturer of natural personal care products — owned by Estée Lauder — was awarding more ad buys to a competitor's magazine because it was printed on recycled paper.

Refkin's ire was raised. "I said, 'Hey, hold on here a second. We're promoting magazine catalog recovery with our ReMix program. We're measuring our carbon footprint. We're doing all this stuff. These other people [the other magazine] don't show up at a conference. They don't speak. They don't do anything. But they just went and bought recycled paper, and they're getting ad pages and we're not?'"

"When I get upset about something, I get very energetic," Refkin continues. "The publisher of *InStyle*, Stephanie George, and I went out to Minneapolis to Aveda, and we went to the CEO, Dominique Conseil, and we said, 'Let me tell you what we're doing, let me tell you our story.' We told them our story. For the first time in five years, we got Aveda."

This experience made Refkin realize that, while it was not possible to make green a differentiator at the newsstand or with subscription sales among readers, it *was* possible to turn the company's eco-friendly initiatives into a distinct marketing advantage with advertisers . . . especially advertisers that themselves claim to be eco-conscious.

Refkin realized that spreading the green message to advertisers would also be aiding his cause within the company. "If a CFO sees that we're bringing in more ad dollars, I'm going to get more support, I'm going to get more dollars to do my job."

The message Refkin spreads is simple: "If you're a company that's trying to promote an environmental message — if you're talking about the environment and about how your products are green — don't you want to be presenting your message in a media that is similar? We're the leaders in our industry. Do you want to risk advertising in a magazine where the environmental practices aren't so good? With us, you don't have to worry about placing an ad that's green in a magazine that's pillaging the forests."

Rallying the troops at the Time-Life Building.

Part of Refkin's mission involves getting people behind him in his own company. "I've talked to more publishers in our building in the past six months than I have in twenty years," he explains.

Says Liz Greenburg, sales development director for *InStyle*, while sitting at her desk on the twenty-sixth floor of the Time-Life Building, "I feel like an ambassador for David, which is great. I'm happy to do it. If you're interested, he is excited to educate you and take you into the fold of what he's doing."

"The more support David has in the building, the better. He's made a lot of progress. He's definitely been chipping away. We all want to help him because he's such a nice guy, extremely smart, extremely approachable. He's tireless. And he doesn't care who I am or where I am in the building. The fact that I'm passionate about what he's doing, able to help articulate what he's doing . . . to another pool of people . . . makes him better off."

Greenburg sees herself as a conduit between Refkin and the *InStyle* advertising sales team, making sure they receive Refkin's updates on sustainability issues. "I want to help David have the opportunity to share his message."

"I don't believe the overall message is coming across fast enough," she says. "We're doing so much more, we're the good guys, but we're not getting as much visibility."

"People don't know we're using paper from sustainable forests, that we're not bleaching our paper with chlorine bleach. If you look at how we promote recycling, if you look at the fact that we've measured our carbon footprint, we're ahead of our time in some ways. We're doing the best we can within the world we're in — paper.

"Other titles aren't doing anything with respect to more sustainable practices," she says about other magazines, such as *Vanity Fair* and *Elle*. "Sure, they talk about it — every single publication has something devoted to greenness. But we do it from a production perspective. We're talking the talk and walking the walk. Otherwise, it's just words, not substance."

In fact, some of the advertisers are approaching Time Inc. about this issue themselves, high-end jewelry designer John Hardy for one. "Their commitment to the environment translates to their media choices," explains Greenburg. "They have given themselves a mandate to advertise in environmentally friendly or green-oriented media" such as *InStyle.*

"They can put that in their marketing campaign and share it with their customers." With other publications, where the carbon footprint figures are not available, this wouldn't be possible. "No other company can say that they're doing what Time Inc. is doing," Greenburg continues. "It's truly incredible."

In this, the company has turned its participation in the Heinz study into a distinct marketing advantage by using its findings in presentations to advertisers. As Refkin points out, the study indicated that production of an average copy of *Time* results in approximately 0.29 pound of greenhouse gas emissions released into the atmosphere, and that it would cost about twenty-five hundred dollars to offset these emissions. This information allows an advertiser hoping to purchase ad space in the magazine to know exactly how much it must pay to offset the emissions associated with that particular space.

Sticking with the mission for the duration.

"If you look at the predictions, they're pretty scary," Refkin says of the environmental crises. "We haven't even heard that much about the fact that the ice caps of Greenland are melting at a much faster rate than anticipated . . . that the polar ice is going away, that the permafrost is melting in Siberia."

"We're going to see a rise in tropical diseases," he continues. "There's going to be enormous impacts people aren't even thinking about now. Not just more hurricanes, but you have drought issues, malaria . . . you name it."

"I don't want to be eighty years old and have my children and my grandchildren say, 'Grandpa, you were in a position to do something about this . . . look at the world we're living in now. What were you doing back in 2007?'"

"Somehow we're going to have to try and find a way forward," he says, noting that Americans make up 4.5 percent of the world's population but consume well over 25 percent of the world's resources. "There's going to be pressure on us to consume less. We're going to have to consume more efficiently. Whoever figures out that efficiency solution will be a winner in the future. It will be an interesting marketing challenge."

SUMMARY: LEVERAGING GREEN EXPERTISE

For both Mohawk Fine Papers and Time Inc., most end users are unaware of the unprecedented efforts made by these companies to be environmentally responsible. Most readers of material printed on Mohawk paper and most readers of Time Inc.'s many magazines simply don't get the message. However, using energetically and personally deployed education programs initiated by corporate sustainability officers, both firms are delivering their eco-advantage message to print specifiers in the first case and to advertisers in the second. The advantage for Mohawk is that it adds value to paper, which is essentially a commodity. In Time Inc.'s case, it puts a thumb on the scale when advertisers make those budget-critical choices among similar publications with similar reach and demographics.

What should be an important arrow in the CSO's quiver of communications tools is the Gort Cloud. This community thrives on accurate and unflinchingly honest information. CSOs can leverage the power of this communications medium by understanding the complex, interactive, and viral qualities of the larger green community. The Gort Cloud thrives on frankness and can appreciate an honest discussion on difficult trade-offs. It's a medium that doesn't rely on sound bytes. There's patience built into the Gort Cloud, with acceptance for long-term business objectives and transitions.

Selling Activism

Ben & Jerry's Homemade, Green Mountain Coffee Roasters, and Stonyfield Farm

THE CHALLENGE

The birthplace for many of today's green brands is the verdant hills and valleys of New England. This is where Tom's of Maine, Ben & Jerry's, Stonyfield Farm, Green Mountain Coffee Roasters, Burt's Bees, and others were founded. These companies grew out of the counterculture backlash against corporate America and were bred on the philosophies of the *Whole Earth Catalog*, rural communes, food co-ops, and a belief that less is more, simple is smart. All of these companies believed in making healthy, earth-friendly products and that profits should serve a purpose higher than simply returning dividends to investors.

This chapter studies Ben & Jerry's Homemade, Green Mountain Coffee Roasters, and Stonyfield Farm. Each shares a commitment to producing products that are natural and, in the case of Stonyfield Farm and Green Mountain Coffee, also organic. They share one other differentiating quality. Each is committed to social activism as a mechanism for grounding its culture, ennobling employees, raising awareness, and building customer loyalty.

Two of these companies were bought by multinationals that recognized their value and the growing demand for healthy and sustainable products. How they managed to escape mission dilution is explained here. All three have experienced rapid growth despite growing competition — both within their green foods category and from without, following the entry of mass retailers into the natural and organic marketplace.

So how did they get where they are, and how do they deal with a changing competitive landscape?

THE SOLUTION

Each of these businesses has been an eco-pioneer and built alliances within the natural foods and LOHAS consumer movement. It's been a cooperative effort that has led to the growth of health and wellness retail channels, making their products more accessible and easier to buy.

Stonyfield Farm and Ben & Jerry's have become adept at the shelf space dominance game, so crucial to survival in the highly competitive grocery store business. Both have been acquired by multinational food giants, presenting special challenges, but so far parent and acquired brand have both recognized the importance of maintaining integrity.

All three have aligned environmental and social issues with their individual corporate missions. Despite becoming mainstream brands today, they continue to use an anti–Madison Avenue marketing style.

The food industry is the birthplace of the sustainable market. This should come as no surprise: We put food in our bodies. The idea that some of the things that we eat could be toxic or otherwise detrimental to our health has spurred a multibillion-dollar industry in natural, organic, local, and/or additive-free foods. These health foods are not necessarily grown, packaged, and delivered sustainably, but most are less demanding of the earth's resources than similar products from mega-farms and corporate food giants.

The health food movement has its origins in the hippie communes of the 1960s and the bulk food co-ops that became the trading posts of this culture. It grew slowly, getting a boost from the LOHAS (Lifestyles of Health and Sustainability) crowd with their "love the earth, heal my body" message. The LOHAS phenomenon grew at an 18 to 25 percent annual clip into a mainstream market segment that saw $13.8 billion in consumer sales in 2005, representing a 284.4 percent jump in eight years, according to CNN. The humble and sometimes funky food co-ops spawned Whole Foods, Wild Oats, and similar chains, while mass food marketers also began to take notice.

Organics, with the certified organics label, have become the preferred choice for natural foods because of mass marketers' misuse of "all-natural" claims. With its higher margins and huge growth, all food retailers are scrambling for organic product, which has limited supply. Alongside Costco, Trader Joe's, and many of the big supermarket chains, Wal-Mart now calls itself a distributor of "organics for everyone," recently doubling its organic offerings at 374 stores nationwide. Food-sector giants such as General Mills and Kellogg's have become players in the sector, and many veteran organic food makers have been purchased by multinationals.

In fact, the health food movement has had so much success that suppliers have become overwhelmed. Given the limited number of certified farms and ranches, demand is outstripping supply, with production going to the strongest players. This has made it increasingly difficult for the smaller health food makers to remain competitive and profitable.

Three brands that have ridden the health food wave and are synonymous with *natural and sustainable* are Ben & Jerry's Homemade, Green Mountain Coffee Roasters, and Stonyfield Farm. All three have developed far-reaching environmental and social responsibility agendas and are now benefiting from the fact that "perceptions of environmental, ethical, and social stewardship are the fastest growing contributors to consumer brand value," according to Z + Partners, a consumer research group.

These three are reacting to the growth and challenges in the health food industry in different ways. Two have been purchased by multinational conglomerates headquartered in Europe — Ben & Jerry's by Unilever and Stonyfield Farm by Groupe Danone. Green Mountain Coffee remains independent.

Ben & Jerry's Homemade: Aligning the Corporate Mission with a Marketing Strategy

Ben Cohen and Jerry Greenfield have positioned their business as an activist food company since 1978, when the partners opened their first Ben & Jerry's Homemade ice cream scoop shop in a renovated gas station at the corner of St. Paul and College streets in downtown Burlington, Vermont.

Cohen and Greenfield were determined to build a company that was different and have since done an extraordinary job fashioning a brand around ethical consumerism, which includes an ever-evolving list of social, health, and environmental commitments. The financial benefits have been enormous, first as an independent enterprise, and now as part of the multinational conglomerate Unilever. Although the company does not release specific information, sales ranged between $250 and $500 million annually as of 2007, according to Rob Michalak, Ben & Jerry's director of social mission and public elations (no, that's not a typo).

Targeting and differentiating with a creative product.

Ben Cohen believes the Ben & Jerry's market "is anyone who has the money in their pocket and would enjoy our product," according to Rob Michalak. Ben & Jerry's appeals to a fairly narrow demographic that "has been loyal and consistent over the years — young, well educated, professional, twenty-four to forty-five," he explains. It's a group that some demographers refer to as the cultural creatives. This market also dovetails with a description of LOHAS consumers, who are interested in personal wellness and the health of the environment.

The company's focus has been on maintaining these customers and increasing their purchases, rather than on significantly expanding the demographic. Michalak stresses that "creative flavor innovations" with fun names tied to a specific cause are critical to keeping these customers happy, pointing to the well-received 2007 introduction of two new flavors: Steven Colbert's AmeriCone Dream and Willy Nelson's Country Peach Cobbler. "People liked the flavors and the stories behind them," he says. "There's that kind of emotional relationship between the customer and the flavor. It just resonated."

Andrea Asch, Ben & Jerry's manager of natural resources, believes that although the primary reason for choosing Ben & Jerry's over other brands is "because we make a fabulous product," the social and environmental mission appeals to these customers and makes them "feel good about eating the ice cream."

Indeed, according to studies done by GollinHarris in 2006, over two-thirds of Americans interviewed agreed that, doing well by doing good is a savvy business strategy. The same study found that "Baby Boomers and Millennials (children of Baby Boomers, also referred to as 'Generation Y') are twice as likely to associate their own personal values with companies and brands."

"We ask ourselves what we should be doing as a company that is socially and environmentally proper," explains Michalak. "If we do that and get it right, and then tell that story, it becomes part of the marketing."

Social action before it was fashionable.

Ben & Jerry's assumed its corporate social responsibility mission early in its history with the sponsorship of a variety of local Vermont events, such as an autumn Fall Down Festival and a free outdoor movie festival. In 1985, Cohen and Greenfield formalized their social mission with the 1985 launch of the Ben & Jerry's Foundation, allocating 7.5 percent of annual pre-tax profits toward the funding of community projects.

As the company's Web site explains, "Capitalism and the wealth it produces do not create opportunity for everyone equally. We recognize that the gap between the rich and the poor is wider than at any time since the 1920's. We strive to create economic opportunities for those who have been denied them and to advance new models of economic justice that are sustainable and replicable."

If we examine Ben & Jerry's corporate history, a pattern emerges of self-promoting good deeds in exchange for positive PR and customer loyalty. The following tracks the connection between altruism and profits in an unmistakable way:

1979: Marking its first year in business, Ben & Jerry's launches a Free Cone Day, a giveaway that will be enshrined as an annual event.

1984: Häagen-Dazs's parent, Pillsbury, tries to limit distribution of Ben & Jerry's, prompting a lawsuit and the now famous PR campaign, "What's the Doughboy afraid of?" Sales reach $4 million.

1985: The Ben & Jerry's Foundation is established to fund community-oriented projects. It is subsequently provided with 7.5 percent of the company's annual pre-tax profits. Sales now exceed $9 million.

1986: Ben and Jerry personally go on the road driving their Cowmobile around the country and giving out free scoops of ice cream. Sales exceed $30 million.

1987: The Ben & Jerry's founders visit Wall Street following the October 19 crash to distribute That's Life and Economic Crunch ice cream. The company begins feeding food waste to Vermont farm pigs in a cradle-to-cradle earth-friendly scheme. Sales exceed $31 million.

1988: Ben & Jerry's helps establish a new no-profit initiative known as 1% for Peace, its goals to redirect 1 percent of the national defense budget to fund peace-promoting projects and activities. Ben & Jerry's rescues Rhode Island's legendary Newport Folk Festival from oblivion by becoming its sponsor. Sales exceed $47 million.

1989: Ben & Jerry's comes out against bovine growth hormone (BGH) on concerns about adverse economic impact on family farming. The company introduces Rainforest Crunch ice cream to indirectly benefit rain forest preservation efforts. Annual sales top $58 million.

1990: Ben & Jerry's introduces Chocolate Fudge Brownie in partnership with Greyston Bakery, which employs disadvantaged people from the local community. The company protests New Hampshire's Seabrook nuclear power plant with a billboard declaring STOP SEABROOK. KEEP OUR CUSTOMERS ALIVE AND LICKING. Ben & Jerry's prints a SUPPORT FARM AID message on eight million packages. Total sales in 1990 are $77,024,037.[1]

Phew! And I can keep going, as each year the list grows longer . . . but instead I'll refer you to the Web site for the complete story. Clearly, the company's activism and constant inventiveness have contributed to its sustained, unbroken growth.

Product campaigns based on innovative flavors, celebrities, and a cause.

One successful Ben & Jerry's marketing scheme involves identifying a social issue the firm can support, then finding a celebrity partner, and finally creating a custom-made, custom-named product to tie a campaign together. With the AmeriCone Dream flavor named in honor of Steven Colbert's political satire show, Ben & Jerry's was fortunate to make a connection with the *Daily Show* celebrity "just as he was rising up the celebrity marquee," Michalak says. "He has an irreverent sense of humor and political edge just like we do." Colbert donates proceeds to charity through the Stephen Colbert AmeriCone Dream Fund. In a similar tie-in with a celebrity, Ben & Jerry's created the Country Peach Cobbler flavor, with proceeds going to Farm Aid: "Willy Nelson has the whole connection to Farm Aid and farmers. His personality, his identification as a country icon — it all worked out."

According to a post in BuzzSugar, an entertainment blog, "Willie Nelson appeared on *The Colbert Report* to discuss his new Ben & Jerry's flavor, Country Peach Cobbler. Seeing as how Stephen just got his own AmeriCone Dream ice cream, he used the interview as an opportunity to confront his celebrity-dessert competition. Colbert calls out Nelson's nefarious agenda with an attack ad, in which an 'ice cream expert' (read: little kid) asks: 'Why would I want to eat ice cream the pot man told me to eat?'" Ben & Jerry's sense of humor and the celebrities it partners with to create it are key components of the brand personality. The resulting video clips and posts on YouTube also echo around the Gort Cloud.

"We're a product based on agricultural production," Michalak continues. "We've always supported family farms, and we've also expressed our support by paying a premium to use rBGH-free milk. People like the association with Willy Nelson, they like that we give back to the community by sending the royalties to Farm Aid. We're continually trying to put our money where our mouth is and also to [launch] campaigns relevant to the brand's core mission and values."

Michalak explains that with celebrity flavors, the company makes sure that it's an appropriate match between the personality and the product before moving forward. This further strengthens the fulfillment of the three primary goals included in the Ben & Jerry's mission statement: superior product, profitable growth, and social responsibility. "The idea is that those three are supposed to work in harmony." When they do, "then we're cooking."

"We live our company values as often as we can and as close to the truth as we can. Consumers see that . . . and that's what creates loyalty and that's what keeps a company successful. When you start deviating from that, you lose their trust and the loyalty."

Creating partnerships with sympaticos.

The Ben & Jerry's brand benefits from partnerships with like-minded companies, such as its recent venture with Patagonia. In the outdoor clothing company's 2008 catalog, an insert from Ben & Jerry's champions the Sanders-Boxer Senate legislation on global climate change. Explains Andrea Asch about the legislation, "We're asking Patagonia consumers to take action, and when they take action, they get a free-pint coupon."

Ben & Jerry's maintains close ties with other activist companies in New England, with Green Mountain Coffee Roasters perhaps the best example. There's a synergy between the two that works on both a product and a mission level, a recent example being sponsorship of a rally to urge Vermont legislators to override the Republican governor's veto of energy-efficiency legislation.

"To me, it was just the epitome of grassroots organizing," says Michalak of the rally. "One could certainly say that you're preaching to the choir, but then the press picked it up and we were on TV that night. And, you know, that's how things happen."

Beginning in 2002 and continuing on to the present, Ben & Jerry's has joined Green Mountain Coffee, along with Stonyfield Farm of New Hampshire, in building wind turbines on Sioux Nation land in Nebraska through an alternative energy company, NativeEnergy. In addition to providing a renewable energy source and new jobs to an underemployed region, it presents the three New England companies with the opportunity to obtain renewable energy credits to offset factory carbon emissions. It also has an incremental effect on the air quality in the Northeast by reducing air pollution drifting downwind from Midwestern coal-fired energy plants. By funding these wind turbines, the New Englanders are improving their own air.

Asch, who attended a Native American ceremony to dedicate the first wind turbine, says of the 2002 event: "When we drove up to the reservation, it was starting to rain and they'd been in the midst of a drought, so that's a very spiritual component to this whole thing. And when the last blade was up, a bald eagle happened to fly over. There was a lot of power behind that event."

Aligning operations with the sustainability objectives.

When Andrea Asch assumed her role as Ben & Jerry's director of natural resources in 1992, no one knew what her job title meant. "The company recognized that they'd been doing environmental things as part of how they do their business, but they wanted to give it a bit more focus," she explains.

"I'll never forget my first day at work, when they proudly told me they had a 30 percent energy-reduction goal. So I said, 'That's awesome. What's your starting point? Have you measured how many kilowatt-hours you're using now?' And they said, 'Well, no.'"

Asch's first task was to develop baseline numbers, and she's been measuring ever since, from recycling to energy use, solid waste levels, carbon dioxide emissions, and compost. "And based on what we measure, we establish goals on an annual basis," she explains.

Much progress has been made in other areas as well. Since 2001, all of Ben & Jerry's pints have been packed in unbleached paperboard Eco-Pint containers, and all Ben & Jerry's scoop shops use a variety of unbleached paper products. Efficiencies also apply to new methods for making product. "Instead of getting five-gallon pails of cherries, we get twenty-five-hundred-pound totes of cherries," Asch says; a hose pumps the cherries into the ice cream eliminating heavy lifting. The tote is returned to the vendor, washed, and recycled for other use. The process reduces waste as well as workers' comp claims.

To further progress toward sustainability with the pint containers, the company recently transitioned to a board certified by the Forest Stewardship Council, which means that all pulp used is from sustainably harvested forests. All Ben & Jerry's US pints will now carry an FSC certification logo. Asch is hopeful the logo will pique the curiosity of consumers, who will then go to the Ben & Jerry's Web site, where "we'll have the whole story written for them."

Asch says, "The hope is to influence the industry to want something better. So that's our goal going forward — to really communicate the benefits of using renewable resources so we're not relying on petroleum that exposes us all to global political and environmental conflicts."

Expressing brand personality through words and deeds.

"We're not afraid of expressing our opinion," says Asch, recalling the giant, melting baked Alaska the company sent to the Senate Chamber in Washington during the ANWAR debate on drilling in the Alaskan wilderness.

"I think it's cool that we talk about [the dangers of] dioxin on the back of the vanilla pint container. I mean dioxin! That's nasty stuff," she exclaims. "And we're talking [about putting this message] on the back of the happy pint of ice cream!" The important thing, Asch says, is that it raises awareness about eliminating dioxin, which "is an important issue to us."

Even when the subject is dioxin, the company refers to these packaging messages as "romance copy," explains Asch. "If our customers read the back of the pint, they know that we do good things and they support it. They may not know all the projects we do, but they know we have a soul and that matters to them."

"We're a values-led company," she continues. "We don't do a marketing campaign on environmental issues because we know it's a good marketing opportunity. We [take on specific] initiatives and then we talk about it to our consumers."

"We're asking our customers to take action," urging them to "write their senator or congressperson, or the governor of their state, to support a specific piece of legislation that we believe is important for the environment."

The company also uses the Internet in a variety of ways to get the message out. It sends out "Chunk Mail" to an extensive list of "core consumers who really get our brand," Asch says. "We'll target them with surveys, opinions . . . all types of things." Chunk Mail also directs its customers to the "Cool Your Jets" page at www.benjerry.com, where page visitors can offset the carbon emitted from jet flights they've taken with renewable energy credits via NativeEnergy. "It's very easy, very quick. You'll get a nice certificate thanking you for your purchase," explains Asch.

Michalak points out, "We're always trying to tie this back to our business, [asking] what we can do that's associated with our business. This year we're looking at investing in biomass projects on farms in Vermont . . . looking for ways to have a collective biomass project where there might be a facility that could be used there to generate energy."

A corporate culture rooted in sustainable family farms.

Ben & Jerry's goes a long way to support sustainability on family-owned dairy farms by giving them a self-assistance tool kit that "looks at economic, social, and environmental attributes of dairy farming," explains Asch. It's part of collaboration between Ben & Jerry's, the St. Albans Co-op, the University of Vermont Center for Sustainable Agriculture, and the Vermont Agency of Agriculture.

"The tool kit gives the farmers a traffic-light system of scoring themselves as to their farm's sustainability, helping them identify challenges," she says. The kit includes a soil sample test, which will tell the farmers how much synthetic fertilizer they have to add to the land, allowing them to avoid overuse and hence assisting in the cleanup of the Vermont water supply that is contaminated by farm runoff.

Battling for shelf space in the superpremium ice cream segment.

While there is a premium ice cream segment, Ben & Jerry's, as a pioneer in the superpremium segment, shares shelf space in markets and convenience stores with its main competitor and past adversary, Häagen-Dazs. "It's pretty much a fifty–fifty split" between the two, says Rob Michalak. "Every year, you want to get a little more of that market share. Generally, it comes down to putting out creative flavors and continuing to do that on a regular basis."

"Shelf space is about performance," he continues. "If you have a flavor that's selling . . . if you're creating flavors that have a high turn, you have the leverage to go in and make a case for another spot on the shelf. It comes down to the sales force making presentations and your marketing team working that as well."

"It's also about continuing to express a company culture that people have come to both recognize and expect from you. Anytime you have a product that has a social mission element, it keeps the brand lively and keeps the customers loyal."

Michalak notes, that while "Häagen-Dazs positions their brand on a luxury experience," Ben & Jerry's is positioned as "a real good ice cream with creative flavors and a personality." This "company started by two guys" and "established with real values and a connection to the community" delivers "brand equity, a brand awareness, and a brand loyalty over time," Michalak continues. "Häagen-Dazs took a different approach. They went [for] a different emotional appeal."

"I think both companies have done well to establish their place. It's up to us both to continue to figure out ways to express it. In our case, it's creative flavor combinations and [our] social mission, the way we make and market our products, and through the associations and partnerships we make over time. We're going to continue to be an activist brand . . . with an irreverent sense of humor."

Preserving a mission after an acquisition.

Both Asch and Michalak insist that the acquisition of Ben & Jerry's by the European corporate giant Unilever in 2000 has had no impact on the social messaging. "I'm still here," Asch explains. "They didn't compromise my values. As soon as they try to compromise my values, I'll move on."

In fact, Unilever is known in Europe for its aggressive pro-environment positions. It owns the US brands Breyer's, Klondike Bar, Good Humor Bar, and Popsicle; Ben & Jerry's moved in as its superpremium brand.

Ben Cohen and Jerry Greenfield assured their employees at the outset that Ben and Jerry's would continue to be run entirely independently. "Unilever bought us because we represented something," says Asch. "They may not have understood just how far we want to take things sometimes, but we still push the activism as far as we can."

Ben & Jerry's is one of the emerging global brands in the Unilever universe, and it's important to the conglomerate that there be world-wide "consistency and continuity" in the brand, as Michalak explains. "We're still evolving as a global brand. A lot of the work we're doing right now is to build a stronger structure that can carry on the brand's mission statement globally."

Rooting the brand in foreign soil.

How does this particular and unique Yankee activist brand translate into foreign tongues? "We try as we grow to hire people who are native to the area, who understand how to best actualize an activist brand within that country," Michalak says.

It might be worth going to www.benjerry.com to sample the international links. Each country has a page on the site done in the style and humor of that particular culture and language. You may not understand the particular languages, but you'll catch the drift.

Although the regional taste for ice cream flavors may be different, there is worldwide convergence on many of the Ben & Jerry's social and environmental agendas. Considering the recent uptick in the global awareness of climate change, Michalak says, "I think the important thing is to stay true to your values and true to your goals. Just like Patagonia, Seventh Generation, Timberland . . . it's all the companies that have been in this space for a while. Their messages have been consistent with their actions. So now their brand credibility stands a little bit higher than many others, and that can [instill] brand loyalty [in] the customer."

Green Mountain Coffee Roasters: Turning Coffee into a Cause

Across Vermont, sustainability seems to be on almost everyone's mind. In the west-central part of the state, around Burlington, there seems to be a virtual Gort Cloud stretching for miles, companies and NGOs connecting in all directions.

In Waterbury, where Green Mountain Coffee Roasters is in the center of town and the Ben & Jerry's plant is up the road, the two like-minded companies often come together to promote social and environmental causes. Today a press conference is under way in the Green Mountain Coffee parking lot. Green Mountain Coffee employees hand out free cups of Fair Trade Rain Forest Nut, while Ben & Jerry's employees serve their Fossil Fuel ice cream flavor from a trailer-turned-ice-cream-dispenser that has been pulled here by the Ben & Jerry's Lick Global Warming Ford Escape hybrid. It's a very warm day, and the ice cream melts quickly. Several representatives from Vermont-based NGOs are also in attendance.

The rally has been called primarily to urge the Vermont legislature, in Montpelier just twenty-three miles to the south, to override a recent gubernatorial veto of progressive energy legislation. Green Mountain

Coffee Roasters has also chosen this moment to cut the ribbon on its new biodiesel tank, which will be used to fill its Waterbury delivery trucks.

The premium coffee landscape.

Paul Comey, Green Mountain Coffee's VP of environmental affairs, calls GMCR "a medium-sized company," with more than a thousand employees and 26.8 million pounds of coffee roasted and shipped annually, as of this writing. It has ridden the wave of growth in the premium coffee segment at the same time that overall consumption of coffee in the United States has been flat. In 2006, Green Mountain Coffee accounted for 1.2 percent of the 2.2 billion pounds in US coffee sales, 7.1 percent of specialty coffee sales, and approximately 10 percent of Fair Trade coffee sales.

The growth in the specialty coffee market is attributable to its spread to fast-food restaurants and convenience stores as well as to the increased demand for specialty coffee in the workplace. Green Mountain Coffee has taken advantage of these trends. Its coffee is featured at bagel shops, delis, and restaurants that compete against large national chains such as Starbucks, and it provides its coffee to offices through distributors, most often using the Keurig single-cup coffee-brewing system.

The total revenue for Green Mountain Coffee Roasters, Inc., in 2007 was $341.6 million, with two-thirds coming from the coffee division under the Green Mountain Coffee and Newman's Own Organics labels, and one-third coming from Keurig, Incorporated. Of the 26.8 million pounds of coffee shipped by Green Mountain Coffee, 7 million pounds went through office coffee service distributors, 6.4 million pounds went to supermarkets, 5.6 million to convenience stores, 5.4 million through food service at restaurants and institutions, 1.2 million through Green Mountain Coffee's Web site and catalog sales, and 1 million pounds through resellers.

"Part of the complexity of our business is that we operate in more channels than most coffee companies," explains T. J. Whalen, Green Mountain Coffee's vice president of marketing. "It's part of our strength — we try to surround the consumer with opportunities to buy our products."

Each channel has its own set of competitive dynamics. When it comes to sales of packaged coffee in supermarkets, Starbucks was on top at

$358 million in sales in 2007, but it has recently scaled back retail stores partly due to overexpansion, while McDonald's seems to be ramping up its premium-coffee service.[2] Seattle's Best was at $68 million. Peet's was at $61 million; Green Mountain Coffee, $32 million. Dunkin' Donuts, a brand that is considered halfway between premium and commercial, was at approximately $63 million in sales.

Competition from nonpremium, commercial brands comes primarily from Folgers, with $892 million in 2007 revenue, and Maxwell House, with $486 million. While Green Mountain Coffee's sales increased last year, Folgers and Maxwell House saw a decline.

"Consumers in general are trading up," Whalen says. "They're understanding the value of specialty products."

Pushing the environmental agenda for twenty-two years.

"If you're a facilities manager, you're looking at environmental components whether you like it or not," says Paul Comey, who joined the company in 1986. "How do you recycle, how do you deal with the waste stream . . . it's ingrained in you as an integral part of your day-to-day business."

"The bigger you get, the more you understand the scope of your impact. Idling of trucks is bad, but when you look at the number of trucks we have, then you see it's something that really needs to be addressed."

Comey's initiatives have included modification of energy systems to reduce waste, companywide recycling programs, and changes in packaging procedures. Green Mountain Coffee offsets 100 percent of its documented emissions from operations and transportation as well as a portion of indirect emissions related to outbound freight. The offset funds go to varied sites depending on the year. Supported projects have included the Rosebud Sioux Tribe Wind Turbine in South Dakota, a methane-recapture project on a family farm in Pennsylvania, family-farmer-based renewable energy projects, Midwest farmer-owned wind turbines, and Vermont farmer-owned methane digesters. The funds have also helped retire CO_2 offsets that have been generated by the Des Plaines Landfill Project, owned by the Archdiocese of Chicago.

In 2006, Green Mountain Coffee partnered with International Paper to bring to market the Ecotainer, the first petroleum-free disposable to-go paper cup for hot beverages made from renewable materials. The company also offers an eco-friendly to-go cup for cold drinks.

"One of the challenges with this business is that when you get the best packaging for the coffee, odds are it will be bad for the environment. If you get the best packaging for the environment, odds are the coffee will go stale before it's used, unless you're a micro-roaster with very small distribution," Comey explains. "So you're caught between a rock and a hard place."

The company is looking into biopolymer packaging alternatives. "It's something we're tracking very closely," Comey says. Green Mountain Coffee recently introduced new packaging for its Single Origin and Newman's Own Organics lines. The bags use a layer of polylactic acid (PLA) made from corn to replace a petroleum-based layer.

Finding a corporate voice in a social mission.

The company's founder and chairman, Bob Stiller, discovered Green Mountain Coffee Roasters, then a Waterbury coffeehouse, on a trip to Vermont in 1980. Impressed by the coffee's great taste, he purchased the establishment a year later and spent the next twenty-six years growing the coffeehouse into an international coffee supplier. In May 2007, he stepped out of his role as CEO, but unlike Ben Greenfield and Jerry Cohen of Ben & Jerry's, he did not sell to a conglomerate. Under present CEO Larry Blanford, the company continues to use social action as a platform from which to market its product.

GMCR donates 5 percent of pre-tax earnings toward its good works. "We are motivated to achieve success because the more profitable we are, the more good we can do in the world," the company's Web site states.

"The first part of our mission is to create an exceptional coffee experience from tree to cup, making sure that all of the stakeholders, from growers to consumers, benefit from that," says Whalen. "The second part of the mission is about changing the way the world understands business. That's something we take seriously. We're trying to communicate to the consumer that these issues are part of who we are, and that as a consumer you have the power to do something about them."

Coffee production presents unusually fertile ground in terms of opportunities to do good. First, coffee is the world's second most heavily traded commodity, trailing only oil. As the Green Mountain Coffee Roasters Web site states, "With 25 million coffee farmers in the world and an estimated 100 million people working in the coffee industry in total, we have a remarkable opportunity to positively touch the lives of so many people through our work."

The site also talks about the "Coffee Crisis" of 2002, when a collapse in coffee prices "drew attention to the ongoing plight of coffee farmers." According to the site, "The Coffee Crisis threatened entire cultures and communities as well as the stability of long-term supplies of high quality, specialty coffees." Things have grown better since '02, but farming conditions remain poor and much technical assistance is still needed.

The Web site, which doesn't spare any detail when it comes to reporting on the company's socially responsible activities, goes on to say, "Millions of coffee-farming families continue to lack basic necessities such as healthcare, education, and food, forcing them to either reduce their investments in environmentally sound practices, abandon their land, gather more debt or switch to illegal agricultural crops."

Green Mountain Coffee makes a case that the Coffee Crisis mirrors the global human rights and environmental crises and cites the following statistics pulled from a variety of sources: "Every 14 seconds, 5 children younger than 5 years of age die of hunger and other preventable causes . . . Nearly 3 billion people live on less than $2 per day . . . Nearly 852 million people worldwide are undernourished . . . About 1.2 billion people worldwide — 400 million of them children — do not have access to clean water."

Many of these points are touched on at the company's visitor center, housed in Waterbury's Amtrak train depot, just adjacent to Green Mountain Coffee Roasters' headquarters. A multimedia presentation about the company's connection with indigenous coffee producers around the world is projected on the ceiling as well as on seven screens placed around the room. It is a powerful piece that takes the viewer around the coffee-growing world to such places as the Huatusco Cooperative in Mexico, the Koakaka Cooperative in Africa, and the Gayo Organic Coffee Farmers Association in Indonesia.

The company's consumer education initiatives also involve a great deal of instruction on the nature of coffee production. Extensive Web site sections are devoted to the history of coffee as well as the company's manufacturing processes. The unique nature of Green Mountain

Coffee's methods is emphasized, including a description of Appropriate Roast — the trademarked name of the company's roasting technique.

The challenge of communicating to disparate stakeholders.

Michael Dupee is one of the Green Mountain Coffee Roasters execs at the rally this morning. "You do these [social and environmental action initiatives] because it's the right thing to do," he says. "You do the programs, hopefully you get results, hopefully you know what those results are, and then you've got to talk about them. You need to share them with people in a way that doesn't oversell it, doesn't undersell it . . . but is communicated in a way that people hear you and are able to connect it with their own experience."

Telling this story is complicated "because there are so many stakeholders," he notes. "You've got to connect with your community, you've got to connect with your customers — with that business or that restaurant selling your coffee — and you've got to connect with the consumer who goes into the bagel shop and says, 'I want that coffee.' You've got to connect with your supply chain, you want to connect with your employees. That's a lot of people to tell a complicated story to, and it's a real challenge."

"Any company that's doing this kind of stuff will tell you they don't tell their story well enough," Dupee continues. "We're not sharing enough of what we do in enough ways. And that's really the frustration, that's the tension. For example, two years ago we made the decision to align our social responsibility work with our Millennium Development goals, which is great, but where do we go with that? How do you tell that story? Even after you figure out how to put it into five hundred words or less, there are a very small number of people who are going to want to hear that. And there's probably some way to say it in eight seconds, ten seconds, twelve seconds, but we haven't figured that out yet."

Building markets or serving trends?

Dupee believes that too many companies today are jumping onto the sustainability bandwagon with skin-deep credentials. "It's people using code words and buzzwords to try to communicate some level of virtue that may or may not be true. It doesn't do justice to the kinds of things that we're all working on here."

"I think if you really want to be engaged and if you're really interested in creating a forward-looking vision and realizing it, surfing market waves and waiting for consumers to tell you what to do is not the way to do it," he continues. "That's not where the real thinkers are. That's not where real progress is. That's not where true inspiration is."

"Business is the most potentially powerful agent for change in the world," he continues. "It used to be community, and then it was religion, and now it's business. That's what we need to use as the tool."

Creating a direct relationship with the consumer.

"We don't do a lot of traditional media," says Whalen of the company's marketing priorities. "What we do a lot of is grassroots events and sampling — our coffee is served in tens, if not hundreds of thousands, of individual locations."

The company also communicates with consumers through direct mail, catalogs, and brochures, as well as its Web site. Like Ben & Jerry's, it places socially and environmentally responsible messages on its cups and bags of coffee.

"We change the message on our cup about every three or four months, and we probably have a dozen different messages at any given time," explains Whalen, holding a cup that details the company's efforts to be carbon-neutral, including its Gort Cloud connections with other New England companies and the connection to the Sioux Nation NativeEnergy project.

"Through our communication effort, we hope that people will begin to understand these messages, internalize them, and frankly do something about them," Whalen says.

Connecting products to causes.

Again like Ben & Jerry's, Green Mountain Coffee connects products to specific causes, hence its Rain Forest Nut selection and its Gombe

Reserve coffee, which was developed in collaboration with the Jane Goodall Institute. Other socially conscious products include National Wildlife Blend, introduced in cooperation with the National Wildlife Federation to help support Fair Trade and organically certified family-owned farms in Central and South America that raise shade-grown coffees while providing habitat for migratory songbirds.

The success in promoting the positive connections made between Green Mountain Coffee and its indigenous suppliers has inspired the company to expand its product offerings. At the visitor center in Waterbury, you can purchase everything from Indonesian masks to Kenyan beads to pottery from Peru and Colombia. At the Web site and through the catalog, other food and beverage products such as Fair Trade Organic Cocoa, Mexican Vanilla, and Tanzania Chocolate Sauce are also available, as are Vermont-based products such as Maple Butter and Woodstock Cranberry and Maple Walnut Granola.

Media-shy or media-savvy?

"We have a long history of instances where we've tried to raise the bar a little," Comey says about environmental and social initiatives. "Some people would come in, see what we're doing, want to write a story, and we'd say no, because next thing you know people will accuse you of greenwashing."

"We don't say, 'Look at us, we're green.' We are green, and then we tell the story. There's a subtle difference," explains T. J. Whalen. "Successful green marketing comes from the inside and works out."

Sustainability increases sales.

Whalen says there is a definite link between Green Mountain Coffee Roasters' rising coffee sales and its image as a company concerned about sustainability issues. "We track it through consumer surveys, which measure and monitor what consumers think of us and what they think of our competitors," he says. "The coffee market is a big complex game, and we try to play it with as much information as we can."

The research is "telling us we're on the right track," he continues. "Increasingly, consumers understand and value the message of sustainability."

An infectious culture of environmental respect.

As Green Mountain Coffee Roasters' VP of environmental affairs, Paul Comey is leading the way toward sustainability and is responsible for originating the rally today.

"There's a level of environmentalism in the company that kind of wells up from within," he says of the people who work here. "You have an obligation to society to act responsibly." Comey points to Don Ostler, a GMCR route supervisor who has been part of the biodiesel truck introduction today. "He's been such a champion of it, he's made it work. That's the kind of employee base that makes the company great," says Comey.

Todd Jones has been in charge of Green Mountain Coffee's anti-idling program, which instructs the company's truck drivers to cut off their engines during delivery stops. "I was one of the skeptical people at first," Jones says. "But unless it gets down to fifteen below," it's doable. "It's truly astounding how much fuel is wasted. If everyone just stopped their unnecessary idling, there'd be a huge impact."

Growing more productive employees.

Whalen says that most environmental and social initiatives at the company, which are ultimately what the marketing department uses to promote the products, "come from bottom up, as opposed to top down." "You're encouraged to make a positive difference," he notes of the Green Mountain Coffee Roasters company culture. Referencing Comey's transition from facility VP into VP of environmental affairs, "It can take you into a different role, but that is encouraged."

"Bob Stiller believes that when an individual is allowed to follow his own passion, it will work better," Whalen continues, hence the extensive continuous learning and development seminars offered by the company. "At Green Mountain Coffee, it's about what you're passionate about. And when that's sincerely carried out, it leads to great business results . . ." and ideas, apparently.

Rick Peyser, the company's former director of public relations, "cultivated a passion for helping coffee growers," Whalen says. "So he was
able to move into a role where that was his full-time focus."

Elected board president of the Specialty Coffee Association, Peyser
was responsible for bringing a guest speaker to the organization's
convention. "He realized there had never been a woman speaker, so he
brought in Jane Goodall," explains Whalen. "She gave a rousing presentation about the relationship between chimpanzee habitats and coffee
around her preserve in Africa. Many of the area farmers were engaging in negative impact practices, leading to deforestation and reducing
chimp habitat."

As a consequence, Lindsey Bolger, Green Mountain Coffee's director of coffee sourcing and relationships, traveled to Tanzania to forge a
partnership that would create a new market for the coffee grown in the
region, improve the livelihoods of area farmers, and preserve chimp habitat. The result was Green Mountain Coffee's Tanzanian Gombe Reserve
coffee, made from beans grown by members of the Kalinzi Cooperative,
a group of twenty-seven hundred small-scale farmers who live near
Gombe National Park, the home of Goodall's chimpanzee study site.
The company clearly benefited from the press attention received thanks
to the Goodall connection when the flavor was launched.

Stonyfield Farm: The Price of Organic Success

Stonyfield Farm, founded in Wilton, New Hampshire, by back-to-the-
land advocate Samuel Kaymen as an organic farming school, has spent
the past twenty-five years inching its way from counterculture outpost to
the world's leading brand of organic yogurt. The man behind this huge
success story is president, "CE-Yo," and well-known eco-capitalist Gary
Hirshberg, who joined Kaymen in 1982 and convinced him to begin selling the full-fat plain yogurt the farming school was locally famous for.

"Our mission — the reason we founded our company from the very
beginning — was actually from a very authentic and genuine social
concern: the demise of family farmers," Hirshberg says. "Farmers don't
have any voice in our society, no political clout. Organic is the only way
to give farmers better and more sustained advantageous pricing."

Forging a path on a rocky road.

Growing Stonyfield Farm has not been an easy task. Hirshberg's wife, Meg, an organic farmer when she met him, refers to the early period as the couple's "bad old days," and the farm as "cold and crowded, with a road so perilous that suppliers often refused to come up."

"We had a wonderful business," says Gary. "The only problem was that we had no supply and no demand."

"Twenty-five years of struggle has brought us to where we are today," says Erik Drake, Stonyfield Farm's director of marketing. "Twenty-five years of having a mission has brought us to where we are today."

In founding Stonyfield Farm, "we were creating a category," Hirshberg explains, noting that it took nine years to make a profit. "If you're creating a category, you've got at least twice the marketing costs of someone who joins the category once it exists." He's referring to what brand analysts call predatory second-to-market competitors, who try to knock off category innovators. Success often goes to the company with the most marketing muscle, not necessarily the best or most innovative product.

To emphasize the point, Hirshberg continues, "Being first is not always an advantage. I always say a pioneer is someone who is facedown in the mud with an arrow in the back."

Sustainability = loyalty = word of mouth.

From the beginning, Stonyfield Farm has made its social mission a vital part of its world and image. It donates 10 percent of its profits "to organizations and projects that work to protect and restore the Earth," its Web site states, listing literally hundreds of organizations it has assisted over the years.

Stonyfield Farm has been very active in children's nutritional issues with its Good2Go and Menu for Change programs, and between 2003 and 2005 the company placed healthy vending machines in schools across the country until it was overwhelmed with requests and revised the program to a do-it-yourself vending machine makeover. "It all started because I had a then junior high school kid who was eating absolute crap in school," Hirshberg explains. "It horrified me. All the adults who made the decisions had surrendered to the idea that if it's healthy, kids wouldn't eat it, which is completely ridiculous."

Here again we have a social mission driving the branding agenda. Hirshberg helped the kids, which in turn helped the company's image by associating Stonyfield Farm with children's good health. And putting smoothies and squeezers into vending machines automatically introduces a whole lot of kids to Stonyfield Farm who most likely aren't getting it at home.

"Our Yo-Kids line has, at various times, been *the* yogurt for the school systems, including the New York City schools," Hirshberg explains, although it's a "tough market for us" because "invariably school systems are under fire for money." Stonyfield sometimes loses to lower bids.

The yogurt company's efforts to clean up its manufacturing act have contributed to its image as well. It maintains stringent reuse and recycling standards and in 1997 became the first US manufacturer to offset 100 percent of CO_2 from its facility energy use. Back in 1997, "it wasn't a distinct advantage. It was just the right thing to do," Hirshberg says of the emissions offsets. "People thought I was crazy. Now everyone's talking about it."

Measuring the business payback of sustainability.

The payback of sustainability in Stonyfield's case has been substantial. For example, from 1995 to 2005 Stonyfield Farm reduced facility energy use and the associated CO_2 emissions per pound of product by one-third, saving more than $1.7 million. Reducing packaging and converting from plastic to foil lids have also saved hundreds of thousands of dollars.

"The consumer payback on incorporating sustainability can be a little bit intangible to most people," Hirshberg explains. "But it's extremely tangible to me . . . and that's the loyalty you get, which fuels word of mouth."

Nevertheless, this is "hard to concretize it in a temporal sense," he says, the growth is "much more likely to show up in longer-term trends" than in a direct burst of business due to any specific sustainable action or campaign.

"What I can tell you is that we are in our nineteenth consecutive year of over 24 percent compounded annual growth rate . . . and the yogurt category in the same period has grown 3 percent."

Gary Hirshberg: Eco-capitalist among eco-capitalists.

Erik Drake remembers the first time he saw Gary Hirshberg while a student at the University of Michigan Ross School of Business. "He's an amazing public speaker — very captivating. He was speaking to five hundred students [at the business school] and four of them ended up working for Stonyfield."

"He's a very real person," Drake continues. "He doesn't edit himself — he says what he believes. If we could get Gary to talk to each one of our consumers, there would be no more Yoplait out there." Yoplait is the company's chief competitor.

Stonyfield gets a steady flow of publicity in the press, Drake explains, because "if there is something in the news about organics, they'll reach for Gary as a reliable source who will say what he believes and is passionate. The core of who we are goes back to that passion." *BusinessWeek* describes Hirshberg as the "industry's philosopher king."

This constant source of publicity has helped Hirshberg maintain what he feels is "a very intimate connection to our consumers" — something that also comes from the prominently displayed letter from Hirshberg to the consumers on the homepage of Stonyfield Farm's Web site. The fact that every cup of Stonyfield Farm yogurt bears Hirshberg's signature has also helped," says Drake.

"We are saying that we are personally responsible for our product. And you as a consumer can trust that there are actually real people here making this stuff."

Selling with a personal connection.

In the beginning, Stonyfield Farm's marketing technique consisted of Hirshberg and Kaymen standing in the aisles at grocery stores, cajoling shoppers into sampling the product. The method seemed to work, at least when it came to spreading the word about Stonyfield Farm locally; the target customer at that time was "anyone within twenty miles who liked the taste of our yogurt," says Drake.

"We've always believed in grassroots efforts — opportunities where we can have a one-on-one connection," Drake continues. "Organic isn't sold with a slogan, it's sold with a handshake . . . We have a deeper story . . . We need more quality interaction with the consumer to drive the difference. We have to explain why we are paying a premium to make the product and why they should be paying a premium to buy it."

Of course, as the company grows larger, it is increasingly more difficult to have that "one-on-one ten-minute conversation with every consumer," Drake says. The company is obliged to tell its story other ways. "A lot of our efforts are about telling that story, whether it's through event marketing, the Web, through PR. We get the message to people by telling our story."

"We've done some mass media," he continues, "Some regional TV, some print. But at the end of the day, we won't have the marketing budget of our competitors, because so much of our resources goes into buying ingredients." The good news according to Drake? "If you're making a great product, you don't have to spend a lot of money on marketing."

The Yo-competition.

Stonyfield Farm is now the number-three yogurt maker in the United States, after Yoplait and Dannon. "There's a big jump from Dannon to Stonyfield," says Drake. "But we're always trying to make that gap smaller." As a point of clarification, Stonyfield is number three to Dannon, the product, not Groupe Danone, its parent. Because Stonyfield and Dannon are both owned by Groupe Danone, Stonyfield Farm finds itself competing against its corporate sister.

In the organic world, Stonyfield Farm is not only number one, it is king. The company is four times larger than all of its organic competitors combined. The two largest competitors are Horizon and Wallaby.

High on the Whole Foods wave.

After growing up in "local smaller supermarkets," Stonyfield Farm "rode the wave with the growth of Whole Foods and Wild Oats," Drake says.

"It acts as a badge of acceptance when your product is in those stores," he explains. "Having a presence in Whole Foods makes a consumer who may not have heard about us try us out. They trust Whole Foods, so they trust us. It helps consumers understand what we're all about." And that works both ways, he says. When consumers go to Whole Foods in search of Stonyfield Farm product, Whole Foods naturally benefits.

Stonyfield Farm sales have grown further as more traditional grocery stores, expanding their offerings into natural and organic, look to the shelves of Whole Foods and Wild Oats when deciding what it is they should offer. Marketers would describe Stonyfield Farm as an icon brand representing an entire category, in the same way that the Prius is an icon brand among fuel-efficient cars.

Adjusting to a more mainstream clientele.

As Stonyfield Farm has grown, so, too, have the tastes of its customers. Gone are the days of servicing only those craving high-fat plain yogurt. "You almost have to be a foodie to appreciate that," says Drake. "It's delicious, but it's not what the whole country's grown up on. Many more people were introduced to yogurt in small cups with high sweetener levels, with fruit on the bottom. We have to deliver on their taste buds."

"We've always tried to have a very diverse group of products for a company our size," Drake continues. "We need to be close to our core consumers, who go more for the plain varieties, as well as to a broader audience that's looking at broader diversity . . . We strive to meet the needs of both types of consumers."

In terms of message crafting, the company has always looked for "a simple and positive way to explain organic," says Drake. "Yes, organics means no hormones, no antibiotics, no toxic, persistent pesticides. But it is also the probiotic cultures, being a great ingredient for cooking . . . that's a message that people can absorb."

The next frontier for marketing Stonyfield Farm is the club stores such as Costco. According to Drake, customers at these stores began asking for the Stonyfield Farm product quite some time ago. "For the last four or five years, we've had great success with the club channel," he says. There's also been "a lot of growth with Wal-Mart. Every year we double our sales there. Wal-Mart will play a big part [in the organics and sustainable goods market] in the future."

The climb to all-organic.

Stonyfield Farm has not always been an all-organic label. According to Drake, the company was organic "on day one" but soon had to go to "natural product" due to the lack of sufficient organic milk supply. After twelve years of manufacturing all natural, the company began introducing some all-organic product again, and by the mid-1990s it was 85 percent organic. With the onset of the organic milk shortage in the early 2000s, organic content was cut back, dropping below the 85 percent level until it was finally brought up to 100 percent organic in October 2007.

The USDA's organic certification system includes various levels of organic. The topmost is 100 percent organic, made with 100 percent organic ingredients. The next highest ranking is organic, made with at least 95 percent organic ingredients, with strict restrictions on the remaining 5 percent. Today all Stonyfield products are organic.

According to Sarah Badger, communications associate at Stonyfield Farm, "Organic farming has long been associated with the ideal, pro-sustainable goal of purchasing locally grown food products. Yet that ideal is hardly possible given the explosion in the interest in organic food. Many organic food companies, including Stonyfield Farm, import some ingredients from global sources due to a lack of adequate domestic sources to meet the demands of a growing organic market. We also use the sound business practice of multiple sources to ensure an adequate supply year-round and to avoid the potential calamity of drought or other weather-related crop failure with one supplier in one location."

She continues, "While all of the organic milk Stonyfield purchases annually comes from family farmers in the United States, other ingredients are sourced outside the US. Stonyfield sources over two hundred million pounds of organic ingredients annually — fruit, sweeteners, grains, spices, et cetera. Those ingredients annually support over fifty thousand acres of organic production. Stonyfield always sources locally in the US first, but some ingredients like organic cocoa, banana, and vanilla do not grow in the US, so Stonyfield imports them. Only a small amount of organic sugar is grown in the US, so virtually all organic food companies import organic sugar."

As for the local versus organic debate, a lot of discussion on this issue stems from concern over the climate footprint, a concept Hirshberg himself studied back in the 1970s. However, in some cases, local sourcing can result in a bigger footprint — in other words, a larger adverse impact on the environment — than sourcing from greater distances. For example, a truck with a fuller load of product traveling a greater distance can be greener than a half-full truck traveling a shorter route.

Explosion in organics: A dream come true . . . or not?

"The explosion of organic is my life's dream come true," says Hirshberg. "If you'd asked me ten years ago, would I ever expect to see an organic Raisin Bran on the shelves, I would have laughed at you." Now there's a rush of "organic private-label coming. Safeway, Trader Joe's, Tesco will do a private-label organic line. Kroeger will do a private-label organic line."

"Of course, some of my friends are horrified," he continues. "The fear is that large companies with lots of purchasing power and lots of money to spend on marketing will dilute the standards. And that's not a bad thing to fear. It's for us to keep our eyes on the ball." Which, as I've noted in an earlier chapter, is something that Dr. Bronner's grandsons are doing.

Hirshberg explains that the present situation makes it imperative for the industry to maintain strict standards. "The organic food industry is the only industry to fight for more regulations," he says. "We can't let the word *organic* become as meaningless as the word *natural* has become."

Increased demand stresses the market.

In many cases, it is becoming increasingly difficult to find organic ingredients, *BusinessWeek* noting that such shortages have in the past forced Hirshberg to cut the percentage of organic products in his line.

"Dairy producers estimate that demand for organic milk is at least twice the current available supply," at a time when "the number of dairy farms has shrunk to 60,000 from 334,000 in 1980," *BusinessWeek* states. "And almost half the milk produced in the US comes from [nonorganic] farms with more than 500 cows, something organic advocates rarely support." Organic dairy farmers can actually reduce herd size while maintaining profits precisely because they are earning a premium price for organic milk.

Differentiating in an organic world.

Gary Hirshberg and others like him, are now finding themselves faced with the question of how to differentiate their products in an increasingly organic world where prices are going down and private labels are coming on. "Organic is a model for a new type of agriculture in the US, but to many, organic is really just the absence of negatives," Hirshberg says. "It's an increasingly difficult brand proposition. It's the reason a lot of people come to organic, but it's not the reason they're going to stay with us."

So how does a company like Stonyfield Farm differentiate itself, especially when its commitment to family farmers means it cannot drop its purchase prices? Well, first of all, the yogurt has to taste better than its competitors, Hirshberg says. And aside from that, "We have to be damn sure that we're communicating that authenticity to the consumer."

"It's essential that you are honest, that you're factually correct. You're pulling a superiority pitch [with organic], where you're inviting the consumer to trust you. And if you breach that trust with an exaggeration of the truth, then it's game over."

"If we continue to overdeliver on the consumer's expectation with a 360-degree commitment not only to sustainability, but also to a superior product proposition, then these are the things that really add up," Hirshberg continues. "We're fueling the word-of-mouth machinery."

The *360-degree commitment to sustainability* is a phrase that Hirshberg uses often, and it peppers the company's literature and Web site. "Organic is just one aspect to sustainability. How we treat the waste in our plant, how we derive our energy, how we reduce our carbon footprint, the hundreds of things we do, provides credibility as to our authenticity. That will keep a lot of consumers coming our way," he says.

Just like many other firms across the Gort universe, Stonyfield Farm is partnering with like-minded companies and institutions in other clusters. Specifically, Stonyfield has entered into collaboration with TerraCycle, a maker of household cleaning and garden products created from and packaged in trash. In this program, used yogurt containers are collected and shipped to Trenton, where TerraCycle is using them as material for planting pots. TerraCycle will then sell the pots to large retailers, which can use them in their gardening sections. It's one more example of Stonyfield's 360-degree commitment.

Crafting a fit with a new corporate parent.

Between 2001 and 2003, Groupe Danone, a $17 billion European conglomerate, purchased approximately 85 percent of Stonyfield Farm. Among its many brands is Dannon Yogurt. Hirshberg's motivation for the sale was, in part, to allow his product to reach a larger market. As he recently told *BusinessWeek*, "The only way to influence the powerful forces in this industry is to become a powerful force."

"In Groupe Danone, we've found a partner that provides cost-saving efficiencies and growth opportunities, while allowing us to manage ourselves autonomously and remain true to our mission," he went on. The parent "brought a lot of new knowledge and talent to our company . . . helping us manage our rapid growth by sharing their expertise in food research, production, operations, logistics and distribution."

Hirshberg has been fortunate in that the conglomerate has seen no need to make any management changes. "We have a unique partnership," Hirshberg says. "They made no changes to our company's environmental and social missions." According to the Stonyfield Farm Web site, "We still use the very best environmental practices we can find. And we're still as committed as ever to increasing the number of organic family farms in the world."

Yet purchase by Danone has put pressure on Hirshberg. According to *BusinessWeek*, the way the agreement is set up, in order to "retain management control he has to keep Stonyfield Farm growing at double-digit rates."

SUMMARY: SUCCESS ON THE LONG MARCH

Stonyfield Farm, Ben & Jerry's, and Green Mountain Coffee Roasters have each built their business on the growing awareness of and demand for healthy food products. The companies have grown exponentially because they also invest heavily in corporate social responsibility programs, which become the anchor of many of their seasonal marketing and product development campaigns. All three were early adopters, embracing social responsibility and environmental business practices, which has paid off over time. They are now considered the real thing with intense brand loyalty, having weathered the ups and downs of a highly competitive market and, in the case of Stonyfield Farm and Ben & Jerry's, the demands of corporate parents.

The interconnected green community is also well aware of Stonyfield's and Ben & Jerry's good works — and those of Green Mountain Coffee to a lesser extent. All three reach out to this community through their Web sites, e-mail blasts, in-store communications, and stories about customer and vendor experiences. When there's news to report, they often include their NGO and social activist partners, which in turn become stories broadcast by the green news organizations and food bloggers. While there is no conscious exploitation of the Gort Cloud, messages from these companies move around quickly and fluidly — generally more quickly than within traditional media with its limited space and need to serve a broader audience.

Sustainable Living

Interface Inc. and YOLO Colorhouse

THE CHALLENGE

Paint and carpet are not the first things that spring to mind when it comes to environmentally friendly products. Paint, after all, comes from chemical companies and has long been a pollutant from one end of its life cycle to the other. Carpet often uses toxic glues and petroleum-based fibers and represents a huge portion of unreclaimed urban waste.

Two companies, one from each of these industries, are bucking the trend. Interface, the giant carpet maker, is setting an eco-friendly example for the textile, carpet, and furnishings industry. YOLO Colorhouse is mixing up a fresh palette with paints that don't stink up the home and poison the lungs.

How are these companies using sustainability to differentiate and create share in an impossibly competitive, price-sensitive market?

THE SOLUTION

Each of these companies has created innovative products that also differentiate through good looks and environmental performance. So, in addition to a green pedigree, these firms make products that meet the desires of the design community.

They actively partner with architects, designers, builders, and the eco-aware within the Gort Cloud's green community to increase awareness and build sales channels.

They benefit from the USGBC's sustainable building program by contributing to LEED credits. A choice of their products adds to LEED certification of homes and businesses and thereby enhances the value of those building projects.

In the case of Interface, the company benefits from the tireless efforts of CEO Ray Anderson to use his personal awakening to motivate other corporate leaders to follow his example.

Interface Inc.: A Traditional, Conservative, For-Profit Company Leads an Eco-Revolution

The United States supplies nearly 45 percent of the world's carpet, most manufactured in the Southeast, a region where textile and furniture mills have long dotted the landscape and have often scarred it. One company that has reversed this trend and now has a goal to reach a zero environmental footprint and to eventually be "restorative" is Interface Inc. Chairman Ray Anderson founded the company in 1973 in LaGrange, Georgia, when he saw the opportunity to manufacture and distribute carpet tiles for what was then the emerging "modern office."

The carpet tile idea is simple. Instead of tearing up all the carpet when one area is worn, you can replace sections. Carpet tiles are much simpler to transport and install with a smaller number of workers. Cutting and piecing are also easier without those giant rolls. The concept was initially developed by Heuga Home Flooring of Holland. Ray brought it to America by way of England.

"It just seemed like efficiency . . . efficiency is good," Anderson says of the modular concept. "And it sold."

In the thirty-five years since, the company has become the world's leading producer of soft-surfaced modular floor coverings. Acquiring close to fifty companies along the way, Interface now works under an umbrella that includes the Heuga and Bentley Prince Street labels. The flagship carpet tile company, now branded as InterfaceFLOR, is now the only part of the company in LaGrange. A spin-off residential carpet tile division, FLOR, was founded in Elmhurst, Illinois, in 2003. In all its forms, Interface maintains manufacturing locations on four continents and offices in more than a hundred countries.

In the early years, Anderson was about as far from an environmentalist as he could possibly be. He had no concept whatsoever of the environmental damage his company was causing with its manufacturing processes. Ray has since described himself as a recovering "plunderer of the earth."

He also didn't realize that modular tile was, in fact, a very eco-friendly concept. He had moved the country a step toward sustainability without even knowing it.

The changing floorscape.

The global carpet industry shipped 2,057 billion square yards of product in 2005. Nearly 45 percent of that was supplied by the United States, 80 percent of it coming from the state of Georgia, where the four largest carpet companies are headquartered. Shaw of Dalton, Georgia, owned by Warren Buffett, is by far the biggest, followed by Mohawk in Kennesaw, Georgia; Templeton in Dalton; and then Interface, headquartered in Atlanta.

According to Joyce LaValle, InterfaceFLOR's senior vice president of marketing, Interface doesn't take a whole lot of stock of where it is in the carpet business pecking order because it considers itself to be in a separate category.

"To measure our progress, we only look where we compete," LaValle says. "The other big companies are primarily in residential, in broadloom. They are a hundred times more in that industry than they are in modular."

That's not to say that the competition isn't growing. Many companies are launching modular divisions because they see it as the future. "They're all way behind us in terms of volume," says LaValle. "They entered the market way after we created it."

For many years, Interface made product solely for commercial space. But due to a downturn in the flooring business in 2000, the company was forced to diversify to keep itself afloat. "Today, instead of 100 percent of our business being in corporate America, now 50 percent of our business is in corporate America and 50 percent of our business is in other segments," LaValle explains, pointing to the home, educational, retail, hospital/medical, and hospitality markets.

"We have hotels buying our product that never would have looked at carpet tiles before."

Alone in the global arena.

Interface is the only company that manufactures carpet internationally. "The reason it makes sense to us is that we're into modular goods," LaValle says, noting that the firm is now looking to build a plant in China. "That would be solely for the Chinese market," she explains. "It doesn't make sense to manufacture and then ship carpet globally because you can't overcome the freight costs."

LaValle attributes the company's global growth to the multinationals on its client list. "If you're doing the carpeting for a Citigroup or a Goldman Sachs, they have offices all over the world. Our expansion is about customer satisfaction."

Building a market from scratch.

In 2003, InterfaceFLOR introduced carpet tiles for the home through its new FLOR brand and packaged it in do-it-yourself kits. "We've been creating a brand from absolute scratch," LaValle says.

"Carpet tiles are the fastest-growing segment of the residential soft floor covering market. It's taking more and more market share away from broadloom. And that's because carpet tile looks better than it ever looked. People think of it as a smarter, better way to cover the floor." Although LaValle believes that the growing environmental consciousness has factored into the success of FLOR, "what plays is 'smart,'" she says. "It makes more sense from a financial standpoint" because it is easily shipped and easily moved and reused.

"We were looking to segment our business," she says of the decision to go into the home market. "For many years we'd have architects and interior designers asking, 'Can I have some for my house?' And then you had a lot of people moving into lofts, people more design-driven, people thinking they wanted to do it themselves and being involved in design."

"So our strategy was to really go after this key group of people who are real influencers, who could 'get' carpet tile in the house. It could be graphic designers, anyone who has an interest in design as a subject — young, hip, professional people who have a sense of taste."

To attract this market, Interface focused on Web strategies. "Because it was a carpet tile, for the first time people were able to go online and in forty-eight hours it was delivered to their home in a box, and they would be able to put it on the floor. From the design standpoint, they could shift things around and move color" — a reference to the ability to make custom designs with different tile colors and textures, just as you can do with vinyl, ceramic, and stone floor tiles.

The FLOR brand has caught on very quickly despite the fact that "we advertised very little," LaValle notes. It relies mostly on PR and appearances at trade and home shows, where the product is well received. When customers see it on the exhibit floor "it looks fabulous."

"Once you capture the early movers — the people with design interest or education — then you move to the next level, which is just people with good taste," LaValle says. Recently, Martha Stewart joined with Interface to create a Martha Stewart line of modular carpets. Says LaValle, "She's going into KB Homes with it."

Ray Anderson: A change of heart, a change of course.

When the history of the Age of Sustainability is written, Ray Anderson will no doubt go down as one of its pioneers.

Anderson is one of the most influential role models anywhere for corporate America and has solidified the Interface brand around this image. He has been successful in influencing others to go green because corporate executives see him as one of them. He is determined to make Interface "the first company that, by its deeds, shows the entire industrial world what sustainability is in all of its dimensions: people, process, product, place, and profits." Anderson is now in his seventies, and his wisdom, southern charm, keen perspective, and tremendous communication skills have kept him going stronger than ever in his quest to climb what he calls Mount Sustainability.

The conscious phase of Anderson's career began in 1994, when he had what he refers to as his "environmental awakening" at the age of sixty.

That's "when we began to hear questions from our customers we'd never heard before, especially from interior designers and architects," says Anderson. "The question was, 'What's your company doing for the environment?' And we had no answers. And the company was twenty-one years old at the time. And I for one had never given one thought to what we were doing to the environment, or for the environment . . . you know . . . nothing."

"We're a very customer-intimate company, and we felt obliged to find some answers for our sales force. So a group of us said maybe we ought to create a task force, and bring people from our businesses around the world, and get them all together, and see what we're doing."

It was decided that Anderson should speak at the task force conference about his environmental vision. "Well, hell, I didn't have an environmental vision," he says. "I started to sweat because I could not get beyond 'we obey the law.' That was my environmental vision. Compliance.

"So, it's a week or so before the appointed day. I have not a clue as to what I'm going to say and I'm really sweating. At that propitious moment, Paul Hawken's book *The Ecology of Commerce* lands on my desk. It was sent to me by Joyce LaValle."

"I got it from my daughter," LaValle says. "She'd been one of those kids who was just wired" into environmental issues.

Ray says, "It was like a spear in the chest. I got it in a heartbeat."

"It was just like the book was put there by the hand of God," he continues. "I had no idea what it was about, who Hawken was. I just picked it up and started thumbing it and on page nineteen, I came to a chapter heading 'The Death of Birth.' That's an arresting chapter heading. I began to read, and I quickly found out."

Ivan Handler, a founder of the Third Wave Study Group, describes the chapter this way: "'The Death of Birth' refers to the enormous extinction rate now occurring and explains the fearful consequences of exceeding the carrying capacity of the biosphere. Here as with the rest of the book, Hawken attempts to bridge the gap between environmentalists and business people by pointing out that finding a solution to this crisis is in everyone's interest. Good environmental policy, in other words, is also optimal business policy. However, Hawken also insists that the current structure of the world's industrial economy is what pits business against the environment. Changing this structure is really what this book is about."[1] Paul Hawken is a founder of Smith & Hawken gardening supplies and is both a successful entrepreneur and an environmentalist.

Anderson was especially struck by Hawken's point that the "biggest culprit" in the decline of "the living systems and the life support systems of earth" is "the industrial system."

"There's only one institution on earth that's big enough, and powerful enough, and wealthy enough, and influential enough, and pervasive enough to really change all that and that's the one that's also doing the greatest damage — the corporations. The internationals. That's my institution . . . so the spear went deeper," Anderson says.

Toward a restorative company.

"I really just stunned this task force," Anderson says of his address to the group of Interface employees who had gathered together. "These people met for two days and their heads were spinning." It was felt that "if we could get a really clear idea of what sustainability is for our company, we might influence somebody else to go in that direction, too. And that's how we become restorative, not just through what we do, but what we influence others to do. So that's been our mission now for fourteen years, to become a restorative company."

A transition to sustainable business practices by corporate America is the single most important change needed to address the environmental crises. That Anderson took on this task before many others is particularly notable.

Under Anderson's leadership, Interface began to transform. It

- Eliminated toxic substances in its manufacturing,
- Began to use renewable energy and recycled materials,
- Transitioned to resource-efficient transportation,
- Redesigned commerce to create new business models, and
- Created a healthier corporate culture.

"The business case (for moving toward sustainability) is crystal clear," says Anderson. "Cumulatively we can show $353 million of cost savings over the years, more than paying for all of the rest of the effort. Our products are the best they've ever been. And it's made all the difference in the world in product design."

Influencing fellow CEOs.

Anderson, seeing a great need, began to spread his message about his conversion to sustainability and how it had brought so much in savings.

Anderson notes that to be an early mover is not always easy — many of his colleagues questioned his sanity. "I had my chief competitor, so help me, ten years ago, look me in the eye and say, 'Well, you're a dreamer.' And since then he's been retired by his company, and his company is scrambling to catch up. We left them in the dust. And, of course, it feels wonderful to realize the competitive advantage out of doing the right thing."

Whether the market is the public at large or corporate buyers, Anderson believes there's a lot to be said about portraying a corporation as responsible. Citing Wal-Mart as an example, he remembers when the company's CEO, Lee Scott, told him going green was "the smartest thing we ever did. Because people just galvanized around this initiative."

"Anytime a paradigm shifts, early movers win," Anderson explains. "And the earliest of the early movers win the biggest," he adds. That's what's happening right now.

Differentiating with a higher purpose.

The Interface move toward sustainability "has helped immensely as a brand differentiator. It's not only the thumb that goes down on the scale of decision making, it's the whole arm," Anderson says.

"It's become a cliché, doing well by doing good, but it's real. There's a positive feedback loop there . . . the more well you do, the more good you can do . . . the more good you do, the more well you can do . . . and it builds and builds and builds."

"The galvanizing effect on people is just amazing," he continues. "At the top of this hierarchy of human needs is this thing for self-actualization, and that translates into higher purpose. So you've got people galvanized around a shared higher purpose. You can't beat it for bringing people together to climb the mountain. This has helped with all stakeholders. The goodwill in the marketplace is just astonishing."

Targeting green-aware customers.

When it comes to the Interface target market, Anderson immediately identifies interior designers and architects. In fact, almost all of the company's commercial business is specified business, meaning that an architect and/or interior designer is involved in choosing the product.

"One of the things that has enabled us to have gone as far as we've gone as quickly is the fact that we're operating in a very receptive marketplace heavily influenced by interior designers and architects, the people who want to do the right thing," he says. "If they can find the companies or products that they feel make a difference, they'll specify them."

"We [found ourselves] in the business of educating the design community fourteen years ago," Joyce LaValle explains. "We brought them on board because they saw the sense of it all." As for those who didn't have the time or patience to listen, "you'd have to parcel it out little pieces at a time, and then attach it to the product. That was certainly a very laborious way, but one that probably in the long term has been successful."

"People do remember who it was who started to educate them," LaValle continues. "Our hope in those [early] days was for the architects or interior designers or end users to join the journey, because if they join the journey, in the end it's good for Interface because there's a match in value system."

Well, this is happening. A very large and vocal component of the Gort Cloud includes the green building community, spurred on by the US Green Building Council and the American Institute of Architects' green initiatives. Designers, trendspotters, bloggers on architecture, design, and building technology, as well as industry and green building news groups frequently comment on Ray Anderson's company, its products, and its good works.

The company's best marketing tool.

Ray Anderson's outreach is a "huge part" of the company's rapid expansion, according to LaValle. He is able to tap into market "segments and people we would have never touched before" because of "the power of the press," the many speeches he has made, and documentaries for which he's been an interview subject, such as *The Corporation* and Leonardo DiCaprio's *Eleventh Hour*.

Anderson brings attention to Interface with his many honors, such as his 2007 inclusion on *Time* magazine's list of "43 International Heroes of the Environment." He also makes headlines in the political arena, most recently through his work on the President's Council on Sustainable Development, which originally met during the Clinton years and as of this writing was coming together again to work on an agenda for the first hundred days under the next president. "It's vetted, it's based in deep science, and it's even been through legal," says LaValle.

"We will never know or ever understand the reach that Ray has. I can go to university campuses and it's amazing [how many] young people . . . have heard of him or are reading his book." This book, *Mid-Course Correction: Toward a Sustainable Enterprise: The Interface Model*, documents his journey from businessman and polluter to late-life awakening and environmental action.

Greening the building industry.

InterfaceFLOR contributed to the formation of the US Green Building Council in 1993 and has been heavily involved with the 13,500-member organization ever since. The USGBC created the Leadership in Energy and Environmental Design (LEED) Green Building Rating System to reward designers and builders for making the right eco-choices. It has become "the nationally accepted benchmark for the design, construction and operation of high performance green buildings," its Web site explains, giving "building owners and operators the tools they need to have an immediate and measurable impact on their buildings' performance."

The Green Building site goes on to explain that "LEED promotes a whole-building approach to sustainability by recognizing performance in five key areas of human and environmental health: sustainable site development, water savings, energy efficiency, materials selection and indoor environmental quality."

LEED buildings are going up all over the country and in forty-one countries globally. In New York City alone, the Bank of America Tower, the *New York Times* headquarters, the Hearst headquarters, the Bronx Library Center, and the visitor center at the Queens Botanical Garden in Flushing are just a few examples of many recently opened Gold and Platinum LEED-certified structures. The certification system has now expanded to include interior design accreditation and residential reward systems.

When it comes to floor covering, LEED ratings require that carpet systems meet or exceed the Carpet and Rug Institute's Green Label or Green Label Plus requirements. InterfaceFLOR receives approximately 50 percent of floor covering orders originating from LEED buildings, with the company clearly reaping the benefits of its forward-thinking practices.

Reaching the end user.

With InterfaceFLOR, the end user is generally a corporate or institutional organization. To reach that customer, the company sends account executives to meet with key management personnel. "These are mostly MBA grads," says Joyce LaValle of the Interface reps. "Our story connects with these customers because all of these companies are awakening to sustainability." Again, Interface now finds itself reaping the benefits of what it has long been sowing.

The company also relies on mass e-mails to reach its customers, sending out a blast whenever there are technological breakthroughs at Interface or other newsworthy items. "We may create new Web sites if we want to draw people to a particular place where they may learn something," LaValle says.

Smart marketing begets innovation.

The tremendous innovation that Interface has achieved has helped with marketing its products, and marketing the products has helped with more innovation. It's a continuous loop. "That's one of the ways the company has grown," says LaValle.

Take one of the latest innovations — manufacturing carpet out of recycled material. Although InterfaceFLOR has been making carpet backing from post-consumer waste for several years, "the face, the actual fluff [now made out of recycled carpet fiber] is brand new," LaValle explains. "It's extraordinary — an amazing breakthrough for us and for anyone in the carpet industry. No one's been able to take first-quality nylon and turn it into first-quality nylon again."

Where did this concept come from? InterfaceFLOR developed the new process in its R&D division, but the idea came from outside the Interface family. "Like anything else, because of our reputation, somebody on the outside who came across the technology – somebody not involved in a carpet company – made the phone call here," LaValle says. "It was someone who understood that the only company that would see value in this would be Interface. It's that halo effect in marketing, when your reputation is such that outside people know that you'd be interested."

Marketing an uncomfortably honest message.

When Ray Anderson speaks about the future, there's no sugarcoating. He simply states the truth as he sees it. "The basic economic problem is the gap between what we have and what we want, not what we need," he says. "No matter how much we have, we always want more. And that is the economic driver . . . the basic economic problem. What is wrong with this picture?"

"The whole economic system needs to be turned upside down," he continues, identifying the "two trends we're living with . . . the bad one is the decline of the biosphere, biological decline. The good trend is the growing awareness, ethical awareness. And where those two intersect is where the fate of humanity lies."

This may strike some as curious because his message seems to suggest *Consume less*, which is not typically a business message. Also, bad news is not typically considered a useful marketing message. But it seems as if Anderson can get away with it, perhaps due to his image as a man of independent thinking and common sense. The bottom line is that Interface appears to have benefited from his public warnings.

Mission Zero: A repositioning effort.

A few years ago, it was decided that brand repositioning and alignment were needed because "Interface appeared across the world in disparate ways," LaValle says. This rebranding effort resulted in the "journey to the top of Mount Sustainability" concept as well as the journey to Mission Zero.

"It makes a big difference from a marketing standpoint," LaValle goes on. "Mission Zero is the marketing emblem that appears on everything that's Interface. So it's a little bit about coming out of the closet and saying to the world, *This is our journey*." States the Interface Web site, "What we call the next industrial revolution is a momentous shift in how we see the world, how we operate within it, what systems will prevail and which will not. At Interface, we are completely re-imagining and redesigning everything we do, including the way we define our business. Our vision is to lead the way to the next industrial revolution by becoming the first sustainable corporation, and eventually a restorative enterprise."

The company is now designing www.missionzero.com, hoping it will become a destination site around which a social network will form, becoming a holding spot for dialogue about Mission Zero. Says LaValle, "It will be the place people go to learn talk, argue, discuss" sustainability and will "encourage others to join us in the mission."

The Interface name will most likely be left out of the Mission Zero site to keep the information neutral. "We hope to build it as a legacy," she continues. "So it's different than marketing. More about reputation and the halo effect that it creates."

YOLO Colorhouse: An Entry-Level Product for the Green Home Improvement Crowd

YOLO Colorhouse is a growing Portland, Oregon, firm that strives to supply artist-designed house paint colors with virtually none of the toxicity of paints past. It is housed in a southeast district warehouse taking up ever more floors as it ships paint out to a growing number of customers in the United States.

"We're an entry-level product to the green building world," says cofounder Virginia Young. "It acts like other paint, and it's pretty and beautiful and relatively inexpensive in the remodeling process . . . the building process . . . so it's an easy one for people to get on board with."

YOLO Colorhouse was founded by Young and Janie Lowe in 2005. The paint is distributed primarily by green decorating and home improvement stores such as Livingreen, which has outlets in Culver City and Santa Barbara, California. "When we started two years ago, there were just a handful of [these green] stores across the country, maybe twenty," Lowe explains. Today "there's more than 130," in all the places you'd expect to find them, plus "in surprising places, too."

Promoting paint that doesn't stink.

When conventional paint is applied, it emits a breathable gas accompanied by an unpleasant odor coming mostly from the high levels of solvents, or volatile organic compounds (VOCs), that are required to give the product its consistency, viscosity, and durability.

We thought we were rid of unhealthful paint when lead was outlawed, but the problem has persisted in both oil-based and water-based paint.

Paint cleanup adds to the problem, as it often requires toxic solvents that release additional VOC pollutants. These solvents have been proven to diminish regional air quality, can be detrimental to health as an indoor pollutant, and are thought to be contributors to the depletion of the ozone layer. Alternative manufacturing techniques have allowed the development of low- and zero-VOC paints that are virtually odor-free. There are even natural paints made from milk protein, clay, lime, and earth pigments that avoid the toxic chemical issue altogether, but application and performance offer significant challenges.

So, while many states have mandated cleaner paint and the industry is responding, public awareness of the risks has created an opportunity for small green paint makers, like YOLO Colorhouse, Mythic Paint, Best Paint, and others, to go toe-to-toe with Benjamin Moore, Sherwin-Williams, and the other chemical coating makers. And it's not just paint. There's a growing list of green building materials makers — offering everything from denim insulation to bamboo flooring — that are carving out niche markets where the big boys once dominated.

As green as it gets.

Virginia Young and Janie Lowe, the YO and LO of YOLO, understand color theory. Self-described color nerds, they are both trained artists. They met in New York City when Lowe was doing her graduate studies at the School of Visual Arts and Young was an art director for J. Walter Thompson.

"We just got a little sick of the grind," Young says of their move from New York to Portland. "We're campers and skiers, bikers and hikers. We moved to Portland because we wanted some quality of life." And in the process, Virginia and Janie may have unwittingly joined a burgeoning green movement in the "People's Republic of Portland," as local residents mockingly refer to themselves.

In 1996, the women founded YOLO Paint, a custom paint and plaster finishes company. They worked with designers, architects, and homeowners and became known for doing custom color mixing on the site.

"We know that color is relative," continues Young, "and it depends on what space you're in, and it depends on the light, and it depends on a lot of things. So we would go with our colors and paint right there on site . . . put it up and tweak it if we needed to, one way or the other." When the color worked well, harmonizing with other colors, it would become part of the YOLO Paint palette.

The women enjoyed their work, but there was a cost. "Our throats would be sore at the end of the day and we'd get grumpy," says Lowe. "Just that indoor air quality and the fumes from the paint were so bad, we started looking into what was in that paint. Once you know too much, it's like you can't turn back and keep using that stuff."

"So we thought, 'Let's take this color palette we've developed, and this idea about a healthier paint, and see what happens if we combine the two.'" YOLO Paint became YOLO Colorhouse.

Cultivating a green, upscale core audience.

YOLO Colorhouse knows its audience. It brands itself sophisticated for a customer who is design-savvy. And unlike Martha Stewart, who skews her branded paint toward women, or Ralph Lauren, who skews his paint toward the fashion-conscious, YOLO speaks intelligently about color to home designers and decorators.

The label on the YOLO cans has a no-nonsense, informational quality about it. A handwritten scrawl in what looks like penmanship from centuries ago reads, CREATED BY SCIENTISTS AND ARTISTS WITH NATURE IN MIND.

The interior color palette is broken into families — Air, Grain, Leaf, Water, Stone, Clay, and Petal — and is "organized to reflect how the eye sees color in the landscape, reflecting the natural surroundings that have inspired humans since time began." This is part design, to reflect the culture of the sustainable market, but also a necessity, because some human-made saturated colors will contain toxic coloring compounds such as cadmium, chromium, and lead. In turn these toxic compounds must be held in liquid solution with even more toxic compounds like dibutyl and diethyl phthalate, mercury, formaldehyde, benzene, and other petrochemicals. Nasty stuff.

Nevertheless, YOLO is struggling with its earth-friendly identity. "On the one hand, we're catering to this independent green market, and part

of being green is really supporting that small business. At the same time
... to really touch the masses and to educate them more quickly, it would
be better to go into the Home Depot," Lowe says, explaining that attain-
ing this balance "is a little hard for us. It's about being able to support
these green dealers while still serving a bigger market."

The solution, at least for now, is that YOLO will continue to launch
new products through the green stores and then serve the wider audiences with products that have already been tested in the marketplace.

A woman's place is in the paint store.

When it comes to homes, and very often in workplaces, too, women
choose paint. YOLO has conducted studies with all-women focus groups
where the Colorhouse paint was preference-tested against that of other
manufacturers.

"The women were drawn to our packaging," explains Young. "They
felt like they were being treated like intelligent people who could make
a wise choice. We respected them, and that's exactly what we wanted to
come across. Good taste, good design."

It is women "who usually choose the bulk of color," explains Lowe
regarding the all-women study. They're the ones who seem to love the
fact that with YOLO product, "you can literally paint a room, sleep in it
the same night, and not smell a thing," says Young.

This plays into YOLO's attraction to young mothers hoping to protect
their children from environmental damage. They've also introduced
Little YOLO, a line of paint for children's rooms, reinforcing their brand
image as child-friendly. The tagline the company is using for this product is, "Created by artists and scientists with Little People in Mind."

"We're trying to grow as fast as we can because the market [for zero-
VOC] has become a lot more crowded," Lowe says.

"I think there are two things that differentiate us," she continues. First,
"it's the authenticity that our whole brand is built on this idea. We don't
have fifty other paints that *do* have VOCs. We have one, and it doesn't.
And the other differentiator is the color."

A shade of difference.

YOLO differentiates with colors. It does so not only by offering colors that are very distinct, but also by offering so few of them. Its narrow "artist-selected palette" differentiates the company from other paint manufacturers, low-VOC or not.

During the recent development of the company's first exterior paint line, Lowe and Young tested and retested the colors on a shed in their North Portland backyard. "You have to see color outside. You have to see it in context," Lowe explains. "We put the color up on all sides of the little shed to see how it changed throughout the day. Then we mixed trim colors to harmonize."

"I don't think other big companies are going outside and putting their paints on the wall and tweaking them. I think that color really differentiates us."

YOLO makes it a habit to set the trends in color rather than to follow them. "We're always observing color," adds Young, noting that the founders are both members of the Color Marketing Group, an organization of color professionals from all over the world who set color trends.

"We like to think of ourselves as a little bit ahead in pushing the consumers rather than following the trends more," says Lowe of YOLO. "We think about what's next" in color, as well as "how we can go even cleaner and greener with our paint formula."

"We pull them in with beauty and then say, by the way, this is going to be better for you and your family. As artists, we believe environmentally responsible products can offer good design."

Networking in the development phase.

Hoping to leave the fume headaches of their original business behind and seeing a need for color design in the green space, Janie and Virginia hooked up with the green building community in Portland and elsewhere. They began to experiment, making paint with "old recipes," as Lowe calls it. They worked with clay, even collecting it from road cuts in the Painted Hills of central Oregon.

"We created a clay-striped wall in our studio," says Young. "It pays homage to the beautiful colors of the earth." Lowe adds, "We started making small batches of clay paints and plasters and using those for our jobs, which was not at all economical."

Lowe and Young's contacts in the green building community eventually became an important marketing outlet, serving as their first customer base. One example is their partnership with the architect Michelle Kaufmann, featured earlier in this book.

Creating a thoroughly custom look designed by artists.

By the time they launched YOLO, Young and Lowe had forty core colors, all of them evocative. The Earth's Color Collection palette is based on natural elements, from earth to foliage, and includes colors designed to work together. Since launch, the company has added three or four colors every spring.

YOLO has further built up the sophisticated nature of its brand by offering design kits with samples that are actually painted onto the paper. This further reinforces the identification of the paint product with the artist founders. The poster-sized sample sheets are created in an enormous warehouse basement space just across the street from company headquarters in southeast Portland. They're cut from long rolls of paintable wallpaper, which are stretched down the length of hundred-foot tables and rolled out with paint.

With these unique samples, YOLO has found another way to brand itself as custom and, more than that, as conscientious. The samples tell consumers that YOLO is ready and willing to help them get exactly the color they want and exactly the color they need. Repositionable tape on the back of the posters enables the customer to move the color samples from wall to wall, room to room — without ever using a brush. As the YOLO literature claims, "No more discarded sample quarts of paint cluttering up the garage and creating a disposal problem. No more walls with patches of sampled paint to have to deal with at a later date. And no more tiny color chips printed in ink."

And the posters can be "reused as wrapping paper, art paper, party hats . . . use your imagination."

A focused marketing budget.

YOLO spends little money on traditional advertising. What advertising it does is "precious advertising," meaning that it's restricted to business-to-business paint dealer publications.

The firm has also made an effort to market itself directly to architects, builders, facility managers, NGOs, and student designers by appearing at the Greenbuild Expo, "the world's largest conference and expo dedicated to green building." Greenbuild is sponsored by the US Green Building Council. Using YOLO paints and other earth-friendly materials adds points toward LEED certification, which translates into regional tax credits and/or increased market value.

When it comes to promoting the company, nothing beats a one-on-one presentation. "We were on a schedule for a while every month where we would go to an architect's firm here in Portland and give a little twenty-minute spiel," says Young. "We need to keep doing that kind of thing."

Otherwise Young and Lowe depend on PR, employing a public relations expert who once worked in the organic food space. "She makes a lot of connections for us," explains Lowe. "She's helped us talk to the consumer in a really transparent way."

This is something that I've run across in similar interviews. The organic (or natural) food business was the pioneer in sustainable marketing. The most effective marketing and distribution tactics that other green industries now use were first tested and deployed by health food brands some ten to twenty years ago.

YOLO has received a good amount of press, with the first important article published in *Sunset* magazine in September 2005. "*Sunset* has amazing power," says Lowe. "We knew the article was coming out, so we installed three more phone lines. There were four of us here in the studio, and the phones were just ringing. And then we got four little notebooks to take the orders; and, so whenever the phone would ring, we'd run to get a notebook or slide it across the floor to each other."

All that press, she adds, "helped raise awareness, particularly with interior designers."

Expanding markets.

"The biggest motivator of going into a place like the Home Depot is to be big enough be able to impact the way the whole industry runs," says Young. "If we could be big enough that everybody has to start using [recycled] plastic cans [like ours] and everybody has to start shipping with biodiesel [trucks like ours], if everybody had to make changes in the supply chain — well that would be the ultimate goal."

And perhaps this sea change has started. All through the building and home improvement industry, upstart companies like YOLO Colorhouse are sprouting up to produce sustainable countertop materials, recycled gypsum wallboard, floor tiles made from discarded bottles, gray-water reclamation systems that reduce water consumption, and furniture made of wood waste. There are literally thousands of companies entering this industry, and each is making a name for itself in the Age of Sustainability.

SUMMARY: BUILDING MARKETS BY BUILDING GREEN

The construction and decorating industry is one of the most intensive consumers of the earth's limited resources. Interface and YOLO are examples of companies — each working in a different sector of the industry — that are incrementally making a difference. Today these two are joined by many other eco-conscious and sustainably minded manufacturers that are making money by differentiating their products from the wasteful practices of the past.

Of course, Interface and YOLO are but the tip of the iceberg when it comes to the gigantic building and decorating industry. Connecting manufacturers to distributors, designers to patrons, and new products with customers is the Gort Cloud. There are now countless clearinghouses and nexus points for building and design news, each of them connecting green consumers with sustainable brands.

Think Big or Go Home
TerraCycle

THE CHALLENGE

A Princeton University student gets the idea of making fertilizer out of worm poop using garbage as the feedstock and garbage as the packaging. Next thing you know he's dropped out of school, set up shop in a depressed area of Trenton, New Jersey, and — with gardening products only the beginning — set his sights on becoming the next Procter & Gamble, producing a wide range of household products. How does he plan to do this?

THE SOLUTION

Tom Szaky and his partners will develop a key market-entry product that performs at least as well as the dominant competitor's, without playing the green card. They will brand all of their earth-friendly products TerraCycle.

To ensure the broadest possible customer base, they keep production costs and product price as low as possible They focus only on mass-market retailers to keep quantities high with margins low. To help deliver recovered packaging for reuse, they turn schoolchildren and others into willing partners and spokespeople for the brand. To fuel a steady stream of free media exposure, they hire an army of in-house publicity agents at a fraction of the cost of a traditional advertising budget, and Tom joins the eco-capitalist speaking circuit, appearing wherever and whenever asked. When challenged by the market's leading competitor, they turn a lawsuit into a marketing advantage.

Urban renewal via worm poop.

A message is spelled out on the sides of the bridge that connects Pennsylvania to Trenton, New Jersey. Spanning from the top of the bridge to the bottom, the old and tarnished letters boast an eighty-year-old claim: TRENTON MAKES. THE WORLD TAKES.

That was true back in 1928 when Trenton was a bustling industrial town in a newly rising industrial America. But in the past forty years,

Trenton has become another casualty in industrial America's decline. It is depressed, the companies gone, the economy perpetually sour, the crime rate high. It's quite a fall from its place in history as the site of Washington's first victory in the Revolutionary War.

Now another revolution is trickling into Trenton. TerraCycle, a producer of organic fertilizer made from worm excrement and distributed in recycled containers, moved in four years ago from nearby Princeton. Housed in a compound covered with graffiti that's there by design, TerraCycle makes Trenton part of its personality, and hence its branding message, casting itself as a provider of jobs and a beacon of hope in a long-neglected city. In the company's annual summer graffiti jam the more gifted locals, as well as other graffiti artists from around the country, are invited to spray-paint every exterior surface available, spreading goodwill in all directions. This year, TerraCycle is launching a new line of graffiti-decorated ceramic pots, designed by some of the same local artists.

"Graffiti artists can have a really negative rap," explains Michael Avale, twenty-two, one of five young TerraCycle publicists. "We try to get something positive out of that . . . take something negative and turn it into good. That's how it is here at TerraCycle. Everything we use is recycled . . . We see trash as a treasure."

Turning a negative into something positive.

TerraCycle's CEO and cofounder Tom Szaky, a twenty-five-year-old Princeton dropout, says that his company will one day be the Procter & Gamble of a sustainable world. The worm poop fertilizer is just the first of a long line of products the company is planning to offer. He is positioning TerraCycle as ambitious, and he's positioned himself that way, too.

Perhaps the most interviewed of the younger generation of ecopreneurs, he is exceptionally media-friendly and has his sound bites down cold. "We have the world's first product where everything is made out of garbage," says Szaky. "This is not hyperbole. No exaggeration. We are *the* most eco-friendly consumer product in America today, period." The *New York Times* apparently agrees, calling it "the most eco-friendly product ever made."

In addition to the interviews, Szaky speaks around the country. "We get a request every two days . . . so I do a very selective number," he says. "I try to spread it around and get as many people in the company to do as many as we can handle."

It is interesting to note that at the same time Szaky brands his company as eco-friendly, he also downplays this aspect. "I don't consider myself an environmentalist," he explains. "I don't want [TerraCycle] to be considered the next Tom's of Maine or the next Seventh Generation. Their markets are the premium, forward-thinking people. That's sort of the LOHAS crowd" — a reference to Lifestyles of Health and Sustainability, a consortium of companies that, according to their Web site, are committed to "practice 'responsible capitalism' by providing goods and services using economic and environmentally sustainable business practices."

"I hope my target customer is the person who doesn't give two shits. I want my customer to be the blue-collar worker who goes and bowls at night, who lives in the Deep South," Szaky says.

"I know for a fact that the average person doesn't care," he continues. "Oh, let me rephrase. They care, but they are not willing to do a single thing about it. So if you give them a product that is cheaper, then they'll choose that. They won't spend more money on an eco-friendly product. They are the anti–Whole Foods shopper." Indeed, with Tom's audience, the drivers of preference are price and performance. Some of these customers may not care a whole lot about a company's sustainability and corporate social responsibility commitments.

TerraCycle is able to offer its product at a price below that of standard chemically based fertilizers because of the low raw material cost of making product from waste. "It's not a premium-priced item like most organic, eco-friendly products are," he explains. "That's where we really differentiate."

As opposed to most organic products, TerraCycle's Whole Foods business represents just a fraction of its overall revenue. "Our focus is Target, Home Depot, Wal-Mart, Sam's Club . . . you know, these big colossal retailers. If they agree to carry a product, then it's worth making. And because we're launching [new] products insanely fast, they're the best retailers to work with."

Szaky maintains that when typical customers realize that the TerraCycle product is not only cheaper than anything else on the market, but also packaged in used soda bottles collected by children, it will push them into the zone of having no reason not to buy it. Eco is the firm's added advantage, not the primary advantage.

This financial-bottom-line approach to environmental and social activism is what's been driving TerraCycle's development all along. The company's policy of packaging all of its product in recycled containers, for example, was originally implemented because "we couldn't afford packaging at the time," Szaky explains. "We went to people's recycle bins and took their used soda bottles."

Similarly, the company's relocation to Trenton was less about social justice and more about finances. "We moved to Trenton because it was cheap," Szaky says. "We were living hand-to-mouth for a long time." Not only are rents very low in the Trenton area, but TerraCycle is intentionally located in an Urban Enterprise Zone where New Jersey state income taxes are waived.

Explains Tom, "We're saying that if you do the most eco-friendly thing, the most socially responsible thing, you'll actually be making more money. It's a completely different paradigm."

It starts with one product.

Tom Szaky, born in Budapest, is intense, strong-willed, and energetic. "People often want to know how much caffeine he's had that day," says Alysia Welch-Chester, thirty-three, a Trenton native who is very thankful that TerraCycle came to town. Serving as the company's special projects manager, she shares a small office with Szaky and company cofounder and chief information officer Jon Beyer. "He's running all over the place," she says of Szaky. "He's very high-energy . . . He wants things to be done yesterday."

Szaky is clearly a young man who accomplishes a lot in very short time spans. At the age of fifteen, having moved to Toronto with his family eight years previously, he founded an award-winning Canadian Web design company, Flyte Design, which employed three associates and earned the teenager a five-figure income. Also while in secondary school, Szaky bicycled solo from Toronto to Vancouver to raise four thousand dollars for the Ontario Naturalists organization, setting a national speed record of twenty-one days. By the time he was eighteen, he was engaged in the start-up of three dot-com companies: Werehome.com, a home improvement site; Priority.com, an online fund-raising school; and StudentMarks.com, offering a grade-tracking software.

It was during these late teenage years in Canada that Tom first discovered the idea for his future worm fertilizer company. On a road trip to Montreal, he was "partying out of my friend's house where my buddies were growing ganja in the basement," he explains. "But they were having a hard time with it. The [marijuana] plants were not working out too well because [they] were feeding chemicals to them. [Then] they started feeding the plants worm poop. It got the plants going really, really well. But what was really interesting was the way they were making the worm poop. They were taking garbage and feeding it to the worms. That was the genius of the idea. Feeding worms organic waste."

As a freshman at Princeton University, Szaky remembered what he had seen in Montreal. He and his friend Jon Beyer began experimenting with worm poop in the cluttered basement of a campus office building. It worked so well as a fertilizer that the two wrote up an initial business plan and submitted it to a business plan contest sponsored by the Princeton Entrepreneurship Club. They won.

The two freshmen convinced Princeton Dining Services to allow them to process the dining hall waste in their prototype Worm Gin. Within a few months, they found their first investor, who helped finance their move into office space on Princeton's Nassau Street. In 2003, Szaky dropped out of the university to concentrate his efforts on growing the company. "My parents weren't too happy that I dropped out of Princeton to shovel poop," he says.

Szaky entered another business plan contest, this one sponsored by Carrot Capital Healthcare Venture, which focuses on giving seed and early-stage investment opportunities to companies across a broad spectrum of the health care industry. TerraCycle won the million-dollar seed reward, but then Szaky turned it down because he didn't care for the direction Carrot planned to take his brainchild.

He began searching for other angel investors, finding it a tall order. "We were asking for a million dollars to be given to a twenty-year-old dropout," he explains. To make ends meet, he entered seven additional business plan contests in succession, scraping by on the winnings, keeping the company afloat month to month. All the while, he was personally pitching the big-box retailers with his worm poop fertilizer.

In 2004, TerraCycle landed its first major account with Wal-Mart

Canada. A second major breakthrough came later that same year when the Home Depot Web site began selling TerraCycle Plant Food. In 2005, Whole Foods, Home Depot Canada, Wild Oats, and Do-It-Best began carrying the TerraCycle line. Since then the company has been quadrupling its gross revenue every year, with the help of approximately seven million dollars raised from angel investors.

It hasn't been an easy road. "We've been almost bankrupt four times," Szaky says candidly. In the beginning, "we bankrupted all of our credit cards."

"We made mistakes all the way through," he continues. "Some of these ideas that you think will be so great just turn out to be complete failures. But you know, the trick is to spend as little money as possible to test an idea, and then you're okay if it fails . . . The trick is to learn from the mistakes and keep going." In a sense, he's turning his mistakes into an advantage.

Growing up to meet demand.

Szaky eventually moved the operation from Princeton to nearby Trenton. Cofounder Jon Beyer, still a student, stayed in Princeton while Tom successfully recruited interns from all over the planet to work for the company in exchange for room and board at the rented Trenton house where he also resided. When Tom came home one day to find a hole in the wall and realized that it had been made by a bullet, he and the others vacated the premises and moved into the surrounding area.

As the company grew, more seasoned employees were hired. William Gillum, a PhD chemist and twenty-three-year employee of Lucent Technologies, was brought in by an old friend serving on the company's newly formed board of directors. "He told me the company needed someone with experience, someone with gray hair, and someone who could say no," Gillum explained.

The chemist was put in charge of conducting experiments to verify the TerraCycle claims. A lab was set up at a greenhouse in Burlington County, New Jersey. Plants were grown with the TerraCycle compound alongside plants fed with Miracle-Gro and plants fed with just water. In almost every category, the TerraCycle product outperformed or equaled the Miracle-Gro. "We got more marketable peppers, more flowers, taller plants," Gillum says. "It worked."

Of course, this was no double-blind study, but it gave Szaky the confidence to go head-to-head with the market leader in the garden fertilizer business. Scotts Miracle-Gro is the premier product of the Scotts Miracle-Gro Company, itself a merger of Miracle-Gro and the Scotts Company. Their product has an estimated 59 percent dominance in the home fertilizer market. Competition over critical shelf space would put TerraCycle, the organic upstart, and Scotts, the old-school chemical-based giant, on a collision course.

Naming a brand versus naming a product.

Tom Szaky has done all the design work for the TerraCycle product labels since the beginning. But when it came to finding the right name for the company, it has been more of a group effort.

"We initially called ourselves the Worm Project," he says. "That was the first name. And then we just started brainstorming new names. It was called Terra Environmental for six months. Then Terra Earth, Cycle, Recycle, and that's sorta how the name TerraCycle came up."

In terms of branding, Szaky and company moved from a purely descriptive product name, Worm Project, to an umbrella brand name that can house any number of products and conveys a brand message. In this sophisticated brand architecture vision, the actual product names are purely descriptive — TerraCycle Drain Cleaner, TerraCycle Fire Log, et cetera.

The naming process helped these young entrepreneurs discover their core brand message. "We started to figure out what we really stand for. We stand for 'Better, greener, cheaper.' And so that's what will embody all of our products," says Szaky.

The power of publicity.

TerraCycle has worked hard on getting this core message across to its potential customers. With no advertising budget whatsoever, the firm has put all of its marketing resources into publicity — hence the five young publicists presently employed at the company. "We average about two to three articles every day. And that's what our PR team drives . . .

we have more articles about us than the big consumer product companies have about their products," Szaky says.

He instructs the young publicists to work the phones, "because that's how to be successful." Each publicist generates three articles a week on average, and each is paid in the vicinity of thirty thousand annually. "So if you divide it out, I pay about a dollar for every five hundred words in circulation I get," he explains. "It's a great deal . . . What do you get for thirty grand in advertising? Thirty grand gets you a [one] page ad in *Better Homes & Gardens*." In fact, a single-page four-color ad in *Better Homes & Gardens* runs upward of four hundred thousand dollars, per the magazine's Web site.

Three years from now, Szaky hopes to employee thirty full-time publicists in what would essentially be a "PR agency in-house."

"We had a profile done by the biggest Christian magazine in the country, *Guideposts*, and the same day an article ran by the biggest marijuana magazine in the country, and if you look at both articles, they are almost identical. It's the power of the angle of our story. It appeals to everyone. We're going to be in an article in *Stuff Magazine*, which is as close as you can be to soft-core porn, and it's going to be the same article as everything else." As I listen, I wonder about the demographics of horticulture. Do pot smokers, Christians, and porn lovers all share the same love of gardening?

"We're solving waste problems [and] in the process that generates great stories. One of the things that TerraCycle is in no short supply of is stories. And that's the one beautiful thing," Szaky says.

Sometimes a company can benefit from PR generated by a competitor. In TerraCycle's case, that's what transpired when Scotts Miracle-Gro sued, claiming that the upstart's packaging infringed on the "distinctive and famous trade dress" of Miracle-Gro."[1]

"What they've done by suing TerraCycle is to bring TerraCycle's name into circulation even more. We have some fun with that," Szaky explains.

Indeed, TerraCycle is casting itself as David going up against Goliath. It created a special Web site to make its case, SuedByScotts.com. As the site states, "The Scotts Miracle-Gro Company, a $2.2 billion assets giant which has at least a 59% share of the relevant market, has sued tiny TerraCycle, Inc., an inner-city company founded by college students to create an eco-friendly business."

"We think they've sued just because we've taken so much shelf space,"

Szaky elaborates. "As we get more of our fertilizers in stores, almost by definition Miracle-Gro loses. And again, it's because we're playing in the major retailers. Wal-Mart gives us a foot, somebody loses, and it's usually Miracle-Gro. I think that's where this all came from."

"They claim that our product is confusingly similar to theirs, which is a load of horseshit quite frankly," he continues. In order to win the lawsuit, Scotts must prove that a customer would not be able to tell the two products apart when making a purchasing decision. "There is just no confusion here," Szaky maintains.

"We're actually fighting back with a big PR campaign. We're getting a lot of articles on it. It's really great. It's building our brand awareness, which is really excellent . . . A blessing in disguise."

At the close of writing this chapter, I heard that TerraCycle and Scotts had settled. "TerraCycle has agreed to change certain advertising claims and its package design to avoid possible consumer confusion, and Scotts has agreed to dismiss its false advertising and infringement claims," according to TheEnvironmentalBlog.org.

What I find interesting about Tom Szaky's PR approach is that he mines both traditional media and the Gort Cloud with equal intensity. His team will reach out to print editors and green bloggers equally with the result that his stories, particularly his dust-up with Miracle-Gro, appear everywhere. You'll find the same story in Organic Gardening Tips, a gardener's blog; on Ecopreneurist.com, a green business site; and in the pages of the *New York Times*.

Packaging that communicates the brand message.

Piles of enormous plastic bags stuffed with used plastic bottles are visible over the walls that surround the TerraCycle headquarters in Trenton. Inside the compound, the bags are stashed everywhere — overflowing from garbage bins, stuffed into warehouses. The recycled bottles have come from close to four thousand schools, churches, and other organizations across the United States, that make up TerraCycle's Bottle Brigade. For every bottle donated, TerraCycle sends a penny to a charity of the organization's choice.

Says publicist Michael Avale: "It saves a lot of energy. Instead of melting down all these plastic bottles, we're just reusing them over and over."

The bottles, he explains, are washed and then fitted with a TerraCycle label that is slipped over whatever label was there before, be it Aquafina or Coca-Cola.

"Our collection programs are massive in scope. We have half a million people right now collecting bottles for us — actively," says Szaky. "And that leads to big PR, that sort of thing. So that's [one way] we build our awareness."

Inside the TerraCycle offices, all of the furniture is recycled, most of it discarded by other corporations. In the production area out back, bags of worm excrement that have been sent to TerraCycle from worm farmers in the area await processing. "That's our money. That's our black gold. It's full of nutrients," says publicist Avale of the excrement as he demonstrates how the very fine substance is placed into tanks and brewed into a tea. The material that's left behind becomes the TerraCycle-brand potting soil.

Once in the tea form, the excrement travels by pipe into a neighboring room where it is bottled by machines that were once used by more mainstream companies to fill bottles of soda. The caps used for the bottles, whether sprayhead or regular, are castoffs from more mainstream companies. So are the boxes in which the fertilizer is shipped. "Our boxes are every other company's misprinted waste," explains Avale, again emphasizing the company's personality.

The mismatched shipping boxes, containers, and caps all add to the brand's mystique. There's a kind of beautiful chaos in this, a brand chaos that is communicated from the shelf to consumers. Once they understand the reason for the inconsistency, they buy into the whole TerraCycle mission. They become brand loyalists.

These decisions to buck the norm have not come easily. Take the objective to keep the price low and competitive. "I get a lot of stress in the company, because even people internally say we should be charging premium pricing," he says. "[I believe] we have to go right down to the cheapest price and get it into the biggest stores."

"I could be completely wrong in this," he continues. "It will shake out over time. If I'm still around in five years and still growing, then I'm right. If not, then I was wrong."

Exploiting established sales channels by expanding product lines.

TerraCycle plans to launch ten new product categories in 2008, which include, in addition to the aforementioned ceramic pots, a line of cleaners, a line of composters, a line of bird feeders, and a line of fire logs. Most of the new products are "made entirely from garbage and packaged entirely from garbage, and are 'better, greener, cheaper,'" Szaky says, reiterating the company's core branding message.

"We try to take the garbage thing as far as possible," he continues. Hence, the new fire log is made from recycled wax cartons, wood chips, newspaper, and glycerin — which is a by-product of biodiesel. The composters and bird feeders are also made entirely of waste.

"In some cases, like the cleaners, you can't pull that off, so we try to take it as far as absolutely possible. The cleaners contain the most eco-friendly contents available today . . . from microbes and enzymes . . . the packaging and the triggers are made from waste products."

The cleaners will be retailing at $2.99 for a one-liter bottle. "It's roughly half the price of Seventh Generation, which is the big eco-friendly cleaner, and our contents will actually be more eco-friendly than theirs . . . Our goal is to enter into every single product category we can, and get it as close to that made-from-waste and packaging-from-waste paradigm as we can."

Co-marketing schemes.

TerraCycle is beginning to market in partnership with some of its retail customers. Home Depot will be selling the TerraCycle drain cleaner under its new Eco Options brand. "It will be the first product to have Eco Options on the label itself," Szaky says.

The company is also entering into agreements with other natural product companies. One such arrangement is in the works with Stonyfield Farm, which will be funding a collection program administered by TerraCycle. "There are ten billion yogurt containers thrown out every year," explains Szaky. "We [will] make planting pots out of them." Both Stonyfield and TerraCycle have broadcast this story from their corporate Web sites, and the Gort Cloud has spread it around.

"What we're trying to do is create this idea of sponsored waste, where big companies come to us to drive a marketing platform to reuse one of their waste chains, ideally their most visible ones, and return it into a brand-new product by reuse," he says.

"I think one of the big things that we can accomplish as a company is this unique form of marketing, [drawing] big companies in to fund [programs like this] for us. One of our goals in the marketing department is to actually be profitable. We want our marketing department as a stand-alone unit, to be a profitable entity."

Rebel with a cause.

Tom Szaky portrays himself as a revolutionary, at least for the audience that values a sustainable product. "What's really great about us is that Tom and Jon are changing the face of capitalism," says Avale. "That's why it's revolutionary. It's a product that keeps remaking itself."

In fact, Szaky sees himself as one revolutionary among many, Gary Hirshberg of Stonyfield Farm being another. "The same people keep popping up all the time," he says. "It's quite amazing, actually, that it's a very small group of people who are in this business."

At the same time, Szaky says, there are "thousands of people beginning sustainable businesses across the country. What the green business has right now is a vast number of tiny people . . . doing very interesting things — but in the mom-and-pop size. And that's massive."

He includes self-styled eco-model Summer Rayne Oakes in this group. "Her big platform is that she wears eco-fashions, and she's in a completely different business. She doesn't sell anything. She promotes things. But she's doing it in a big way, too. *Vanity Fair* just did a big spread on her."

Oakes believes that a company must have charisma in order to succeed — and TerraCycle has lots of that. "Who can make worm poop cool?" she questions. "Most people would say, 'Forget about it.'" But "because they're charismatic and cool, you find yourself buying the worm poop on the shelves. Part of that is authenticity. You can't just go into a branding firm and say, 'Make worm poop cool.'" She also believes that to succeed as a sustainable business, "you have to create demand for a category," which is what she did in becoming an eco-model and what TerraCycle has done through its marketing.

Perhaps it's the influence of his fashion-minded friend, but one of Tom's newest projects is a partnership with Honest Kids to collect juice pouches and turn them into handbags. It's one of several of his "brigades" using kids to collect yogurt pots, energy bar wrappers, plastic bottles, and, now, drink pouches for recycling and reuse. To showcase the Drink Pouch Brigade, fashion designer Nina Valenti of Naturevsfuter has designed a full-length gown made from juice pouches for Soyeon Lee, a concert pianist, for her performance at Carnegie Hall.[2]

It's all about timing.

"The environmental movement has come around a couple of times, but this is big," explains Szaky. "Big companies can't do it. So there is this huge opening for the ultimate green brand to go big. It's like a new revolution that's hyped right now, but it's going to hit. We are still before it. In three or four years, five years, down the line . . . it [will] take over."

"Our goal is to get into every consumer product that we can, own 1 to 2 percent of the market — tiny, low percentages — and sit back and grow it," Szaky continues, predicting that "twenty years from now, 95 percent of [business] will be green. If you look at any big revolution, the big mainstays become things of the past. And I think that will happen, but it will take a long time."

For now, TerraCycle will go into the marketplace aggressively. "I guess that's why we are being sued by Miracle-Gro. We want to go head-on, as aggressively as possible, against the biggest and the best. So when we launch our cleaner, we want to go right against Procter & Gamble. And that's the only thing we care about . . . I don't think those other [green] brands launch with [this kind of] intent."

Interestingly, it is the companies that fail to adopt sustainable practices that will increasingly place their brands at risk through lawsuits or public embarrassment.

Redefining garbage as a resource.

TerraCycle is bent on eliminating the concept of garbage. "That's what we're trying to prove, that you can eliminate garbage and the idea of waste," he says. "If you find uses for garbage, you can eliminate the idea of garbage."

"Since it seems as if the current [business] models cannot help save our world, is there a model that can?" Szaky questions. "Can a model exist where all three bottom lines complement each other by allowing a corporation to be wildly profitable, socially responsible, and environmentally sustainable?"

Yes, he says. "Through eco-capitalism, you can be doing the right thing from a profit perspective, and in the process eliminate the idea of waste." To that end, TerraCycle posts extensive comments on its Web site about the eco-capitalist ideas that power its business (www.terra cycle.net/revolution.htm).

SUMMARY: THE PROOF IS IN THE POOP

TerraCycle has made dramatic progress against entrenched competition because its products are effective and its distribution channels are broad, allowing the company to reach a mass audience. Its pioneering use of garbage as the raw material earned it the trust and respect of the green community within the Gort Cloud. It gave the firm access to distribution and media channels that it might otherwise have needed much longer to penetrate, and the timing was perfect. Large mass retailers, like the Home Depot and Wal-Mart, are looking for sustainable products that will help polish their image as being at least nominally proactive about the environment.

And just as there has been a tremendous interest in the sustainable practices of TerraCycle among the citizens of the Gort Cloud, there is also the awareness of what happens to companies that practice less sustainable objectives. For instance, TerraCycle's nemesis, Scotts Miracle-Gro, was recently the subject of a nationwide EPA-mandated recall of certain products with chemical pesticides containing invalid registration numbers. Green bloggers and organic gardening sites spread the story. So while TerraCycle, the upstart green brand, was helped by the Gort Cloud, the opposite can be true for companies wedded to less sustainable business practices.

The Ultimate Gort Cloud Connector: Energy

Southwest Windpower and Bonneville Environmental Foundation

THE CHALLENGE

Southwest Windpower came on the scene when most people associated wind power with creaking windmills next to some derelict farmhouse on the prairie. The challenge – which the founders have deftly navigated – is this: How do you convince homeowners and small businesses that a spinning blade on a slender tower is a good thing, a beautiful thing?

The Bonneville Environmental Foundation is also an innovator that faced a slightly different problem. How do you sell something that you can't hold in your hand, that doesn't benefit you directly, and that has never been tried before in the public sector? I am speaking of the Renewable Energy Certificate, or Green Tag, the carbon-offset mechanism that allows people to invest in clean energy to make up for the carbon emissions they are responsible for.

THE SOLUTION

In the case of Southwest Windpower, the solution has focused on design, performance, channel development, and education. The product is relatively inexpensive, easy to install, attractive, and scaled for different uses. The result is a reliable source of alternative energy that gives customers control over their energy bills. To deliver a steady stream of customers, the company has retained an expert communications agency that gets the word out and then educates the new prospects.

For the Bonneville Environmental Foundation, the trick was positioning the new Renewable Energy Certificate offer correctly from the get-go. The group recognized and leveraged the instant gratification that comes from simply writing a check to do your part.

It touches us all.

I've saved the chapter on energy for last because energy represents both the greatest problem with regard to destruction of the environment and global warming *and* the greatest opportunity to bring relief to the planet by turning to smaller, more distributed suppliers of renewable energy.

For the last century, energy in the developed world has been dominated by the burning of fossil fuels, with their enormous extraction costs; by the construction of dams with related habitat destruction and damage to fish runs; and by nuclear power and the colossal investments associated with technology development, extraction and refining of uranium, disposal of spent fuel, protection against weapons proliferation, safety issues attendant in maintaining the sites and protecting against terrorism, and extremely long deactivation processes required to render a retired plant safe.

Coal, oil, hydro, and nuclear are expensive, so it's no wonder that these primary sources of energy have fallen under the control of huge businesses and the government. There's not a lot of room for the little guy amid the oligopolies' self-preserving desire to control production and fix favorable prices. Coal, oil, hydro, and nuclear are all heavily subsidized by our tax dollars, so the true costs are hidden.

Nevertheless, our modern way of life and, in fact, the ability to support so many people on the planet are directly attributable to cheap sources of energy, primarily from fossil fuels. Some scientists have glumly warned that poorly planned transitions to more sustainable energy sources could actually lead to a population collapse, while on the other hand, failure to control our influence on the environment will surely do the same thing. Doing nothing is not a solution.

So, in the true spirit of American enterprise, many small inventors and ecopreneurs have stepped forward on their own, many without subsidies or large investment, to provide alternative and mostly distributed sources of energy. These companies include the pioneers in solar, wind, geothermal, and biofuel — fuels made from algal fermentation, for instance. Of course, solar and wind are well-known and maturing technologies. The big commercial solar and wind farms have also come under the control of multinational energy companies and the utilities. BP, in its efforts to move "beyond petroleum," has made a big move into solar. Large utilities like Edison International are investing in some of the country's largest wind farms and huge solar plants. With their subsidized profits, Big Energy can delay competitive alternatives while jumping in to control them once they mature and become a threat.

But just as ancient people have traditionally made their own energy by burning wood or dung, we can invest in personal energy production, most notably with photovoltaic systems on our roofs and, where possible, with the latest incarnation of the venerable windmill — the modern electricity-generating wind turbine. One of those independent energy providers is Southwest Windpower, maker of the most popular residential- and small-business-sized wind turbine and the focus of this chapter.

But there is another side to this story: the need for conservation and alternative energy investment. This is where NGOs like the Bonneville Environmental Foundation (BEF) play a role. BEF was founded through a collaboration between the Bonneville Power Administration, a government entity that provides hydro and nuclear energy to the Northwest, and three nonprofit environmental organizations to explore alternative sources of energy and promote watershed restoration.

"The most obvious distributed energy resource that's out there is conservation," says Rob Harmon of BEF. "Almost all buildings hemorrhage energy. There's a huge amount of waste."

BEF is also the inventor of retail Renewable Energy Certificates, or RECs as they are called. You've probably seen evidence of RECs in the form of bumper stickers on SUVs that proclaim, THIS VEHICLE'S ENERGY USE OFFSET BY XYZ. Some have described them as the equivalent of the church's dispensations that can be bought to offset past sins. More importantly, if you buy a renewable energy product from your utility, it is more than likely that the mechanism behind this product is the REC. Hundreds of thousands of citizens across the United States use RECs as a way to ensure that the electricity they use is replaced by renewably produced electricity. RECs have also become an important source of investment capital for distributed, often smaller-scale and independent energy production projects, like methane-recapture systems at a local dairy or solar systems on homes and businesses.

The experiences in building an alternative energy business and providing both conservation information and investment capital are the focus of this chapter. This is the one subject that unites and affects every person and every organization within the Gort Cloud. It's a common thread.

Southwest Windpower:
The Answer Is Blowing in the Wind

Small-scale wind power has been around forever, of course. Windmills have dotted the northern European countryside for centuries and have long been an icon of any road trip through America's heartland. But these devices could be used only to mechanically pull water out of the ground by means of a rod, as opposed to modern electricity-producing turbines.

Southwest Windpower of Flagstaff, Arizona, produces wind turbines, which generate electricity that can be used to do anything from pumping water to charging a battery on a sailboat. The systems deliver a steady output of energy on a fixed investment with minimal upkeep (depending on the wind). They are immune to rising energy costs and deliver power to where it's needed without miles of power lines and the resulting necessity to lease right-of-ways. As a result, Southwest Windpower has become the world's largest producer of small wind turbines and stands to benefit from the emerging distributed consumer-energy market in a very big way.

"Our electricity grid is changing," says Southwest Windpower cofounder Andy Kruse. "It's become much more alive, with technology that allows consumers to participate in their own energy production and then communicate the data back and forth via the Web. It's the beginning of the smart grid, which is quickly evolving."

A rural resource for modern living.

Kruse's partner, cofounder David Calley, has had a lifelong relationship with wind power. He grew up just outside the counterculture center of Sedona, Arizona; his father was a math and science teacher who was "very ideological" and "into all things renewable," Calley says. "All around our house there was solar everything. He built wind turbines out of washing machine parts," eventually purchasing "a commercial machine called the Windcharger," Calley continues. "It was one of those really old designs from the 1920s. It was for running those big old radios in farmhouses."

While still in grade school, David was running the appliances in his room with a small wind turbine he built with his father. By high school, he had started his own company and was building much more sophisticated machines for neighbors. "I had to make everything by hand," he explains. "I didn't have the money for anything else."

In college, Calley studied engineering and physics. "Engineering is how you get it done — I have done a great deal of engineering. But physics is even more important to me. It provides such a strong grounding in theory. I still have a love of all kinds of physics."

Calley was also an art student, studying sculpture, which is a big factor in Southwest Windpower's aesthetically pleasing product. "It's human beings we're trying to serve," he says. "This thing's going to be in their face. It's going to be on their lawn. You might as well make sure it's not offensive."

In the mid-1980s, Calley met Andy Kruse, who was building a solar energy system on a ranch east of Flagstaff. When Kruse saw Calley's latest turbine version, built with a modified Ford alternator and able to produce three hundred watts of electricity, "I said you know, I think there's an opportunity here. There's a market here for this," says Kruse.

Bringing his business and marketing smarts to a partnership that has lasted more than twenty years, Kruse acts as something of a front man for the duo. While he travels the world to develop the business and create the market, Calley continues to focus on technology development. He is more of a purest, living off the grid and riding his bicycle fifteen miles each way to the company's Flagstaff plant and offices.

"For me it was always an ideological thing. I was trying to save the world . . . trying to do something to make a difference," explains Calley about the early days.

"We had credit cards and David's dad gave us a little bit of money to help us along the way," adds Kruse. "We built these things just out of nothing. It was just pure 'out of a garage.' Even our garage didn't have electricity, so some of the wind generators we built were used to produce the electricity that operated the equipment that allowed us to build more wind generators."

"It was an interesting time," he continues. "We got into renewables just as President Reagan was killing the last of the solar and renewable energy credits" enacted during the Carter years. The new company's first product, the Windseeker, was introduced in 1987, with Calley and Kruse "scrounging up a thousand dollars for a booth" at a technology show in Anaheim, California, to test consumers and see if there truly was an interest.

"The machine was a bit crude," Kruse explains. "But instantly people said, 'Wow, that's really cool.' One distributor ordered ten. And we're like, Oh my gosh, now we've got orders. With a few well-placed press releases, we started getting calls from all around the world, and suddenly we were a global business. From day one we were selling wind generators to Israel and the UK and Mexico and Chile. We realized that the market was still very small for this technology in only the US, so we had to be a global business to keep things running."

It wasn't long before Southwest began to sell the bulk of its product through dealers. "We'd find people that would sell our products. We'd sell to them at a discount, and they'd mark it up."

The company's primary distribution is still through dealers. "It's all about the eighty–twenty rule," Kruse says. "You've got 20 percent of those dealers out there that are doing about 80 percent of the business."

Identifying customers: A moving target.

Southwest Windpower's first target customers for the Windseeker, the three-hundred-watt generator based on the modified Ford alternator, were ranchers and farmers living in remote places far off the electrical grid. But this market proved hard to reach. "How do you get to them?" asks Calley rhetorically. "They don't have electricity. How do you find their address? How do you identify them? It quickly became apparent that they were by far the most difficult people to serve." According to Kruse, however, they also became the company's most important first adopters — and the importance of this customer group continues today.

Over the last twenty years, Southwest Windpower has produced well over a hundred thousand wind generators. Discovering new applications and finding new customers to fuel this growth and build the business has been a full-time effort. Competition then and now for the off-grid market is the gas generator. Because Southwest had only minimal resources to market its products, it turned to partnerships with well-funded solar PV companies that shared the same market. "We convinced companies such as BP Solar and Kyocera solar that small wind was a complement to solar. These partners introduced us to their extensive channels of distribution," explains Andy Kruse. This kept the company on an excellent growth path. But in the late 1990s everything began to change.

Around 1998 came the distributed grid-connected market: homes and business that are connected to the grid but offset utility power with power they make themselves. Kruse says, "While we were focused on keeping up with orders partly due to the Y2K fears that the world might come to an end, my solar friends were telling me they were about to change their entire marketing strategy. They saw this new market as the future. We quickly realized the same thing and went to work on a new product" to meet the need.

This new product, Skystream, connects to the home. When the wind blows, the home uses all the energy from the wind generator first, and any extra it needs comes from the electrical grid. At times when the wind generator is producing more energy than the home uses, the electrical meter spins backward. The company's target audience has already grown to include exurban areas in addition to rural areas. The primary domestic target audience is now a very specific thirteen million homes that have enough land (half an acre), enough wind (an average of twelve miles per hour or greater), and the appropriate zoning ordinances to put the product into use. There are great resources that will tell a prospective customer exactly where the best wind power locations are, like WindPowerMaps.org.

"The current half-acre limit requirement will get smaller as we work toward better micro-sighting tools where we can look at a person's home, their property, and better predict energy production on turbulence factors," Kruse says. "We'll go to smaller and smaller lot sizes, which only makes the market larger." A recent post on Inhabitat described a micro-generating scheme using Southwest Windpower turbines in urban settings without the need for a tower. "Dubbed 'Architectural Wind' (made by Aerovironment), the system seamlessly integrates into the parapets of buildings, taking advantage of aerodynamics to catch wind as its speed escalates up a structure's side."[1]

"The concept is to sell the idea that the turbine is an appliance that people put in their backyard," Kruse continues. "The homeowner doesn't think about it, and he doesn't worry about it. It just does what it's supposed to do." Just like your refrigerator or any other appliance.

"Generally, the first thing a customer looks at is how much energy is going to be produced and how much it's going to cost," Calley says. "You have to push those two factors very hard" in developing the product. "Then other factors start to weigh in pretty quickly," he continues. "Clearly, you don't want it to break. You don't want it to make any noise. It's a pretty complex problem from a purely engineering perspective, from a purely functional perspective. There's pretty intense aerodynamics involved."

"And it doesn't end there. Attempting to achieve the correct aerodynamics and at the same time to design a machine that is aesthetically pleasing is also difficult," he says. "But we feel we have it with Skystream."

"The long-term goal for the company is to continue to build innovative products that drive the cost of energy down. As this happens, we'll see that the larger part of the market will start buying them," Calley predicts.

Nonresidential: Starting on water, moving onto land.

Southwest also targets nonresidential markets. In the marine world, the turbines power refrigeration units, navigational devices, and communications gear in sailboats. The company also promotes its products as ideal for offshore oil platforms.

"Close to five hundred platforms located in the Gulf of Mexico use small wind and photovoltaic panels to provide power," says Kruse. Ironically, ExxonMobil, one of the forces behind the climate change disinformation campaign, is a Southwest customer in this sector.

In late 2007, the company began to partner with retailers, working with Coca-Cola and McDonald's to install wind turbines atop light poles in parking lots. "They'll put in slightly stronger light poles, slightly higher," Calley explains. "The installation cost is low and they're buying the turbines wholesale. Once they're up, the maintenance cost is pretty much the same as it would be just for the lights themselves."

It's a bargain all the way around. The per-unit installed cost of commercial systems "can run about 50 percent of what a residential application would cost," says Calley. Other commercial applications are on the near horizon. Turbines can be used to power road and highway lights, and the company is studying how to integrate the machines into office buildings.

Internationally, prospects are bright as well. "We're working with multinational companies," Calley says of the planning stages. "Some international sites are more attractive because of higher power costs and subsidies from governments."

There can be subsidies from state government as well. The company is presently looking to California, where in commercial settings wind power can be installed virtually for free.

Big fish, small pond (but growing).

Southwest Windpower has no competition to speak of in the commercial market. "The market is very new," Kruse explains. "There are people eyeing it, but we're way ahead of the game."

As for the residential market, for years the most important competition has come from the Bergey Windpower Company of Oklahoma. But the Bergey product, because it is a furling machine, creates inherent noise. "Ours are dramatically different in terms of quiet technology," Calley says. In addition, whereas the Southwest turbines are on a thirty-foot tower, the Bergey turbines can be as tall as a hundred feet, which exacerbates the zoning problems.

"The larger the machine, the more expensive the power," explains Calley. "The scale equations drive you to a smaller size, assuming your goal is the lowest cost of energy for a given wind machine."

A number of other smaller companies manufacture residential turbines, such as Solar Wind Works of Truckee, California, Abundant Renewable Energy of Newberg, Oregon, and Wind Turbine Industries in Minnesota. These smaller firms "pop up but they don't last more than a year or two," Kruse explains. "There's nothing quite like us. We're taking a very commercialized approach . . . looking at messaging, looking at the branding, looking at how we communicate with the world, how we say, 'Hey, we can do something here.'"

"However, though we are comfortable with our position, we are always looking at the competition, looking at who may be the next competitor that comes out with something that is as innovative as what we do. At the same time, we are constantly improving our existing products and finding ways to drive down the cost of energy."

A welcome addition to the landscape or an eyesore?

The wind energy business has had to fight neighborhood associations and other interest groups that have registered discontent over what they see as the unsightliness of wind turbines.

"From the focus groups we conducted, we did see the potential for some NIMBY-ism [Not In My Back Yard] out there," says Marty McDonald, creative director and founder of egg, the sustainable branding and communications agency in Seattle that designs and develops Southwest's brand and advertising campaigns. "But the truth is that there are far more people who think wind turbines are beautiful than those who think they're ugly. Some people are attracted to having it in their neighborhood."

"I think everyone responds to simplicity done well aesthetically," says Calley. "There's always a balance that has to be struck between engineering and aesthetics, especially when it's going to be sitting in someone's yard."

"The goal is to make the consumer believe it's an attractive product and that it's the most cost-effective method to obtain energy," he continues. "You want the consumer thinking, *These things are just cool, man, and it's way cheaper, so why don't we do that?* As opposed to, *It costs six times as much and it looks ugly as sin but you should do it because it's the right thing to do.*"

"Small wind turbines deliver a message far better into the consumers' mind than a solar panel does," says Kruse. "Because many people have a difficult time comprehending the technology. The panels don't move. They don't have any kind of visual interactivity." In contrast, "a wind turbine, especially a beautifully designed one, is really a powerful, powerful message."

Wind channels: How to reach the customers.

For residential turbines, Southwest Windpower's primary distribution channel has been distributors, but "that's changing," says Kruse. "We're developing new channels, because we have made the technology very simple." What has always been quite technical in terms of installation is now much easier.

"Skystream is a wind energy appliance," Kruse explains. "It's really simple to put them together — they're designed to be installed by someone who would install a light or a sign for you. Most general contractors will be quite comfortable doing this. A lot of the dealers are now just general construction people. However, that doesn't take away from the importance of training. We have developed a new department that helps new dealers understand how to properly site, sell, and install wind generators. We encourage our new dealers to keep us up to date when they install their first machine. We then bring in the press, make a big announcement, and the dealer gets tons of inquiries as a result. We call this 'planting the seed.' It is incredible. Every new installation is another seed that sprouts new installations."

With the marine business, the company connects with customers through marine retailers. The biggest customer is the country's largest marine distributor, West Marine.

Online: Making sure prospective customers are blown away.

Southwest's corporate site, WindEnergy.com, takes an educational approach by doing a thorough job of informing the visitor on the basics of wind power as well as the dynamics of wind turbines. It also provides maps and other information to help potential customers determine if wind power is appropriate for their particular situation.

Southwest connects with the community of wind power enthusiasts via a third-party Web site, TurningPoint.com. Featured is Southwest Windpower's Skystream hybrid wind turbine, its point product today. The TurningPoint.com site offers, among other things, photo simulations enabling prospective Skystream owners to see a visual of what the turbine would look like on their property.

Promoting product brand over company name.

I was curious why SouthwestWindpower.com is not their active Web site address. "Wind Energy was used as the Web site's name, rather than Southwest Windpower, because Wind Energy is a very easy name to remember," says Kruse. "We had all kinds of variations on how people would spell Southwest Windpower. It was easier for us to get people to remember wind energy. That's what we do — wind energy."

Because Calley and Kruse have long known that they would eventually change the Southwest name, they promote the company's model brand names much more vigorously than they do the corporate entity. "You're not going to invest money in a name that you know is eventually going to fade away," explains Kruse.

As a result of this branding-by-product approach, two of the company's three product lines, Air and Skystream, are now featured on their own Web sites: AirBreeze.com and SkystreamEnergy.com. The third Southwest line, the Whisper, does not have its own site; it's promoted solely on WindEnergy.com.

Southwest Windpower's most venerable product, the Air series, was introduced in 1994. With more than a hundred thousand units manufactured and shipped to over 120 countries, it is the best-selling battery-charging wind turbine in history. "If you go past the end of power just about anywhere in the world, you'll see them," explains Calley.

In 2002, the Air-X was introduced as the first microprocessor-based micro wind turbine. This breakthrough in design improved the performance by more than 20 percent and significantly reduced noise in high winds. More recently, the fourth generation of the Air, the Airbreeze and Airbreeze Marine, have gone even farther in terms of quiet and efficiency, introducing a new technology that produces electricity at a low wind speed of seven miles per hour. As the level of required wind drops, of course, the number of potential customers increases.

The company's larger, more technically advanced Skystream, introduced in 2006, can be connected to a power grid. It will power the home when the wind is blowing, and when it's not, the connection to the local utility company takes over.

The cost of Southwest wind turbines is generally recouped by the customer in four to twelve years, depending on wind speed average, the installed cost, and the cost of electricity. The company estimates that

Skystream can save a homeowner from five hundred to eight hundred dollars per year.

"You'll notice that Skystream doesn't look like any turbine you've ever seen," says Calley. "It has new core technologies, which is why the cost of energy with Skystream is dramatically lower than anything that's existed with small wind before. And it's just barely first generation. Second generation will dramatically change it again. We've pushed the technology very hard."

When the Skystream was introduced, in part from knowledge derived from focus groups conducted around the country, egg "determined that we needed to build a special Skystream-specific Web site to address everything and anything people might want to know or ask about with regard to this product," continues McDonald.

Furthermore, out of egg's research, it was discovered that potential Skystream customers were primarily concerned with "practical matters," McDonald explains. "It turned out that it wasn't about green as much as it was about, 'Wow, I can take control of my energy,' and 'This is cost-effective.' People just don't have any control over their escalating electric or power bills. That's a big thing. That's what attracts them."

From there, McDonald says, "it's a matter of how much does it cost and how quickly can I pay it off and what's the return on investment? We designed the site in a way that addressed the numerous questions culled from the focus groups so that people wouldn't opt out but rather [would] call a dealer or Southwest Windpower [for] further information. It was an information- and education-driven approach to communicating. And it worked extremely well."

Putting wind at the backs of consumers.

Once SkystreamEnergy.com was finished, "we used a combination of advertising and public relations, or earned media, to drive people to the site," says McDonald. This included articles in *Time*, *Wired*, *Popular Science*, and other publications. "It was a fairly easy sell to the media, and we got lots of great press that talked about the company and this product."

At the site, many potential customers e-mailed either a dealership or the company itself asking for more information on the Skystream product. "Once we had developed a database of interested potential prospects, we analyzed the demographics, and some low-level psychographics, and came out with an overall picture of the consumer," says McDonald. "We termed this person the Provider, and they are the individual most responsible for providing for the needs of the household. Typing that person psychographically, we came out with this concept of control. In the end, it's all based on control."

So in a sense, Southwest is targeting consumers who are in control within their household and giving them the opportunity to have more control over energy sources. Control turned out to be the primary driver of preference.

"And the concept of control was a higher-level umbrella theme that supported various lower-level drivers. There were several different issues that got people interested in our product," says McDonald. "We did a series of online banner campaigns to test basic messages as a way to measure which issues mattered the most. The four most important issues that all played into the control theme were national energy security, the cost of electricity, the aspect of renewable power, and cleaner energy production."

All four motivating factors played into Southwest's latest advertising campaign. "We designed a campaign that all of these people can see themselves in and that says there's diversity in the attraction to wind power," explains McDonald. "In one ad, a couple is standing in front of their home with a Skystream in the background. The guy has a big pickup truck and big belt buckle and western shirt and cowboy hat, and next to him is his wife who's dressed in tie-dye garb. The headline says THEY SUFFERED FROM IRRECONCILABLE SIMILARITIES."

Less social responsibility. More enlightened self-interest.

"Generally in brand building, when it comes to creating emotional connections with consumers, it's mainly about storytelling," McDonald says. Today this converges with the fact that "we are in a new era where people are looking behind the company logo and making sure the companies they buy into support their values."

"But in Southwest's case, we're providing a technology — a solution where there's a need. We're saying, 'We've developed this, we've created this technologically progressive product that's going to address the issues. It's what you've been looking for.'" Perhaps that's one reason why the basic Southwest Windpower marketing strategy is less about sustainability or social responsibility and more about "enlightened self-interest," as McDonald calls it.

"This speaks to the always important primary brand drivers, or brand antes," he continues. "The product has to serve self-interest first. It has to deliver on things like affordability, aesthetics, quality and performance, taste, health, accessibility, and convenience. Only then can you create a nice interplay with the secondary feel-good factors. These secondary brand drivers appeal to people's emotions through what egg calls the conscious consumer variables: wellness, environmental impact, fairness, community, philanthropy, authenticity."

With Southwest, "the environmental aspect comes from the fact that it is clean power. You're basically getting electricity for free, from the wind, and creating little or no emissions in the production of it. People love that idea. That's the environmental feel-good aspect, but it's got a lot of self-interest baked right into it in that in the end the price of electricity comes out to be very competitive with what the utilities can offer. And above all, the consumer gets to be in charge, which feels particularly good in these days of sporadic electricity flows and costs."

Selling to public and private institutions.

NASA, the US Geological Survey, and the National Oceanic and Atmospheric Association are just three of the many government agencies that have purchased Skystream units. In Pennsylvania, the Energy Development Authority awarded Southwest a $193,000 grant to place fifteen wind turbines in highly visible locations across the state, enabling Pennsylvanians "to learn and experience alternative energy as part of their daily lives," as Governor Edward Rendell stated when the grant was first announced. It is also, of course, a great way to make the product more visible to potential consumers.

The company offers special pricing for schools, working with the dealers to get the prices down as much as possible. It also sells through the US Department of Energy's Wind for Schools program. "When schools and school systems purchase wind turbines, they are not only doing what's best for their school's energy efficiencies, they are also teaching children about the energy of the future," says Kruse.

"Wind for Schools is about investing in our children so they grow up knowing where electricity comes from," he goes on. "And of course, you can't put a coal-powered power plant in the backyard of your school, but you can install a wind turbine." With the children, naturally, come the parents. It's a great marketing and education tool, encouraging the kids to tell their parents to start thinking about switching to renewable resources.

Riding a slower current toward a bright wind energy future.

The market for Southwest products appears global. Says Rob Harmon of the Bonneville Environmental Foundation on the possibilities in under-developed countries: "There are still many villages without electricity. That's a tremendous growth opportunity for Southwest."

Kruse agrees. "You have two billion people in the world [who] still don't have electricity. You have telecom systems running off diesel, which are becoming very expensive to operate. We're putting our wind systems all over India [in partnership] with Nokia on their communications towers. The diesel systems are just used as backup now."

With the Skystream, "our goal is that eventually it will cost less than a quarter of what you'll pay for normal electricity . . . probably less than a fifth," says Calley. "But that takes a lot of tiny little inventions that have to occur to optimize the product." Look at the washing machine, for example: "For the last two centuries there've been little tiny breakthroughs, and this one part that used to cost a hundred bucks — well, over the course of a series of evolutions, it now costs twenty-seven cents."

"Southwest has an interesting niche," comments Harmon. "Andy said a while back that they needed to be stamping out the product like computer chips. He's done a pretty good job of moving it this way."

Plugging into the Gort Cloud whenever possible.

In a form of outreach to the larger green community, the company's Web site includes glowing customer testimonial stories, as well as media articles about Southwest products and where they've been placed. A recent article posted on the site details a Skystream installation at Walker's Point, the oceanfront home of former President George H. W. Bush in Kennebunkport, Maine.

The company also connects to NGOs, partnering with organizations such as Winrock International to work on projects in underdeveloped countries. In addition, by the end of 2008, Southwest will most likely be connecting with companies such as Bonneville Environmental Foundation to facilitate a carbon-trading program.

"We don't have the systems in place to allow us to aggregate the carbon credits," says Kruse. "But by the end of the year, we'll be incorporating a new generation of wireless technology that will hook up directly with the Net, allowing us to see every one of our machines and what they're doing." This will greatly facilitate the selling of carbon credits to polluters.

Influencing energy policy: The floodgates about to open.

Southwest is also actively involved in attempting to influence federal and state energy policy. "We're looking at how to create rebates, how to get incentives in order to stimulate the market," says Kruse. "We build the distribution networks, and that allows us to create more revenue, which allows us to build the business, which allows us to create a less expensive product."

Says Rob Harmon from Bonneville, "The big problem the renewable industry has had over the last couple decades is that it's competing against heavily subsidized fossil fuels and other traditional fuel sources — the hydro system, the nuclear power industry system — which are also heavily subsidized. Those subsidies are part of the basic tax code."

When legislation to grant tax credits for renewable energy systems comes up for a vote in Congress, Harmon explains, "the tax credit gets used as a bargaining chip, such as in 'You give us the Arctic, we'll give you the tax credit,' and the tax credit gets tabled [or shelved] again."

"We hear a lot of talk from politicians about how important renewables are, but they don't seem to be willing to imbed renewables into the tax code or into basic utility policy nationally."

"I don't care if you're left, center, right, this will be an issue you're concerned about," Harmon concludes. The trick is "to position Southwest

Windpower in this environment . . . to somehow make sure that when the consumers decide they want to make that change, they're going to go to us."

Bonneville Environmental Foundation: The Progenitor of Carbon Offsets

Anyone who grew up in the Pacific Northwest as I did associates the name Bonneville with hydroelectric power. The Bonneville Power Administration is a federal agency under the Department of Energy that operates an extensive electricity transmission network coming from federal dams.

An offshoot of the BPA, the Bonneville Environmental Foundation (BEF) was founded in 1998 under the leadership of Angus Duncan to support watershed restoration programs and small-scale renewable energy development. Soon after Duncan hired Rob Harmon (now BEF's chief innovation officer), Harmon cooked up an idea that has now taken hold across the country. At the time, wholesale renewable energy certificates were traded by power companies. Harmon asked himself, "Why not take these into the retail market? Why not sell the certificates to any company or individual that might want to support renewable energy, thereby allowing them to take responsibility for their electricity consumption?"

BEF proceeded to sell the first retail REC in the country, making carbon offsets available to the ordinary citizen for the first time. It named the product Green Tags, and they are available for purchase on the firm's Web site along with the world's first Carbon Calculator, which enables site visitors to calculate not only their carbon dioxide footprint but also what they emit in the form of other greenhouse gases.

The challenge of selling the intangible.

"We realized early on that selling carbon offsets is a difficult concept for the public to grasp," says Harmon. "We knew that perception would have to be positive out of the gate or it would take five years to recover. So we thought the best way to do this was to run it as a nonprofit."

"Because we're nonprofit, all the money we bring in goes to the mission. If we have any net revenues left over, we put them into solar schools or restoring watersheds, because that's our mission."

Carbon offset facilitators, the majority of which are for-profit companies, have come under scrutiny of late, the media questioning how much of the carbon offset contributions is actually being funneled to fund renewable energy sources and how much is going into overhead and profit.

"The atmosphere embraces the person offsetting their carbon more than the person who isn't. And yet the person who is offsetting the carbon is the one the press is going after," says Harmon about the situation. "Do I begrudge any of our for-profit competitors for spending money on marketing and administration? Not at all." Harmon urges the public to simply compare how much CO_2 is taken out of the air per dollar contributed by one organization against another and then make a choice on that basis.

"We don't have the cheapest ton of offsets at BEF, because we look for really high-quality products and we want money left over to address our mission," he continues. "We hope people will like the other things that we're doing — ancillary things for the environment that we're spending money on."

Bottom line, "what the atmosphere cares about is the total amount of CO_2 that's reduced," says Harmon. "If you ask these [for-profit carbon trade] companies to not spend money on marketing, then the result is that no one knows they exist. No one puts their money in. And the result is we cook the atmosphere. The goal is to bring the maximum amount of money to bear to solve the climate crisis, and to spend it in ways that generate real results."

"The first few years of the launch of a totally radically new product, we should expect overall marketing costs to be high," he maintains. "How else are people going to hear about it?"

Investing in conservation and infrastructure is the answer.

Harmon would rather see consumers less distracted by the questions surrounding carbon offset programs and more focused on the underlying problems. He believes that the United States has been grossly negligent given the lack of investment in infrastructure needed to solve the energy and climate change crises, and that people must get behind the cause.

"You can generate a good chunk of the electricity you need in the US from the wind in South and North Dakota, but the problem is there's not enough transmission," he explains. "There are many people who are suggesting that it's time to build transmission systems again." He is referring to the big government investments in dams and highways at midcentury.

The claim by public utilities "that intermittent wind power cannot be used to power energy grids is ridiculous at this stage of the game," he continues. "We could increase wind power by tenfold before we run into significant stability problems. Smart people who know how the grid works have to be incentivized to make it work with renewables."

"The US has focused its economy on consumption rather than on investing in infrastructure. Investment in infrastructure is good for jobs, it's good for the trade deficit, it's good for the economy, and it's good for the environment. Many people suggest that we should have taken the tax rebates the government sent out [in spring '08] and invested that in our infrastructure instead," Harmon says.

"Why aren't we employing people to do serious energy conservation in every building in America? If done well — and we know how to do it well — it would pay for itself. This is a fabulous way to spend money. But we don't have the political will."

End fossil fuel subsidies for those who don't need 'em.

Addressing the policy question of the subsidization of fossil fuel development, Harmon asks rhetorically, "Should the taxpayers be funding very large subsidies to establish industries in the fossil fuel area? Absolutely not. It doesn't make any sense when we have to reduce carbon emissions."

This point is underscored by a recent *New York Times* editorial. "Peter Schwartz of Global Business Network describes as the true American energy policy today: 'Maximize demand, minimize supply, and buy the rest from the people who hate us the most.'"[2]

The fact that the big energy companies are reaping huge profits and using them to establish themselves as key players in the renewable energy market can look pretty ominous. The multinationals seem to be doing so in order to guarantee the continued oligopoly that has long been the structure of the mainstream energy business. Nevertheless, despite the shady ulterior motives, Harmon makes a worthy point: "Where *should* fossil fuel companies be putting the profits? . . . Exactly where they're putting them, which is into renewables."

As for the overall picture, "there's no silver bullet," Harmon says. "We have to do a lot of everything. It's not an either-or situation."

A four-pronged approach.

According to Rob Harmon and many others, it all boils down to a four-pronged approach: a very heavy emphasis on conservation, a shift toward renewable energy among utilities, the production of energy by consumers themselves, and a huge investment in infrastructure.

Until we do all of the above, he adds, "we'll continue to see a hemorrhaging of dollars in the trade deficit and no change in the carbon problem."

SUMMARY: STREAMING PROFITS

Southwest Windpower made a preemptive entry into the distributed energy business well before others saw the opportunity. The founders carved out a niche in a smaller-scale, affordable wind turbine market and have adeptly built multiple customer bases. They've built a brand architecture around different lines of brand-named products under the umbrella of a master site designed to educate and win over prospective customers. Although Southwest does not directly benefit from the REC market founded by the Bonneville Environmental Foundation, it enjoys an ever-increasing piece of an ever-increasing pie made possible by greater public awareness — and public awareness is where the Gort Cloud comes into play.

The people most likely to purchase wind turbines as well as energy credits are found among the eco-aware. These policy advisers, NGOs, energy experts, tech bloggers, manufacturers, and distributors and their customers use information as their primary currency. It's the honesty and clarity of this information that have raised the awareness of earth-friendly options offered by Southwest Windpower and BEF.

Ten Key Observations for Successfully Building a Green Brand

There it is. Take it.
— *William Mulholland*

A s this book goes to print, numerous articles are being written about the difficulty green brands are having in reaching and compelling their audiences. Of course, some of this has to do with the ups and downs of the economy. With strained wallets, consumers are likely to cut back on everything, including green products; some return to traditional, not-so-green buying habits. But there are other things. The *New York Times* published an article titled "That Buzz in Your Ear May Be Green Noise" bemoaning the confusion among otherwise eco-conscious consumers. Too many messages. Too many claims. Too many conflicting choices. The article quoted Carl Pope, executive director of the Sierra Club: "We worry about it. We all understand that today's media environment is an extremely crowded one, and message overload is the order of the day."[1]

A 2007 study by the Shelton Group offered a similar analysis of the green home market: "69 percent of respondents said that they would choose one home over another based on energy efficiency — down from 86 percent in 2006. 56 percent said they felt positively about the term 'green,' though focus groups also indicated skepticism over such terms in packaging or positioning."[2]

Still, GreenBiz.com has noted a Porter Novelli study that resoundingly endorsed the power of the Gort Cloud. The study "identified about 4 percent of the population that the company labeled 'greenfluencers': environmentally educated, politically active and socially connected individuals that are driving trends and shaping what green products make it off the shelves into individual homes. This group are the people that friends ask for expert advice, are almost three times as likely as the general population to read and participate in blog discussions, and 41 percent of whom write to their political representatives. As a result, they are the tip of the iceberg to reaching newly green consumers, Porter Novelli said."[3]

What Porter Novelli is describing, of course, is one aspect of the Gort Cloud.

So if the premise of this book is correct — that there is an invisible force driving the success of green brands — what should an honestly committed ecopreneur do to win friends and influence people? I have come away from this project with ten primary observations.

1. Honesty isn't only the best policy . . . it's the only policy.

The Gort Cloud is driven by an honest exchange of information. Truth is the currency in this dialogue, and woe unto those who underestimate the number of truth seekers in the Gort Cloud. Outright lies will bring down the greenwashing hammer, as will exaggeration.

But the Gort Cloud is also surprisingly understanding and tolerant of companies that make an effort to be more green, to change incrementally over time. The best policy is to honestly make your case. "We are not perfect, but we are better than we were or better than the alternative for the following reasons . . ." Then state your proof points with outside support and open your findings to a transparent dialogue. Think of your advertising claims as a PhD dissertation subject to peer review. Gary Hirshberg did this when he argued that shipping evaporated milk in bulk from New Zealand produced a smaller carbon footprint than importing liquid organic milk from domestic dairies. He didn't underestimate the intelligence of his customers, and he didn't lie to them. You could make alternative cases, but the point is that his claim was transparent.

2. Green is not the primary driver of choice. For most products, it's just icing on the cake.

Slapping a green label on a product is not going to guarantee success. In fact, it may simply place your product in a crowded and highly undifferentiated category of "green stuff." Method distinguishes its eco-friendly cleaning products with distinctive packaging that is beautiful enough to leave out on the counter — for all your friends to notice how green you are. When Marty McDonald of egg conducted focus groups, he determined that the primary driver of preference for Southwest Windpower's turbines was "freedom" — freedom from the "man," from the utility companies. As with tattoos, consumers' choices were driven by a sense of independence. The primary driver of preference for Tesla's rather expensive Roadster is not so much its electric motor as the raw power of that motor. It's the zero-to-sixty thing — the fact that you and your Tesla can smoke a Corvette. That you never have to pull into a service station is simply having the cake and eating it, too. Likewise with sustainable clothing that must also be fashionable, or eco-friendly furniture that is also comfortable and stylish, or an energy-efficient washing machine that really gets the dirt out . . . and on and on.

3. Price and performance really are important.

The belief that "your dollar's worth more when you walk through the door" applies only to nongreen products sold at Kmart and not to well-heeled greenies is a mistake. As the economy has corrected in recent months, many eco-conscious consumers have been quoted on NPR and other media outlets saying they can no longer shop exclusively at expensive groceries like Whole Foods — sometimes referred to as Whole Paycheck. They're beginning to shop around, buying a bit at Trader Joe's, a bit at Wal-Mart or Costco, a bit at the local farmers' market, not so much at premium grocers. Even among product categories, consumers will comparison-shop to find the best deal. Maybe it's the store label instead of the branded product. Maybe it's a bulk-packaged green product. Even the demand-driven price of the Prius has caused many consumers to hold off on dumping their SUV despite record-high gas prices. Price and performance matter. If the value isn't there or the performance isn't up to snuff, consumers will not respond.

4. Green consumers are not a demographic but a psychographic. It's a way of thinking.

Early studies of the green consumer focused on age, sex, race, education, income, and other measures of demographic profiling. This tended to produce a picture of mostly white, college-educated, liberal, upper-middle-class folks living in major metro areas. The problem with this profile is that it also describes nongreen consumers. Worse, it's exclusionary and leaves out important greens among the young, the not-so-well-off, people of color, conservatives, those in rural communities, and all the others that make up this diverse consumer group. It also says nothing about why people buy a particular green product. "Traditional means of marketing by demographics simply will not work for green consumers," argues Danny Bradbury of BusinessGreen.com. "You need to be able to identify how they behave."[4]

The better approach is a psychographic analysis that pairs a product with a defined user group. That definition should measure the lifestyle, values, and emotional desires of the customer. For a mom of any demographic group, the desire might be to provide natural, additive-free food to her child. For a small-business owner, it might be the desire to make an incremental difference by choosing an EPEAT-rated computer or an Energy Star–rated appliance. The impetus to invest in an expensive home solar system might be about setting an example for your children, rather than some payoff in the distant future. This is part of the reason that green labels, like the US Green Building Council's LEED rating or the Cradle-to-Cradle certification, are so important. These labels tell the values- and emotion-driven consumer that someone has carefully looked over the product and endorsed the claims. It's not unlike the gold medals you find on imported olive oil bottles. It's a mark of assurance and an affirmation of personal commitment.

5. The power of convenience.

Charles G. Mortimer, the former director of General Foods, has been quoted as saying, "Convenience is the success factor of just about every type of product and service that is showing steady growth."[5] This is supported by a recent Green Mountain Energy study, which noted: "Nineteen percent of city dwellers, versus 12 percent of nonmetro residents, say they would be more likely to make environmentally conscious decisions if what they had to do to carry out their decisions could be made easier and less time-consuming." Hence the growth of Whole Foods. The message is, "Everything in here is safe and healthy, so you don't have to think about it." The downside, of course, is the cost. As mentioned, price is still a barrier for many would-be green consumers.

6. It's easier to speak to the choir . . .

Making a brand connection is easier when consumers are already riding the green bandwagon and embracing the green movement as a lifestyle change. Thus it helps if the product represents a badge of membership into this club of like-minded green believers. Buying green and being able to show it off expresses personal ownership in the green agenda. Consumers get bragging rights.

7. . . . and easier still if a product looks as green as it claims.

This leads to a related point: it helps if green products are visibly green. Take the Prius (again): It has a strange body shape that helps it stand out. Everyone knows that this driver is walking the talk. In the same way, people are proud of their residential wind turbines because their neighbors can see their green investment spinning in their yards. They get kudos that help offset possible neighborhood association complaints.

8. The fear factor.

Immediate fear seems to have more effect on purchasing decisions than the fear of something ten or twenty years out. Thus, the fear that toxins in paint, or plastic, or shampoo could begin to kill us today works better than the idea that we'll be killing off the polar bears by 2050. That's why the most green traction has been made in the arenas of food, personal care, home furniture and finishes, and plastic items, especially toys — all things we come into physical contact with. We don't come into contact with landfills, so it's harder to feel an elevated sense of concern about our trash. On the other hand, a high heating or electric bill can drive consumers to economic and eco-friendly alternatives.

9. It's what you don't pay for that may count most.

Among the hardest decisions businesspeople make deal with marketing and advertising strategies. It is expensive to get the word out, and the efficacy of traditional media continues to decline year after year. The alternative media of click-through ads and search engine posts can focus on a more specific audience, but these come with a price and a good deal of experimentation. The true cost per impression (CPM) is one of those "known unknowns."

And then you have the Gort Cloud. Much of it is free. The viewers of any given site can often be narrowly defined. The green social networks, advocacy groups, trendspotters, and business media are constantly trolling for new product stories and readily pass them around. This has provided a leveling of the competitive landscape that enables a small upstart to outperform a category giant. It can also lead to ever-more-specific product differentiation — say, between Seventh Generation and Method, both eco-friendly cleaning products. Best of all, unsolicited PR and endorsements are the most credible of all, and it's credibility that will power an aspiring green brand.

10. K.I.S.S.

Finally, we should not forget Carl Pope's concern about information overload. A product maker may have a lot to say, but consumers have only a limited time to listen. The solution? *Keep It Simple, Stupid.* Knowing your customers and what will drive them to your product takes effort, but once you discover that formula, your brand message should be clear, simple, and unambiguous. Keep in mind the two-second rule as well: You have exactly two seconds to make an impression in the grocery store, on a Web site, or in a magazine ad. If you don't catch your audience then, it's gone. The key is to craft a message that gets to the primary driver of preference and then adds a tangible green reward — *safer, cruelty-free, energy-efficient, locally grown.* Link the green claim to your proof points and let the Gort Cloud argue the merits.

Brand positioning can be defined as *definition + purpose + advantages + audience + personality.* And business leaders can find all the information they need to fill in these blanks in the Gort Cloud. When a business is ready to dive into the green space, it can use the Gort Cloud to tap partners, distribution channels, and markets. And, of course, there are the experiences of the pioneering ecopreneurs who are profiled in this book.

It's all there. Take it . . . and in return, please give us more green choices.

A Passion for Community

*We started off trying to set up a small anarchist community,
but people wouldn't obey the rules.*
— Actor and playwright Alan Bennett

In the early 1980s, when I was creative director at Warner Bros. Records in Burbank and well before I started brand consulting, we were witnessing a lot of change. Of course, there was considerable change and invention happening in the music itself. My team was designing about thirty covers a month. We had our traditional artists like Fleetwood Mac, Frank Sinatra, the Doobie Brothers, Ry Cooder, and George Benson. After all, Warner Bros. was known as a singer-songwriter label. Much of the repertoire was mainstream rock and folk. But we were also beginning to introduce new and unusual stuff. The B-52s, Prince, Devo, Van Halen, Frank Zappa, Laurie Anderson, Funkadelic (father of modern rap), Talking Heads, the Pretenders. It was a very dynamic time, and so, too, for recording technology.

When I joined the music industry in 1977 as an art director for *Rolling Stone* magazine, the majority of releases were on twelve-inch vinyl. By the time I left the industry just five years later, we had seen cassette sales overtake LP sales. Then came the introduction of the first Sony/Philips CD, and then MTV. I art-directed some of the first music videos for Rod Stewart and Sammy Hagar, and it was one of our artists, Dire Straits, that released the first CD to sell a million copies. Our art department was still averaging about thirty releases a month, but we were now producing cover art for multiple formats including singles, LPs, EPs, cassettes, CDs, Beta, and VHS packaging. It was a busy place, with the lights (not so environmentally) on twenty-four hours a day.

The way we recorded music and made artwork was also changing. Although it was still largely a paste-up operation, we composed liner notes on IBM Selectric IIIs, the first of the word processors, or on some of the new desktop computers. The Apple II had been launched in the late 1970s, and some technophile artists were using it. The launch of the first Macintosh with its graphical user interface really got the graphic art community going, but that didn't happen until later, in the mid-'80s.

The very first experiments in digital mastering were under way, and this ultimately led to the digital CD. The very first digital separation of an album cover happened under my direction for a Devo release called *Shout*. And, of course, we had heard about the ARPANET, whose origins date back to experiments in 1969 and promised a future of digital file transfers. I think we even had one of the early thermal analog fax machines. Things were buzzing in Burbank. We were all trying to make Gene Roddenberry's ideas on *Star Trek* come true.

And so it occurred to me that there should be a way to bring the commercial art community together through a shared network. We could post our portfolios, exchange artwork and text, manage accounting, and do all sorts of things via an electronic exchange network linked by the telephone lines. I just cooked this idea up with no clue how it would actually work. After all, we were recording digitally and separating images digitally. We were using computers to set type. So why not an exchange, like a telephone exchange, that stored and shared digital information? All my pals in the design business would use it. Maybe the guys would just share model ZED cards, but they'd use it. I stressed the accounting service because I thought that would be the strongest OBS, or opening benefit statement, for the businesspeople I sought to partner with.

The birth of another Net.

In the spring of 1983, I wrote letters to the leaders of the nascent computer industry describing my idea for something I called the Net. It was basically a description of a digital network like the Internet and of the World Wide Web document-sharing platform long before such a thing existed. In fact, a public Internet would not be available until 1988, with the first World Wide Web browser available in 1993. The people who received the letters included Steve Jobs and Andy Paul at Apple Computer; Arch McGill, Charles Marshall, and Randal Tobias at American Bell; John Opel of IBM; Admiral Bobby Inman, CEO of MCC; Fred Bucy of Texas Instruments; William Norris of Control Data; An Wang, founder of Wang Laboratories; Colby Chandler at Kodak; R. F. Mettler of TRW Systems; and Ken Olson, a director at Digital Equipment Corporation. And here's the surprise — they, or their deputies, all wrote back, mostly expressing support for the idea but also suggesting that such a thing would require computing and transmission power that was not remotely possible anytime soon. At the time, transmission speeds were extremely slow, and there wasn't anything approaching bandwidth. I guess they hadn't read or didn't quite believe in Gordon Moore's famous prediction of a doubling of computing power every two years.

Here's the text of my June 22, 1983, letter to Wang Laboratories proposing an electronic exchange network:

The Net: An Information Retrieval System for the Communication Arts Industry

The Net is a computerized information and accounting service for individuals and businesses in the communication arts industry.

The Net's potential subscribers include art directors, illustrators, photographers, model agencies, typesetters, draftsmen and production artists, prop houses, advertising agencies, stock photo houses, design studios, copywriters, letterers, commercial production companies, animators, special effect studios, printers and separators, camera stores and equipment rentals firms, movie studios, artists representatives, set designers, retouchers, post production houses, stylists, make-up artists and hairdressers, art supply stores, costumers and wardrobe designers, messenger services, location finders, media buyers, stat and print houses, television and radio stations, talent agencies, directors, jinglers, color labs, animal trainers, mailing houses and any client who on a regular basis requires the services of these suppliers. *[This was the definition of the community.]*

The Net offers its subscribers a variety of services including basic accounting, accounts payable and receivable management *[an advanced idea for leased software and distributed computing]*, credit checking, legal advice, tax preparation, billing and bill collection. Because of its unique relationship with so many people, The Net may be able to offer discounts on insurance, airfare or any other bulk purchased commodity or service. *[A kind of*

Priceline?] It may be able to act as or operate a credit union. However, the chief function of The Net is to facilitate the exchange of information. Any supplier to the communication arts industry will have the potential to store a visual file of his services, including his portfolio, in a personal vault at a local Net Exchange. *[Something like iDisc.]* Clients can "call" The Net, ask for access to the vault and view the information. *[Sounds like today's password-protected Web sites.]* Subscribers will be able to locate each other through a coded directory. *[A URL address?]* They will also be able to "talk" to each other visually. *[Sounds like HTML or iChat.]*

The Net offers these services through a system of Exchanges located in every major market in the world. These Exchanges are linked to their subscribers via desktop computers and the telephone lines. All of the Net Exchanges in the various market centers are similarly linked so that any client in the system can reach any supplier in the system at any time. *[The Internet!]*

The Net's basic computer palette consists of a keyboard, a high-resolution monitor, and a telephone modem. Additional equipment could include a black and white or four-color matrix printer, disk storage, a high-resolution video camera, and graphics software packages. With the rapid advances in the quality of digitized visual information, The Net could one day offer a replacement to the use of photographic film and printing papers in the graphic arts. *[Really?]*

Well, the idea just languished in a file in my drawer for years until a 1996 *BusinessWeek* article announced, HERE COMES THE INTERNET. Oh well, one of those missed opportunities in life.

The point is that I've always been interested in how the Internet can be used to connect like-minded communities. I viewed the artists, contributors, and buyers of music as an interdependent community with one group of stakeholders helping another, like the Gort Cloud.

Other Internet community ideas.

Some years later and in a similar spirit, I registered one of the first domain names for a Web site called StyleNet, with the idea of connecting the fashion community to an international style network. I called this type of site a shell site, because it would consist of an edited collection of individual sites catering to a specific audience group. Like visiting a specific section in the library, you could find sites that dealt with the subject you were interested in that were edited by someone with a point of view. The kink in this idea was that it required a "librarian" to search for, select, and list Web sites on the shell site. Yahoo! and Google search technologies would later make this idea irrelevant, but not before I had built and launched some of the very first apparel-industry Web sites, including the first women's high-fashion site for my wife's collection called Product. It was such a fresh idea in the early years of the World Wide Web that Netscape posted it on the What's New list for three years. My guess is that it stayed there so long because it was one of the only sites for women in a sea of sites for men.

This interest in connecting communities emerged again in 1998 when I was working for Caribiner International in New York. At the time, Caribiner was the world's largest live-event media company; I was worldwide creative director. This firm produced the Hong Kong handover event, among others. While I was there, I thought of the idea for a Corporate Knowledge Center with a *.go* suffix. Caribiner.go was a secure place where global staff could collaborate. It would also serve as a primary teaching tool for new hires, giving them access to history, training, job files, and templates. Again, it was an idea for sharing information in a community — in this case, a corporate community.

I realize now that my preoccupation with communities first emerged when I was an architecture student at the University of Washington. I wrote my thesis on the three-thousand-year-old marketplace at Campo dei Fiori in Rome. It was a story about a community — a community of vendors, shopkeepers, residents, and entertainers who have kept this corner of Rome active and vibrant since the time of Julius Caesar. When I returned from Italy, I went to work for the City of Seattle on the Pike Place Market Urban Renewal Project. That, too, is a historic community of small retailers selling mostly locally grown food, and a place that glues the city to its past. Starbucks? Its commitment to community started here.

Some years later, in 1992, I had the opportunity to visit Curitiba, Brazil, home to one of the most ambitious community recycling and mass-transit programs on earth. In another nod to the importance of community, Cuitiba's then young mayor and architect, Jaime Lerner, led the city's rich and poor in a communal effort to reduce pollution while providing safe, economical, and rapid public transportation as well as jobs in the recycling industry for the poorest of its citizens. The client that brought me there was O Boticário, which is today the world's largest perfumery and cosmetics franchising network. Consistent with its interest in natural pharmacological compounds and reverence for nature, the company has also created the Fundação O Boticário de Proteção à Natureza (O Boticário Nature Protection Foundation). This small nonprofit sponsors conservation projects including research, environmental education, and the protection of both wildlife and natural areas.[1]

At home here in Laurel Canyon, I am heavily involved in my community as a board member in the homeowner association. I'm in charge of "communications," but what I really do is knit our neighbors together using our Web site and an e-mail-based information system. Issues regarding development, fire safety, traffic and crime, our local school and park, and community beautification are all discussed in a wired dialogue. Some residents jokingly refer to me as the "Town Crier of Laurel Canyon." Well, I'm not, but I will take credit for helping to connect this historic community of artists and anarchists, musicians and writers.

Building brands is building a community of stakeholders.

The art of building brands is really about knitting a community of stakeholders around a product or service. Someone makes it. Others contribute as suppliers, investors, and advisers. Channel partners are sought out and relationships created with distributors, retailers, and the press. The brand community is further extended to various groups of consumers, right down to a direct and intimate relationship with individual customers.

This personal way of viewing the practice of brand building and marketing is something I've learned from my own clients, who have mostly been in the retail, or customer-facing, world. Retail branding has been my sweet spot. For one of my earliest clients, Gotcha Sportswear,

it was about creating a leadership brand among the professional surf-
ers that made up its core customer base. For Tokyo-Mitsubishi Bank, it
was building connections with banking customers. Our LA–Tokyo team
placed an emphasis on the retail banking experience, which created a
living touchpoint between the bank and its customers. During this
project, I also designed the first credit card to use blood vein recognition technology to enhance security. More recently, I was one of the key
consultants for Tokyo's first experiment in green urbanism, a place I
named ThinkPark. The brand concept was summarized in a tagline with
a community-building message: "Where Ideas Grow."

Seen from the perspective of community, the Gort Cloud is simply
another interconnected group — though one with a mighty cause, the
health and preservation of our planet. But unlike consciously created
brand communities, no one dreamed up the Gort Cloud or organized it
for a specific purpose. In fact, it's not organized. It just exists as a fluid
community. For businesses that recognize its existence, it is a powerful
component to factor into business plans because it can help entrepreneurs and their marketing partners reach out and touch their stakeholders in a credible way. Instead of paid advertisements or stories placed
by PR agents, the endorsement of the Gort Cloud is more credible to the
audience. It's a form of word of mouth bound by the honor system: you
must tell the truth.

This is where the analogy to the Oort cloud returns. Just as we take
notice of an object born in the Oort cloud like Halley's comet when it
occasionally passes by and speculate on what would happen if it were
to strike the earth, the Gort Cloud has the power to come out of nowhere
and make itself known, felt, and, in some cases, feared. There is an old
German proverb: *Fear makes the wolf bigger than he is.* The Gort Cloud,
through its power of collective peer review, has caused most aspiring
green businesses to be very realistic and honest in how they portray their
brands. Unlike the snake-oil salesmen of the past, ecopreneurs work in
a transparent world where claims are very quickly analyzed. In return,
consumers are willing to grant a fair degree of credibility — and empa-
thy — to green businesses in the hope that more and better products will
follow. The Gort Cloud can supply a large rooting section of home-team
fans.

Of course, the Age of Sustainability is still a dream. It may be on the
horizon, but it's not here yet. We continue to produce, consume, and

pollute at an unsustainable rate. Just this month, I read about the near collapse of salmon fisheries here on the West Coast and yet another massive disintegration on the Antarctic ice shelf. Still, the promise of a perpetual state of prosperity without environmental or social costs is so alluring that, like Never Land, it is attracting an army of green Peter Pans. These are the environmental do-gooders who make up much of the Gort Cloud and who also include the pioneering business leaders who are profiled in this book.

Notes

An Interdependent Community of Green Businesses and Their Customers

1. Jasmin Malik Chua, "Is The Swiffer Eco-Friendly?" TreeHugger, February 22, 2007, www.treehugger.com/files/2007/02/is_the_swiffer.php, accessed September 15, 2008; Jill Fehrenbacher, "Greenwash Your Floors with the Swiffer," Inhabitat, March 6, 2007, www.inhabitat.com/2007/03/06/greenwashing-101-the-swiffer-green-or-greenwash, accessed September 15, 2008; Gianfranco Zaccai, "Matching Sustainability with Profits," *BusinessWeek*, February 21, 2007, www.businessweek.com/innovate/content/feb2007/id20070221_603937.htm?chan=innovation_innovation+%2B+design_insight, accessed September 15, 2008.
2. Jennifer van der Meer, "Swiffer Sustainability: The Swiffer Designer Speaks Up," Inhabitat, June 9, 2007, www.inhabitat.com/2007/06/09/swiffer-sustainability-the-swiffer-designer-speaks-up, accessed September 15, 2008.
3. "Poland Spring, Other Nestlé Water Brands Phasing in New Eco-Shape Bottle," Sustainable Is Good, August 21, 2007, www.sustainableisgood.com/blog/2007/08/poland-spring-o.html, accessed September 15, 2008; "Nestlé's Eco-Shape Bottles — Making Plastic Bottles Green? I Think," Change Report, August 20, 2007, www.changereport.com/content/view/106/39/, accessed September 15, 2008; Karen Robinson-Jacobs, "Dallas Plant Makes Water Bottles More Eco-Friendly," *Dallas Morning News*, March 28, 2008, www.dallasnews.com/sharedcontent/dws/bus/stories/DN-water_28bus.State.Edition1.3ad7d6d.html, accessed September 15, 2008; "Packaging, A Commitment to Consumers," Nestlé Waters, Nestlé SA, 2007, www.nestle-waters.com/en/Menu/ResDevel, accessed September 15, 2008; "Nestlé Waters' CEO Counters Bottled Water Criticism," Environmental Leader, September 5, 2007, www.environmentalleader.com/2007/09/05/nestle-waters-ceo-counters-bottled-water-criticism, accessed September 15, 2008; Alex Williams, "Water, Water Everywhere, But Guilt by the Bottleful," *New York Times*, August 12, 2007, www.nytimes.com/2007/08/12/fashion/12water.html, accessed September 15, 2008.
4. Fiji Water, "Every Drop Is Green," www.fijigreen.com, accessed September 15, 2008; Collin Dunn, "Fiji Water Leads Bottled Water Industry in Looking Green(er)," TreeHugger, April 9, 2008, www.treehugger.com/files/2008/04/bottled-water-industry-fiji-water-looks-green.php, accessed September 15, 2008.

The Rise of the Ecopreneur

1. Landor Associates, "New Study by Landor Associates Reveals Most Consumers Don't Care About 'Green,'" July 6, 2006, www.landor.com/?do=news.pressrelease&storyid=464, accessed September 15, 2008.
2. Rob Walker, "The Hidden (in Plain Sight) Persuaders," *New York Times*, December 5, 2004, www.nytimes.com/2004/12/05/magazine/05BUZZ.html?pagewanted=1&_r=1&sq=viral%20marketing&st=cse&oref=slogin&scp, accessed September 16, 2008.

3. Landor Associates, "New Survey Conducted Indicates Green is No Longer a Marginalized Issue in the United States," May 1, 2007, www.landor.com/index.cfm?do=news.pressrelease&storyid=507&bhcp=1.

Visualizing a Network of Shared Interests

1. Christine Lepisto, "The Best Green Search Engines," TreeHugger, July 9, 2008, www.treehugger.com/files/2008/07/best-green-search-engines.php, accessed September 15, 2008.
2. David Wigder, "Green Marketing on Social Networks," Marketing Green, December 1, 2007, http://marketinggreen.wordpress.com/2007/12/01/green-marketing-on-social-networks, accessed September 15, 2008.
3. "Still Made Here," Trendwatching.com, June 2007, http://trendwatching.com/trends/stillmadehere.htm, accessed September 15, 2008.
4. Greg Zimmerman, "The Rise and Significance of Eco-Labels and Green Product Certifications," Facilitiesnet, July 2005, www.facilitiesnet.com/bom/article.asp?id=3087, accessed September 15, 2008.
5. Good Housekeeping, www.goodhousekeepingseal.com/r5/home.asp, accessed September 15, 2008.
6. David Wigder, "Eco-Labels Impact Consumer Behavior," GreenBiz.com, May 24, 2008, www.greenbiz.com/column/2008/05/24/eco-labels-impact-consumer-behavior, accessed September 15, 2008.

1. Marketing Magic

1. Mitchell Clute, "Organic Dilemma: What Rules Personal Care?" *Natural Foods Merchandiser,* May 12, 2008, http://naturalfoodsmerchandiser.com/tabid/66/itemid/1430/Organic-dilemma-What-rules-personal-care.aspx, accessed September 15, 2008.
2. "Organic Trade Association Task Force Kicks Out Leading Natural Soap Company That Stands for Strong Organic Standards, Says Organic Consumers Association," Common Dreams Progressive Newswire, July 23, 2003, www.commondreams.org/news2003/0723-06.htm, accessed September 15, 2008.
3. Jill Ettinger, "Cleaning Up Soap: Why the Bronner Family Is Washing Out a Few Mouths," *Reality Sandwich,* March 31, 2008, www.realitysandwich.com/cleaning_up_soap_why_the_bronner_family_is_washing_out_a_few_mouths, accessed September 15, 2008.

3. Unfuckers United

1. Stephen Filler, "A Legally Enforceable Triple Bottom Line — Nau!" Green Counsel, January 26, 2007, http://nylawline.typepad.com/greencounsel/2007/01/nau_a_legally_e.html, accessed September 15, 2008.

4. Cleaning Up in a Crowded Marketplace

1. Petz Scholtus, "Aveda — Soil to Bottle," TreeHugger, July 15, 2005, www.treehugger.com/files/2005/07/aveda_soil_to_b_1.php, accessed September 15, 2008.

2. "Have You Got Green Fatigue?" *The Independent*, September 20, 2007, www.independent.co.uk/environment/green-living/have-you-got-green -fatigue-402971.html, accessed September 15, 2008.

5. Building Green
1. J. Baldwin, "The Dymaxion Dwelling Machine," Buckminster Fuller Institute, www.bfi.org/our_programs/who_is_buckminster_fuller/design_science/ dymaxion_designs/the_dymaxion_dwelling_machine_by_j_baldwin, accessed September 15, 2008.
2. Judy Reickert, "The Story of Lustron Homes," Lustron Connection, www .lustronconnection.org/whatislustron.html, accessed September 15, 2008.
3. Felicity Barringer, "The New Trophy Home, Small and Ecological," *New York Times*, June 22, 2008, www.nytimes.com/2008/06/22/us/22leed.html ?_r=1&oref=slogin, accessed September 15, 2008.
4. Margot Adler, "Behind the Ever-Expanding American Dream House," National Public Radio, July 4, 2006, www.npr.org/templates/story/story .php?storyId=5525283, accessed September 15, 2008.
5. Brendan I. Koerner, "Bamboo and You: Are Hardwood Floors a Crime Against the Earth?" *Slate*, June 10, 2008, www.slate.com/id/2193239, accessed September 15, 2008.

6. Creating Green Street
1. Paul Hawken, "The New Great Transformation," Long Now Foundation, June 8, 2007, http://blog.longnow.org/2007/06/09/paul-hawken-the-new -great-transformation, accessed September 14, 2007.
2. "Wal-Mart to Source More Local Produce," GreenBiz.com, July 2, 2008, www .greenbiz.com/news/2008/07/02/wal-mart-source-more-local-produce, accessed September 15, 2008.

7. Driving Fast in the Green Lane
1. "The History of Electric Vehicles," About.com, http://inventors.about.com/ library/weekly/aacarselectrica.htm, accessed September 15, 2008.
2. "Eco-Iconic," Trendwatching.com, June 2008, www.trendwatching.com/ trends/ecoiconic.htm, accessed September 15, 2008.
3. Tesla Motors Club Forum, August 2006, http://teslamotorsclub.com/tesla -roadster/535-tesla-mockup-burning-man.html, accessed September 15, 2008.
4. Wikipedia, http://en.wikipedia.org/wiki/Nikola_Tesla#_note-book, accessed September 15, 2008.
5. Michael Graham Richard, "Tesla Motors: Affordable Electric Cars Are Coming," TreeHugger, August 3, 2006, www.treehugger.com/files/2006/08/ tesla_motors_ev.php, accessed September 15, 2006.
6. "Prius May Become a Brand," CalCars.org, December 9, 2006, www.calcars .org/calcars-news/603.html, accessed September 15, 2008.
7. Sarah Rich, "Prefab Friday: Toyota Gets into Prefab Housing," Inhabitat, June

23, 2006, www.inhabitat.com/2006/06/23/prefab-friday-toyota-gets-into
-prefab-housing, accessed September 15, 2008.

8. Robert Gottlieb, *Forcing the Spring: The Transformation of the American
Environmental Movement* (Washington, DC: Island Press, 2005), p. 196.

8. Marketing Your Green Expertise

1. Heidrick & Struggles, "The Emergence of the Chief Sustainability Officer:
From EHS Compliance and Audit Manager to Influential Business Partner,"
GreenBiz.com, March 13, 2008, www.greenbiz.com/resources/resource/the
-emergence-chief-sustainability-officer-from-ehs-compliance-and-audit
-manager-, accessed September 15, 2008.

9. Selling Activism

1. Edited and abridged from www.benjerry.com/our_company/about_us/
our_history/timeline, accessed September 15, 2008.

2. "McDonald's Eyes Coffee as Starbucks Scales Back," VilleVoiceEats.com, July
8, 2008, http://villevoiceeats.com/2008/07/08/mcdonalds-eyes-coffee-as
-starbucks-scales-back, accessed September 15, 2008.

10. Sustainable Living

1. Paul Hawken, Third Wave Study Group, http://thirdwavestudygroup
.blogspot.com/2006/10/ecology-of-commerce-by-paul-hawken.html,
accessed September 15, 2008.

11. Think Big or Go Home

1. Rider Thompson, "Scotts Miracle-Gro Sues TerraCycle," Sustainable Is Good,
April 24, 2007, www.sustainableisgood.com/blog/2007/04/scotts_miracleg
.html, accessed September 15, 2008.

2. Abigail Doan, "NatureVsFuture: Recycled Juice Pouch Gown," Inhabitat,
January 27, 2008, www.inhabitat.com/2008/01/27/naturevsfuture-recycled
-juice-pouch-gown/#more-8160, accessed September 15, 2008.

12. The Ultimate Gort Cloud Connector: Energy

1. Mike Chino, "Modular Architectural Wind Microturbines Take Off," Inhabitat,
June 10, 2008, www.inhabitat.com/2008/06/10/architectural-wind-modular
-wind-turbines/.

2. Thomas L. Friedman, "Dumb as We Wanna Be," *New York Times*, April 30,
2008, www.nytimes.com/2008/04/30/opinion/30friedman.html?em&ex=120
9700800&en=5e50edff9f212b25&ei=5087%0A, accessed September 15, 2008.

Ten Key Observations for Successfully Building a Green Brand

1. Alex Williams, "That Buzz in Your Ear May Be Green Noise," *New York Times*,
June 15, 2008, www.nytimes.com/2008/06/15/fashion/15green.html?_r=
1&partner=rssuserland&emc=rss&pagewanted=all&oref=slogin, accessed
September 16, 2008.

2. Energy Pulse, www.energypulse.org, accessed September 16, 2008.
3. "Most Overwhelmed by Green Marketing, New Studies Find," GreenBiz .com, June 25, 2008, www.greenbiz.com/news/2008/06/25/overwhelmed -by-green-marketing, accessed September 16, 2008.
4. Danny Bradbury, "Are You Targeting the Correct Green Consumers?" BusinessGreen.com, January 25, 2008, www.businessgreen.com/business -green/analysis/2208073/spot-green-consumer, accessed September 16, 2008.
5. ThinkExist.com, http://thinkexist.com/quotes/with/keyword/convenience, accessed September 16, 2008.

A Passion for Community

1. O Boticário, About O Boticário, www.boticario.com.au/shop .php?page=shop/about&, accessed September 15, 2008.

Acknowledgments

This book has been a team effort, with every participant enthusiastically jumping in with both feet. No one held back, particularly among the businesspeople profiled in this book, who have unselfishly opened the door to the many secrets of their success. Everyone who helped with this project understands the need for action and the need for more green options if we are going to change the direction in which the environment is heading. All of us want more players, not fewer; more sustainable products and services, not fewer.

Nevertheless, this project could not have met its extraordinarily swift schedule without the skill and dedication of Scott Fields, who partnered on overall content design, interviews, transcription, research, and writing. Scott is a talented screen and copywriter who is a fellow neighbor in Laurel Canyon. Thanks, Scott.

Thanks also to our wives, Elaine Kim and Lucy Arlene Flesch, for their loving support and encouragement to take on this emotionally, if not financially, rewarding project. Elaine, thanks for letting me do this. To my two children, Tiber and Echo, when you are old enough to ask, "Daddy, what did your generation do to fix the environmental mess you created?" you can look to the good works of the people profiled here.

I would also like to thank my very close friend and partner of nearly twenty-five years, Shi Yu Chen. My life experiences and career path would be very much different today if it weren't for his vision and support. Thank you, Sy.

This book has also benefited from industry experts and communications professionals who have helped make introductions and kept the content honest and on track. They include: Burak Arikan, Will Ayres, Claire Best, Ralph Cavanagh, Katherine Cowles, Chrise DeTournay, Steve Dusek, Andrew Findlay, Robert Jensen, Matthew Jonas, Felix Kramer, Marty McDonald, and Andrew C. Revkin.

Special thanks to my family for their assistance: Dr. Robert Humphrey, Mirena Kim, Serena Kim, Rob Humphrey, and Tessa Humphrey. And with great appreciation to Mila Benedicto, Neka Hite, and Kirta Hartwig for assistance in design, transcription, and research.

Of course, this book would not exist without the support of the ecopreneurs profiled here. Many thanks to: Rob Michalak and Andrea Asch of Ben & Jerry's; Felix Kramer of CalCars.org; Michael Bronner and David Bronner of Dr. Bronner's Magic Soap; Adam Eidinger of Mintwood Media Collective; Rob Harmon of the Bonneville Environmental Foundation; Spencer Brown of Earth Friendly Moving; Marty McDonald of egg; Spencer Beebe, Bettina von Hagen, and Howard Silverman of Ecotrust; Chris Bartle of Green Key Real Estate; Paul Comey, Michael Dupee, and T. J. Whalen of Green Mountain Coffee Roasters; Michelle Kaufmann and Rebecca Woelke of Michelle Kaufmann Designs; Ray Anderson, Joyce LaValle, and Reva Revis of Interface Inc.; Tacee Webb, Logan Lynn, and Mike Akerman of Lovecraft Biofuels; George Milner, Joe O'Conner, and Tom Maddock of Mohawk Fine Papers; Ian Yolles, Chris Van Dyke, Peter Kallen, Mark Galbraith, and Jamie Bainbridge of Nau Clothing; Carsten Henningsen, Leslie Christian, and Amanda Plyley of Portfolio 21; Carlos Salgado of Scrapile; Christie Heimert, Gregor Barnum, Reed Doyle, Courtney Loveman, Stephanie Lowe, Jeff Phillips, and Susan Johnson of Seventh Generation; David C. E. Williams and Erin Fitzgerald of ShoreBank Pacific; Ed Kjaer of Southern California Edison; David Calley, Andy Kruse, and Miriam Robbins of Southwest Windpower; Tom Szaky, Michael Avale, Albe Zakes, and Alysia Welch-Chester of TerraCycle; Gary Hirshberg, Sarah Badger, and Erik Drake of Stonyfield Farm; Darryl Siry and David Vespremi of Tesla Motors; David Refkin and Liz Greenburg of Time Inc.; Tensie Whelan of the Rainforest Alliance; Virginia Young and Janie Lowe of YOLO Colorhouse; Ricardo Bazzarella of Hymotion; Kimberly Danek Pinkson of the EcoMom Alliance; Priscilla Woolworth of PriscillaWoolworth.com; Mary Sue Milliken of Border Grill and Ciudad; Jeff Kovel of Skylab; Mark Buckley of Staples; Blake Mycoskie and Jake Strom of TOMS shoes; and Summer Rayne Oakes.

A very special thank-you to my team at Chelsea Green Publishing: Margo Baldwin, Joni Praded, Emily Foote, Jessica Saturley, Jonathan Teller-Elsberg, Laura Jorstad, Dennis Pacheco, Peg O'Donnell, Allison Lennox, Bill Bokermann, Michael Weaver, Katharine Walton, and Brianne Goodspeed. Thanks for taking a chance on this first-time author.

And most importantly, thank you to the many citizens of the Gort Cloud for their tireless efforts to lead us toward an Age of Sustainability.

The Gort Cloud

The Invisible Force Powering
Today's Most Visible Green Brands

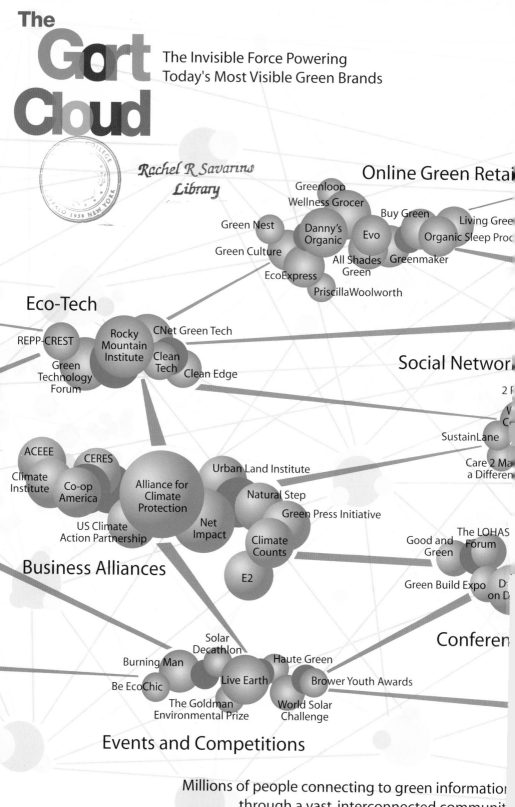

Online Green Retail

Greenloop
Wellness Grocer
Green Nest
Danny's Organic
Evo
Buy Green
Living Green
Organic Sleep Proc
Green Culture
All Shades Green
Greenmaker
EcoExpress
PriscillaWoolworth

Eco-Tech

REPP-CREST
Rocky Mountain Institute
CNet Green Tech
Green Technology Forum
Clean Tech
Clean Edge

Social Networ

2 F
V
C
SustainLane
Care 2 Ma
a Differen

ACEEE
CERES
Climate Institute
Co-op America
Alliance for Climate Protection
Urban Land Institute
Natural Step
Green Press Initiative
US Climate Action Partnership
Net Impact
Climate Counts
The LOHAS Forum
Good and Green
Business Alliances
E2
Green Build Expo
D
on D

Conferen

Solar Decathlon
Haute Green
Burning Man
Live Earth
Brower Youth Awards
Be EcoChic
The Goldman Environmental Prize
World Solar Challenge

Events and Competitions

Millions of people connecting to green informatio
through a vast, interconnected communit